Institutional Change in Theological Education:

A History of Brite Divinity School

Institutional Change in Theological Education:

A History of Brite Divinity School

EDITED BY

Mark G. Toulouse, Jeffrey Williams, and Dyan M. Dietz

A Joint Project of Brite Divinity School and TCU Press, Fort Worth, Texas

TCU Press
Fort Worth, Texas

Copyright © 2011 by Brite Divinity School

Library of Congress Cataloging-in-Publication Data

Institutional change in theological education : a history of Brite Divinity School
edited by Mark G. Toulouse, Jeffrey Williams, and Dyan M. Dietz.
p. cm.
"A joint project of Brite Divinity School and TCU Press."
Includes bibliographical references (p. 232) and index.
ISBN 978-0-87565-406-5 (cloth : alk. paper)
1. Brite Divinity School--History. I. Toulouse, Mark G., 1952- II.
Williams, Jeffrey, 1973- III. Dietz, Dyan M.
BV4070.B84I57 2011
230.071'17645315--dc23
2011019633

TCU Press
P. O. Box 298300
Fort Worth, Texas 76129
817.257.7822
http://www.prs.tcu.edu

To order books: 1.800.826.8911

Cover photograph by Mark G. Toulouse
Cover and text design by Bill Brammer, fusion29.com

Contents

Introduction

When Randolph and Addison Clark founded their college in 1873, Texas had only been readmitted into the Union for about three-and-one-half years. The state (along with most folks living in it) was dirt poor. The state's first steps into public higher education were still three full years away, coming when the Agricultural and Mechanical College of Texas (now Texas A&M University) opened its doors in October of 1876. It would be ten years, 1883, before the University of Texas admitted its first students. The first native-born governor of Texas, James Hogg, wouldn't take office until January of 1891. And the answer to the impoverishment of the state, the discovery of oil, wouldn't be provided until early 1901 at the Spindletop oil field near Beaumont. Like many other universities in Texas, the college founded by the Clarks would eventually reap many benefits from that discovery.

The Clarks believed strongly in the value of education; Randolph recounted that his own life had taught him the valuable lesson "that with right teaching and environment, principles can be so fixed in one's being that the inclinations and tendencies will naturally be for right . . . that when the life is fixed to the right center all actions will be in harmony with God's laws, all things will fall into right relation."[1] Put these two clauses together, and you naturally end up with the importance of a Christian education. The inclination was natural for them. Their father, Joseph Addison Clark, had struggled to obtain whatever education he could at the University of Alabama, and then taught school near Lexington, Kentucky. In 1839, he arrived in Austin, Texas, and found a job in printing for the Republic of Texas. When weather aborted his plans to return to Kentucky in 1841, he found himself in Nacogdoches County. He married and opened a school, which members of the public shut down when they uncovered his proclivities toward the form of Christianity associated with Alexander Campbell. Shortly thereafter, the children came along. Addison was born December 11, 1842, and Randolph entered the scene on August 15, 1844. Throughout their lives, they carried deep within them their father's dedication to education.

Both Addison and Randolph Clark were dedicated to sustaining their family's connection to the Disciples of Christ, a Christian reform movement led by Alexander Campbell on the American frontier in the nineteenth century. Alexander's father, Thomas Campbell, a Scotch-Irish Presbyterian minister, arrived in Philadelphia from Ireland in 1807. Shortly after arriving, the elder Campbell broke with Presbyterian leadership when he welcomed all Christians to the Lord's Supper whether they affirmed Presbyterian creeds or not. Alexander Campbell and the rest of the family arrived by ship in the fall of 1809. Alexander, just twenty-one years old, quickly assumed leadership of a group of Christians who had gathered around his father seeking a return to "simple evangelical Christianity, free from all mixture of human opinions and inventions of men."

From the beginning, these reformers hoped to unite all Christians on the basis of the practices of the early church, the testimony of scripture, and the observance of the Lord's Supper on a weekly basis. Within a few years, they also came to emphasize believers' baptism by immersion, which connected them for a time with Baptists. By 1830, however, Campbell's reformation movement left all Baptist connections behind and increasingly became known simply as the "Disciples of Christ."

By 1832, Campbell's churches began merging with congregations associated with Barton Stone. Barton Stone split from the Presbyterians in 1804 in order to stress the Bible as the only authority for Christians and to express the desire to "sink into union with the Body of Christ at large." Those associated with Stone's movement took the simple name of "Christians" and had grown to some ten thousand in number by the time they merged with the "Disciples." The merger of these two reform movements fueled significant growth throughout the nineteenth century. Known both by the names "Christians" and "Disciples," the congregations associated with this merger eventually formed the American denomination known today as the Christian Church (Disciples of Christ).

Life in the Southwest was hard when Addison and Randolph Clark founded their school with the intention of educating ministers for the Disciples of Christ. The decision to locate their school in Thorp Spring, told briefly in the first chapter of this book, reflected a general desire found among many Christians in the late nineteenth century to protect their youth from the worldly temptations so regularly encountered in the nation's urban settings. Places like Dallas and Fort Worth seemed even more dangerous than New York City or Chicago, filled as they were with trail-driving, hard-drinking cattlemen and gamblers. At that time, the Clarks did not realize that larger forces than these loomed on the horizon, forces that would soon change the face of education in the newly reunited country. Rising concern about the nation's cities was provoked by wide-ranging cultural changes that would far exceed anything imagined by the Clarks in 1873. They included the extraordinary pace of immigration and urbanization; the rise of industrialization and rapid development of concentrated wealth; the creation of a vast underclass, peopled with exploited laborers who sank into deep poverty and even deeper into despair; and by century's end, the emerging power of the nation on the world's stage, defended by an American leadership that created theological linkages between American goodness and the will of God for the world. These social events all took church leaders by surprise. What's more, they could not agree regarding what the events meant. Josiah Strong's *Our Country* (1885) warned Christians of the dangers found in the cities, while Russell H. Conwell's sermon "Acres of Diamonds" (preached thousands of times across the transatlantic world in the 1880s) encouraged Christians to concentrate on the opportunities for Christian wealth.

Educational work that sought to prepare ministers had to take stock of these kinds of cultural developments. That was a bit hard to accomplish in Thorp Spring, Texas. To complicate matters further, these cultural changes were not the most important forces affecting educational and theological work in the United States. Near the end of the nineteenth century, an intellectual battleground emerged, pitting new understandings of science against traditional formulations of religion. Though this battle appeared in the midst of existing cultural divisions (North and South, East and West, black and white, rich and poor, Catholic and Protestant, citizen and immigrant), resulting schisms cut equally across all cultural boundaries. The facts long associated with the hard sciences gave way to new methodologies emphasizing human experience in philosophy, natural science, and the emerging social sciences. The new scientific mantra became "everything changes." As the implications of Charles Darwin's historic work, *Origin of the Species* (1859), were fully explored, theologians could not afford to ignore new scientific conversations. Some theologians railed against them, but others sought to adapt these scientific conversations to theological reflection. Would scientific understanding lead Christians to a better knowledge of matters dealing with both creation and God? What should Christians think of the new departments (psychology, sociology, anthropology, to name a few) increasingly playing central roles in the curriculum taught by the most respected American universities? After all, these departments applied science to every area of human life, including those that had been traditionally left to religion. By the end of the nineteenth century, scientific methodology in universities sought a scientific approach to the study of religion, giving birth to endeavors in comparative religion. Universities were openly questioning the superiority of Christianity itself. What would become of Christian faith?

New forms of liberalism in American Christianity naturally emerged in these years. More progressive theologians paid much more attention to religious experience, to God's immanence in the world, and to the pervasive presence of God in creation, and much less attention to doctrine and creed. By the time Brite Divinity School became separately incorporated in 1914, to preserve the purity of its teaching from the secularizing trends facing universities, including Texas Christian University, a new social gospel found expression in American religion. The new social-scientific approach to religion had begun to produce a revolutionary picture of Christ, whose life, theologians like Walter Rauschenbusch argued, contained profound implications for social and political endeavors. Many would-be faculty members in theological schools studied overseas and soaked up the new scientific approaches to Christ and to biblical materials that had developed by mid-century in Germany. By the late 1800s, the major university divinity schools, located at places like Yale University, the University of Chicago, and Harvard University, hired men (a sign of the times) who utilized scientific methodologies in their approaches to the Bible, theology, and the practice of ministry. These scholars taught doctoral students like Clinton Lockhart, Ellsworth Faris, and James Eskridge, each of whom, following completion of their degrees, arrived at TCU to teach aspiring Bible students in Texas.

TCU and Brite Divinity School, like every other institution of higher learning in the country, struggled with the issues these developments laid before them. In the early years, the two schools seemed disinclined to accept the challenges a new scientific understanding brought to theology and the gospel; over time, however, they seemed friendlier to these new ideas. The story of Brite Divinity School (and that of Texas Christian University's separate religion department once it made its appearance) is one ultimately (though not always consistently) defined not by taking the path of least resistance, but by following the one offering greatest educational benefit. Occasionally, that meant dealing with a good bit of resistance, whether from inside the university itself or from churches and communities outside of the university.

This book documents just how well Brite met, or alternatively how poorly it met, the various challenges facing the school during its history. Well over a century has passed since the founding of TCU (1873) and its early curricular emphasis on educating ministers (1877), and nearly a century has passed since Brite's incorporation (1914) as a distinct school for educating ministers. In its beginning, TCU and the College of the Bible (1895) sought to educate students in middle-class values, confident in an understanding of the nation that connected democracy to manifest destiny and each of these to American aims and purposes. Much of higher education in the United States in those years emphasized a particular kind of moral character. When TCU relocated to Fort Worth in 1911, under Clinton Lockhart's guidance, university students could not go to town without special permission. They were not allowed to smoke and could not own a vehicle. Chapel services were mandatory for all students. Education shaped individual moral character, which was largely defined by the presence of individual virtues and the absence of individual vices. Over the years, definitions attached to genuine moral character changed considerably.

By the mid-1950s, Brite led the way in breaking the color line, admitting black students in 1952, but it would be twelve years before TCU would follow suit (1964), and much longer before Brite hired its first full-time black faculty member (Darryl Trimiew, 1988). Though Brite students used their own lecture series to invite James Cone to campus in 1972, the school's administration did not engage a black adjunct faculty member until 1974. Though TCU, through the leadership of the Clarks, always admitted women, the College of the Bible, with its all-white male Disciples of Christ faculty, educated mostly white Disciples men for the ministry. Well into the 1970s, Brite's all-white male faculty encouraged women to head into missionary or social benevolence work rather than pulpit and preaching ministries. The first woman faculty member (Toni Craven) did not join Brite until 1980, and the first non-Disciples faculty members did not arrive until the late 1960s (Richard Hoehn and George Smith). The school seemed especially slow to respond to feminism and the movement for women's rights.

The Divinity School's faculty, in the early 1990s, finally welcomed increasing numbers of gays and lesbians, who prepared for ministry, many of them seeking ministerial credentials, in a variety of rather hostile denominational locations. Though discussions among faculty had sought changes in these directions throughout the 1980s, changes at Brite only formally occurred near the turn of the decade. In the early 1990s, gay students with partners were welcomed into Brite housing on the same basis as married heterosexual students, and, in time, Brite gained an increasing reputation as a hospitable location for lesbian, gay, bisexual, and transgender (LGBT) students seeking theological education. Brite also welcomed its first LGBT full-time faculty member (Stephen V. Sprinkle) during the 1990s.

In addition to its encounter with changing cultural mores, scientific and historical shifts in methodologies associated with education, and the challenges presented by an increasingly social understanding of the gospel, Brite needed to adjust its own life and work to the changing standards of educational accreditation. Therefore, part of this story uncovers the nature of the common efforts theological seminaries made to improve themselves. In the early years of the twentieth century, the quality of theological education was notoriously low. During the 1920s, for example, schools were "underfinanced, under enrolled, and poorly equipped."[2] Schools admitted students for their tuition, without much regard for previous educational work or their suitability for ministry. Standards defining excellence for theological schools were nonexistent. Most of them granted a Bachelor of Theology by combining two years of college work with three years focusing on theology. During the 1930s, the Conference of Theological Seminaries became the American Association of Theological Schools (AATS) and created an accrediting arm to improve the quality of seminary education; standards for theological education began to appear. Later, in light of the fact that the AATS also accreditated Canadian schools, the AATS became known simply as the Association of Theological Schools (ATS).

From the time of its first communication with the AATS in 1936, to the time of its initial accreditation in 1942 and well beyond, Brite has sought to meet these emerging standards. In some ways, the work of Clinton Lockhart, before the separate incorporation of 1914, had set the stage. As early as 1906, Lockhart had created the Bachelor of Divinity for the College of the Bible at TCU. He defined it as three full years beyond the Bachelor of Arts degree, one of the definitions incorporated into the new standards for accreditation in 1936. In intervening years, however, Brite compromised on this standard and adopted a practice of counting the senior year of college as the first year of seminary education. This approach resulted in a 3/3 program, three years undergraduate combined with three years of seminary, rather than a 4/3 program, a full undergraduate degree followed by three years of seminary study, which was encouraged by the AATS standards. Brite's move toward accreditation revived Lockhart's definition and brought a complete separation between faculty who taught students at Brite and those who taught undergraduate students, in effect creating a new push for a separate undergraduate department of religion at TCU.

Over the years, accreditation has continued to play an important role in the development of theological education, especially in shaping curriculum, areas of study, design of degree programs, and the quality of faculty. Improvements in standards led to automatic certification by the government of chaplains who received the master of divinity (MDiv) degree from accredited institutions. The 1942 accreditation of Brite led to a heavy emphasis on chaplaincy at the school during World War II. In fact, Brite's first black graduate, John Claiborne, graduated in 1955 and went straight into a military chaplaincy position.

Another aspect of Brite's story is wrapped up in the relationship between Brite Divinity School and Texas Christian University. In some respects, the standards of the ATS have been deeply connected to the act of defining this relationship over the years, not only during the 1930s, but in substantial ways during the 1990s. But the themes defining this relationship are wide-ranging and complex. The most important, of course, have always had to do with governance and finance.

In the 1870s, among Disciples of Christ, no clear line existed between founding a college and providing an education for ministers. The purpose of founding a college, in most Disciples circles, had something to do with preparing people for ministry. However, by the early twentieth century, the mission of most universities began to diverge from direct connections to the ministry. The earliest and most significant donor to the school, Texas rancher L.C. Brite, wanted to protect the education of ministers from the inevitable secular influence impinging on university contexts. Therefore, he saw to it that Brite became a separate institution in 1914, with its own board of trustees and in possession of its own legal incorporation.

Ever since, Brite and TCU have both struggled with what that reality means. The struggle no doubt related to personalities as much as to legal realities. In some ways, this is the story of faculties, deans, presidents, and chancellors and their struggle to define either the goals of theological education or the quality of a university and the role of religion within it. This struggle takes place in the midst of changes in both theological education and higher education in general, whether private or public. It involves the evolution of a school's identity through both the halcyon days (through the 1950s) and the cultural disestablishment and, as some would define it, the downright demise of mainstream Protestantism in the United States (from the 1960s). Ultimately, it involves the transformation of the institution itself: from one located in a rural outpost just outside of Waco, Texas, to one found in the heart of a major city and from an institution educating mostly white Disciples men for ministry to a school educating quite a diverse crop of women and men representing a variety of ethnic and international identifications, both gay and straight, for the ministry of at least thirty different denominations, and still others, including Christians, Jews, and other non-Christians, for vocations in social service agencies, academic contexts, and a variety of jobs involving public leadership.

In the spirit that best represents the Brite Divinity School I know from my nearly twenty-four years of association with it, this book is written by Brite students. When Newell Williams, President of Brite, asked me in early 2007 if I might be willing to teach a course on the history of Brite Divinity School with a view toward creating a history of the school out of the student work submitted for the course, I thought it was a wonderful idea. There is a strong history of interaction between faculty and students at Brite in the area of cooperative endeavors in theological research. Faculty members have consistently emphasized the qualitative nature of theological research and how it might be placed in the service of ministry. Faculty in all departments at Brite have helped students develop as scholars who are able to present creative and well-argued theses to a wider public through research and publication. Over the years, a good number of students enrolled in master's programs at Brite have published essays in refereed publications during their time in the Divinity School.

These essays, with the exception of the last one (and it was cowritten by a student), are entirely written by students. They grew out of two courses taught at Brite during the fall of 2007 and the spring of 2008. These students, and one other, Valerie Kuykendall-Rogers, who conducted research and writing that contributed to the book in a number of ways, have made this project possible. Jeffrey Williams, Associate Dean at Brite, agreed to co-teach the course with me during the second semester. He has also helped me to edit this volume. I am grateful for his willingness to contribute in these ways. In addition, I asked my long-time graduate research assistant, Dyan Dietz, to help us finish the editorial tasks associated with the book, a job that required work on her part beyond her two semesters of academic registration in the Brite history courses. Both Jeffrey Williams and I are grateful for her willingness to do so. Though many have contributed to the strength of this volume, they should not be blamed for any deficiencies associated with it; as lead editor on the project, those can deservedly be attributed to me.

Mark G. Toulouse
Principal and Professor of the History of Christianity
Emmanuel College of Victoria University in the University of Toronto

1

Before Brite: Ministerial Education at TCU, 1873–1914

LISA BARNETT

The history of Brite Divinity School began long before the school's separate incorporation in 1914 as the Brite College of the Bible. Brite's history is linked to the founding of Add-Ran College and the subsequent development and transformation of this educational endeavor into Add-Ran Christian University and then Texas Christian University. Founded as an institution dedicated to the cause of Christian education in Texas, Add-Ran emphasized "scholarly instruction and wholesome moral and religious influence."[1] From the beginning, the school made the education of ministers a primary aim.[2]

The school's commitment to nurturing Christian identity and educating ministers evolved in important ways through an integral relationship with Disciples of Christ. Associated both informally and formally with Disciples, Texas Christian University reflected developments and controversies taking place within the Stone-Campbell Movement generally.[3] By the end of the nineteenth century, wide differences of opinion between congregations existed concerning theology, denominational policy, and mission. Alongside cultural divides mostly falling along the old North/South axis in the states, the central issues revolved around the organization of missionary societies, the propriety of having instrumental music as a part of church worship services, and the introduction of modern biblical criticism in the educational institutions. These controversies produced factions in the church characterized as progressive (the members favoring a more liberal view) and conservative.[4]

This factionalizing of the movement also reflected important contemporary intellectual strains, particularly regarding biblical interpretation and the emergence of higher criticism. This new form of biblical criticism emphasized more than just trying to figure out the original wording of the text. Developed in Germany, higher criticism addressed the larger questions of background. Who was the author; when was the text written? What are the literary characteristics of the text? What sources were used in developing the text? How does the text reflect the context within which it was written? Higher criticism called into question traditional Christian assumptions about the Bible, challenging, for example, the historical reliability of the Gospels of Matthew, Mark, Luke, and John.

As M. Eugene Boring notes, Disciples enjoyed "the development and solidification of an indigenous Disciples tradition" in the second half of the nineteenth century, only to find that tradition strained in the late nineteenth and early twentieth centuries through "the encounter between the developing indigenous ecclesiastical tradition and the incursion of higher criticism from the academic world."[5]

Against the backdrop of these challenges within the church, Add-Ran College, which became Add-Ran Christian University and then later Texas Christian University, evolved in three distinct phases between its founding in 1873 and the incorporation of Brite College of the Bible in 1914. The first period, ranging from 1873 to about 1900, featured the efforts of Addison and Randolph Clark to establish a school within the understood Disciples tradition of the mid-nineteenth century. This effort, particularly as it related to assuring the centrality of the authority of the Bible, proved extremely successful.

The year 1902 ushered in a second phase in the school's engagement with broader social, ecclesiastical, and intellectual currents. The university's name changed again, this time to Texas Christian University, and for the first time since 1873, the institution had a president other than Addison Clark. The incursion of higher criticism from the academic world, though not embraced in the curriculum, began to surface.

The third period ran from 1906 to 1914. These years, pivotal in the transformation of the Bible College, tell the story of how the school encountered higher criticism in biblical scholarship and waged a battle over who defined Disciples tradition. Individuals at TCU possessed conflicting views about biblical scholarship, modernism, and liberalism. The scholarly approach to biblical studies and theological education that emerged at TCU around 1906 created suspicion among conservative Texas Disciples. Some within the university's leadership attempted to identify those sympathetic to the promotion of higher criticism, an effort that expanded into a cause to preserve a traditional and

Add-Ran College, Thorp Spring Campus (1873–1895).

conservative approach to Disciples biblical interpretation. The school, which depended heavily upon contributions from members of the church, became a battleground for defining conservative and liberal beliefs in an attempt to protect the Disciples tradition. The financial contributions of L.C. Brite, along with his stipulations and insistence upon protecting certain conservative teachings in the Bible College, not only established the Bible College as separate and distinct from the university, they helped confirm the early triumph of theological conservatism at the College of the Bible and TCU.

The Beginning: Add-Ran College

In September of 1873, Addison and Randolph Clark, along with their father, Joseph, opened Add-Ran College as a private college at Thorp Spring in Hood County, Texas.[6] The predecessor of this educational endeavor, the Clark Private School, began in Fort Worth in 1869.[7] The Clark brothers ensconced their private school and its successor Add-Ran College within the Disciples tradition of the mid-nineteenth century, in part through the influence of their father, Joseph. Randolph Clark wrote of his father's religious conviction in *Reminiscences*, published in 1919:

> At the time of his marriage [January 21, 1842], J.A. Clark had no sure religious convictions. . . . He was led to examine the Bible as

> a system of teaching. . . . He secured the best books of that time on Christian Evidence. . . . In the Old and in the New Testament he found a complete system of teaching, a perfect law designed to restore man's complete oneness with God, and to enlist man as a worker with God to recover the world from sin and its blighting effects.[8]

Joseph also instilled in his sons a firm commitment to education. Addison Clark spent time studying in an academy at Tennessee Colony in Anderson County, Texas, from 1857 until 1860.[9] After returning from service during the Civil War, he spent a short time teaching and then decided to pursue further education to support his career as a teacher.[10] In 1866, both Addison and Randolph went to study with Charles Carlton at his school in Kentucky Town, Texas. The first generation of Disciples influenced Carlton's educational background at Bethany College in West Virginia, where he immersed himself in the teachings of Alexander Campbell, the school's president. Carlton entered Bethany College in 1847 and finished three years' work in two, graduating with his BA degree on July 4, 1849.[11]

In September 1867, Carlton's school moved to Bonham and became a coeducational institution known as Bonham Seminary (chartered in 1881 as Carlton College). Addison and Randolph moved to Bonham with the school and, for a time, both studied and taught there.[12] The educational training they received as students under Charles Carlton influenced their careers as educators.[13]

In 1869, Addison moved to Fort Worth to teach at a school established by the local citizenry. Shortly after Addison arrived, the school lost its building. Recognizing the importance of the school Joseph Clark, Addison's father, purchased land on "the south end of Jones and Calhoun between Ninth and Fourteenth streets" for the school.[14] In Fort Worth, the Clarks hoped to educate young men and women as Christian citizens to rebuild a shattered nation following the Civil War. As individuals who "believed the gospel to be the fundamental power of God in the world," the Clarks saw this work as "an essential part of their great nation-building purpose."[15]

The Clarks envisioned Fort Worth playing a key role in the evolution of the nation. Talk of the new railroad, the Texas and Pacific Railway, coming to Fort Worth began in 1872. Already on the great cattle trail from Texas to Kansas, Fort Worth seemed to be the up and coming city of the Southwest. The town's growth, however, also attracted settlers inclined toward drinking, gambling, and other vices.[16] The Clarks began to wonder whether their hopes for Christian education might succeed in this environment:

> By 1873, [the Clarks] became alarmed at the non-stop pandemonium going on just to the west of the property: the twenty-four hour saloons, gunfire, loud music and whooping cowboys were too nearby. Such a neighborhood was no setting for the quiet life of scholarly pursuits that the Clarks were planning. The location might even discourage respectable families from enrolling their children in the school.[17]

With Addison on a preaching trip, Randolph and Joseph negotiated the relocation of the school to Thorp Spring, with plans to use the Fort Worth property as a means to assume the financial obligations related to the move. Randolph opened Add-Ran College in 1873 with thirteen pupils while Addison and Joseph remained at the school in Fort Worth for its final session.[18] A charter for Add-Ran Male and Female College went into effect on April 11, 1874, with the stated purpose of "the support and promotion of Literary and Scientific Education."[19] The Clarks also hoped "to make a strong academy, in which boys and girls would be taught how to study, would be given a purpose in life, and a foundation on which to build character."[20] These goals seemed to the Clarks best accomplished away from city centers so that "students would avoid worldly temptations," a model used at Bethany College and most of the later Disciples colleges.[21]

In addition to separating students from temptation, the Clarks implemented strict rules governing students' conduct and work ethic. Such behavior codes, as Conrad Cherry observes, "sought to take boys from farms and small towns and mold them into polite middle-class citizens."[22] This commitment to instilling and reinforcing middle-class values appeared in strong doses at Add-Ran College. In 1877, the school incorporated a "Conduct of Students" section into the catalog. The code contained a lengthy and comprehensive list of "nos": "No race course, theatre, circus, billiard-saloon, bar room, or tippling house; No intoxicating beverage; No use of tobacco in buildings of the college; No firearms, a dirk, a bowie knife, nor any other kind of deadly weapon; No profanity; No gaming; No card playing even for amusement."[23] The strict work ethic the Clarks saw as necessary for an education informed the following notice in the 1883 catalog concerning holidays: "We promise none. Parents and children must learn that school life is one of work. Parents will please not encourage nor expect their children to come home Christmas, nor any time till close of session."[24]

The Clarks' interest in developing moral character reflected a key component of the educational philosophy of Disciples. According to Lester G. McAllister, Alexander Campbell was "increasingly drawn to the thought of a college education that would seek to introduce the young to the very best of classical study combined with modern science, practical knowledge, and, at the pinnacle of learning, the development of moral character."[25] Campbell organized the course of study at Bethany College around several "schools": "the School of Sacred History and Moral Philosophy, the School of Ancient Languages, the School of Mathematics and Astronomy, the School of Natural, Intellectual, and Political Philosophy, and the School of Chemistry and Belles Lettres."[26] In a similar fashion, Add-Ran College divided the curriculum into six departments: Ancient Languages, which included Greek and Latin; English Language; Mathematics; Physical Science; Mental and Moral Science; and Social and Civil History,[27] the latter department changing its title in 1875 to the Department of Sacred and Civil History.[28]

Add-Ran College formed a relationship with the Christian Church (Disciples of Christ) from the beginning, though Addison resisted reflecting the relation in the name of the institution. Randolph Clark wrote of Addison's feelings on the matter:

> He would not consent to its being called a Christian college; if it became Christian it would be made so by Christian teachers and would be known by its fruit. He said to call the school Christian in contradistinction to other church schools in the state was to denominationalize the name.[29]

Still, Addison Clark's reluctance to use the title Christian did not mean a neglect of church affiliation. Four months after the school opened, the church body of Texas gave its endorsement to the school "as a College for the Christian Brotherhood of Texas."[30] Additionally, the original charter of 1874 stated "that no one shall be a trustee who is not a member in good standing of the Christian Church."[31] The catalog for 1876–1877 inserted a clear description of the school as "a Christian College."[32]

A specifically Christian education that instilled middle-class values was far from unique in the late nineteenth century, but Add-Ran College paved progressive ground among the Disciples in its practice of admitting both men and women. Bethany College did not admit women until 1877, three years after Add-Ran opened. Kentucky University waited until 1889, and the College of the Bible in Lexington waited until 1904.[33] Interestingly, the Clarks showed more interest in measuring their progressive spirit against other major universities than they did against the other Disciples schools, as reflected in this excerpt from the 1875–1876 catalog:

> The advantages of the coeducation of the sexes are just becoming seen and appreciated. "Mixed Schools" are rapidly increasing in favor among first-class educators and among the people. It is no longer the popular idea that females should be restricted in a literary education to a course of studies inferior to that allowed to males. Many of the first-class colleges have adopted coeducation . . . and Princeton, Harvard, and Yale are preparing to yield to the onward march of progress.[34]

In spite of their comparison to the more established universities in the East, Add-Ran College reflected what had become a Disciples approach to education when it came to curriculum that emphasized reason, experience, and careful thought. Early leaders among Disciples believed in both science and the scientific method, and "from the time of Campbell, Disciples prided themselves on their championing of the freedom to think and teach and their tolerance toward the view of others."[35]

Add-Ran College embraced these foundational principles, but the college's practices placed it firmly in the second generation of Disciples biblical scholarship. In this era, several key figures reinterpreted these traditional Disciples principles, and many of these individuals influenced the curriculum at Add-Ran College. The first published catalog listed the following courses of study for the Department of Mental and Moral Science: "Mental Philosophy, Moral Science, Logic, Milligan's *Reason and Revelation*, Milligan's *Scheme of Redemption*, the Bible: daily readings."[36] Addison Clark, president of the school and faculty-member in the Department of Ancient Languages and Mental Philosophy, taught these courses. Robert Milligan's *Analysis of the New Testament* appeared on the list of texts in 1884.[37] Milligan's works remained listed in the catalogs until 1899. J.W. McGarvey's *Evidences of Christianity* became a standard text beginning in 1886.[38] The curriculum and texts listed in the catalogs for Add-Ran College, however, did not contain any of the works of Alexander Campbell or any other figure of the first generation; rather, Add-Ran College embraced the scholarly work produced by the second generation of Disciples.

A critical event for what would later become the Brite Divinity School occurred in 1877. In that year, Add-Ran added the Bible Course under the leadership of Addison Clark, a fifth course of study that joined the Preparatory Course, the Teacher's Course, the Scientific Course, and the Classical Course. The 1877–1878 catalog described the new course:

> The Bible Course is intended for young men preparing to preach the Gospel. The study of the Bible will be a prominent feature of the exercises of this Course. Colleges do not make preachers, but only help them to make themselves.[39]

The curriculum for the Bible Course included, "Inspiration, Hermeneutics, Reason and Revelation, Latin, Greek, Hebrew, Metaphysics and Rhetoric, Homiletics in practice. A critical study of English may be substituted for Latin, Greek, and Hebrew."[40] The last line of this catalog entry supports Boring's conclusion that "the expectation of linguistic competence present in the First Generation of Disciples biblical scholarship had dwindled in the Second."[41] Nonetheless, a more scholarly and systematic approach to the study of the Bible became the norm for Add-Ran College, reflected clearly in the school's conferral of a degree upon completion of the Bible Course. Study for the Bible Course became a part of the School of Mental and Moral Science in 1888, with a more detailed course of study requiring four years to complete the degree.[42]

During the years of existence as Add-Ran College (1873–1889), Addison Clark assumed the primary teaching responsibilities for the Bible Course. His father Joseph assisted him as a lecturer on biblical literature. G.E. Carpenter, who taught Latin and Elocution from 1880 to 1884, became the first faculty member who possessed a college degree, an SB degree.[43] L.B. Miller, a member of the faculty from 1881 to 1884 as a teacher of Greek, was the first teacher with an AB degree.[44]

In its early years, the college grew in size and reputation throughout the state, but finances did not keep up with this growth. The school at Thorp Spring had just opened when the financial crash of September 1873 created a panic in the business world. The Clarks planned to pay for the school building with the sale of their Fort Worth property, but property values declined rapidly and many in Fort Worth faced bankruptcy. The accumulating interest on the debt for the Thorp Spring property began to mount.[45] The dilemma forced the

Clarks to abandon their plans to purchase the Thorp Spring property. Instead, they agreed "to pay rent at the rate of fifty dollars per month to the close of that session" in 1877.[46] This crisis initiated the first of many financial difficulties that plagued the school over the years to come.

Despite the school's mounting debt, Addison Clark announced that the school would remain open. Randolph Clark wrote about the events that transpired to keep the school open at Thorp Spring:

> A plot of 6½ acres was secured at a cost of $650. . . . The money for the first payment was obtained by the sale of Addison's home and my home in Fort Worth. . . . Another sale was of 320 acres of land belonging to my wife. This land is in Collin County, and the location tells its value, but not what was received for it. Another was wife's childhood home in Bonham, — improvement and five acres of land within two blocks of the courthouse square. . . . Temporary buildings were prepared for the beginning of the session of 1877–1878, and by the end of the first term the new building was ready.[47]

While surviving this financial crisis encouraged optimism, debts continued to accumulate and the financial strain increased. The Clarks believed the establishment of an endowment fund would solve their financial problems. They turned to the church with an offer to hand the college over to its control.[48]

A New Direction: Add-Ran Christian University

In 1889, Add-Ran College became the property of the Christian Churches of Texas, and a new charter changed the name to Add-Ran Christian University.[49] The first catalog for the new institution articulated the significance of the event for the church's commitment to education in Texas when it said, "The University is not so much the outgrowth of Add-Ran College as it is the development of a long felt desire among the Disciples in Texas to have an institution of higher Christian Education. . . ."[50]

The educational endeavor was clearly sectarian in its organization. A later catalog stated, "This is a University for and by the Disciples of Christ."[51] The new charter identified the purposes of the school and the connection to the Christian Church:

> This corporation is created for the following purposes . . . the

> establishment and maintenance of a Christian university, to be conducted for the advancement and education and devoted to the interests of the Christian Church, and it is being declared that the arts, sciences, languages, and Holy Scriptures shall always be taught in said institution of learning.[52]

The new charter also required that each trustee "be a member of the Christian Church in good standing."[53]

With the notable exception of the expansion of the board of trustees to thirteen members and a more clearly delineated financial system, few other changes immediately occurred.[54] Addison Clark continued as president of the university and head of the School of Mental and Moral Science. The curriculum remained the same.[55] However, significant changes began to appear in the 1890s. A master's degree offering came in the 1892–1893 school year.[56] This program of study expanded in the next two years with the addition of Dr. James W. Lowber as chancellor, a position created by the board of trustees in 1893.[57] Lowber "received AB and AM degrees in 1871 and 1874 from Butler College. In 1868, while a student, he was ordained a minister in the Disciples of Christ church. He received a PhD degree from Syracuse University in 1880."[58] The trustees hoped the chancellor would primarily travel to solicit donations for the endowment fund and recruit students, though they allowed Lowber to assume charge of the post-graduate course as well.[59] The *Christian Evangelist* noted the academic nature of this program in 1893: "No one can be a candidate for a post-graduate degree who is not already a college graduate. The post-graduate degrees require a two years course on the part of the graduate, and a thorough examination at the University."[60]

The university also began to address its structure for educating ministers, which since 1877 had assumed the form of a Bible Course. The 1892–1893 catalog contained a section with a plea for an endowment that could support a distinct Bible College within the university.[61] In 1895, the board instructed J.J. Jarvis, president of the board of trustees, and J.B. Sweeney to draft a charter for the Bible College.[62] The trustees adopted bylaws in September 1895.[63] The use of the term Bible College rather than seminary or divinity school followed Disciples tradition, which favored naming "their religious seminaries Bible Colleges."[64] The board elected J.B. Sweeney, who received his AM at Kentucky University, to serve as "President [later changed to Dean] of the Bible College of Add-Ran Christian University at a salary to be paid out of the endowment fund."[65] Sweeney unsuccessfully attempted to raise an endowment of

$50,000.[66] Although funds did not exist for an endowment for the Bible College, the university maintained the Bible College within the larger university, and the catalogs continued to list the College of the Bible as an integral part of the educational program of the university. The commitment to ministerial training now moved forward in a more distinct role within the university.

The most significant change for the university came in 1895 with the relocation to Waco. The board of trustees met on September 13, 1895, to consider this move. James I. Moore, a citizen of Waco, presented a proposal to induce the university to relocate. He read a report of the executive committee from the Christian Church at Waco to the trustees outlining the financial incentives to move the university. Moore proposed giving the university the building of the old Waco Female College, fifteen acres of land, and up to $5,000 in construction costs for new buildings.[67]

Papers from the Waco Commercial Club also indicated the Waco community's desire that the university relocate. According to the minutes of the 1895 meeting, "The Board was unanimous in accepting the proposition."[68] However, complications threatened the move when in November 1895, F.N. Calvin, the pastor of Central Christian Church in Waco, addressed the board of trustees concerning the need for modifications to the original proposal. Calvin admitted that the Waco churches lacked the funds to build the promised dormitories. Instead, he suggested that students rent local housing.[69] The board of trustees accepted the modified proposal, and the university began a new era in the city of Waco, also home to Baylor University.

Unfortunately, the move to Waco hardly solved the university's financial situation. In 1896, the cash-strapped university borrowed $2,500 from the endowment fund, which had supported the appointment of a Bible Chair within the university.[70] The university again turned to the Bible College for funds in 1898 when the trustees appointed J.B. Sweeney to "correspond with the subscribers to the Bible Chair Fund, asking them for authority to turn over said subscriptions and funds to the University to be used in liquidating existing indebtedness."[71] The catalog of 1898–1899 included a report of the board of trustees that identified $4,000 of Bible Chair money loaned to the university, "for which ten percent interest is paid for the furtherance of the Bible department."[72] In spite of the promise of the Christian Church to fund the university, the reality of doing so proved difficult.

With Add-Ran Christian University's move to Waco complete, the college officially opened its doors there in the 1896–1897 school year, with J.B. Sweeney serving as Dean and Professor of Sacred History, Literature, and Hebrew. Addison Clark taught philosophy and evidences and church history, and T. Louis Comparette, who possessed an AB degree from the University of Michigan, taught New Testament Greek and missions. The university required four years of course work for the AB degree with the junior and senior years devoted exclusively to work in the Bible College. Very true to Disciples tradition, the university made clear, "We do not confer nor encourage the title of BD or DD [bachelor of divinity or doctor of divinity]."[73]

The opening of the Bible College occurred during a transitional time as "Disciples began to emerge from their cultural isolation."[74] During this time, a third generation of Disciples appeared. This generation confronted changes within the academic curriculum at colleges and theological seminaries that reflected the societal upheavals brought about by industrialization and modernization. American culture trumpeted progress and civilization, and "universities were thought to be the chief instruments of both cultural progress and social reform, and their divinity schools the religious pacesetters for those educational tasks, . . . shaping the values, ideals, and aspirations of the American people."[75]

Although not yet a divinity school, the Bible College at Add-Ran Christian University aimed for the same role in service to its university. In identifying "What We Study" at the Bible College, the catalog referenced "the Bible from the standpoint of Christ as its center, the Bible's adaptation to the mind and conscience—psychology, moral science, and logic, and application of the word to practical life—good citizenship, sociology."[76] The addition of psychology and sociology brought the Bible College into the emerging ethos of theological education in America that emphasized practical and social Christianity. Glenn T. Miller notes, "Sociology was a new field of inquiry in late nineteenth-century America. For many Americans in this period, sociology was synonymous with social reform."[77] Historians Lester McAllister and William Tucker have observed just how important sociology became to the Disciples: "Young Disciples ministers were encouraged to study sociology, and the subject was a favorite on convention programs well into the new century. . . . By the first decade of the twentieth century this theology had permeated Disciples thinking."[78] The Bible College at Add-Ran Christian University also maintained the connection between curricula and social involvement by acknowledging the "many active churches from which we can learn as object lessons; and in this large city [Waco], many openings for mission work of all kinds, where we can apply good principles as we learn them, and do much good besides."[79]

As the Bible College and larger university adjusted to changes in the broader culture, both the college and university experienced critical changes in leadership that proved integral to their evolution. Dr. James Lowber, who had previously served as university chancellor, became the regent for the post-graduate department, and J.B. Sweeney assumed a very brief tenure as chancellor, in addition to his teaching and administrative work in the Bible College.[80] At the trustee meeting of March 14, 1899, the board instituted a new search for a chancellor and accepted Sweeney's resignation as dean of the Bible College. Symbolic of the transitions underway at the university, Addison Clark resigned as president, though he remained with the university as dean of the Bible College.[81]

The search for a new president for Add-Ran Christian University led to an interesting offer. Chalmers McPherson made a motion at the March 1899 meeting to instruct the secretary to send the following telegram to Clinton Lockhart, president of Christian University in Canton, Missouri: "Will you accept presidency of Add-Ran University, $1200 first year, what chairs can you fill?"[82] Lockhart elected instead to take a position teaching at Drake University.[83] His affiliation with Add-Ran would have to wait almost another decade.

Though the university lacked a president, the trustees named a new chancellor on March 15, 1899. Dr. Albert Buxton, who earned his doctorate at Harvard University, arrived to lead the university into the new century.[84] Buxton's appointment brought a change in the direction of studies at the university, especially for the College of the Bible. Curriculum revisions reflected a more scholarly approach to ministerial training than in previous years. The courses offered by the Bible College now included a theology sequence: Theology I, the philosophic basis of Christian faith; Theology II, the content of Christian faith; and Theology III, the history of Christian doctrine.[85] The use of the term "theology" signified the school's transition away from its earlier roots. According to James O. Duke, "The word 'theology' was rarely used in the early Movement except pejoratively and in reference to the speculative opinions of outsiders. This use was a social protest against the pretensions of theologians and theologies (especially Calvinism) of the day."[86]

Despite the advances in ministerial training, other issues consumed Buxton's time at the school. Before he arrived at the university, he sent a letter to the board of trustees expressing a hope that trustees would clarify the distinctions in responsibilities between chancellor and president, suggesting that the office of the president occupy a role "immediately between that of the Chancellor and the Deans."[87] Buxton viewed the chancellor position as administrative, especially with regard to enforcing rules and overseeing the general working atmosphere of the school, much of what the president of Add-Ran Christian University had been doing. This way of envisioning the chancellor's duties differed considerably from the original role of soliciting money for the school.

Buxton's attempt to clarify administrative roles highlights the difficulty Add-Ran Christian University had in moving from something of a family-owned-and-operated venture into an integrated pattern of organization in line with modern standards for higher education. The fact that the trustee minutes do not record any discussion of Buxton's suggestions indicates a clear unwillingness to change the school's administrative practices. When Buxton arrived at Add-Ran Christian University in 1899, the school was still without a president as the trustees delayed filling that position until they found a proper candidate. It is of little surprise, then, that Buxton sent a letter to the trustees in March 1900 saying, "I wish to place at your disposal my resignation from the double office I am now filling. Its duties are very heavy, and my heart longs for some church work."[88] The trustees made no effort to replace Buxton. Instead, discussion turned to the problem of finding a president. Elbert Snow, a professor of mathematics, became the acting president of Add-Ran Christian University in 1901.[89]

Buxton's resignation had a particularly strong effect on the College of the Bible, and his absence forced the college to alter its curriculum in ways that drew the school back from some of its recent advances. The experiment in a sequenced theology course became the most obvious casualty.[90] Any progress that the College of the Bible made in adapting to recent currents in theological education stalled. Change of a different kind came when Addison Clark resigned as dean in September 1900, and the trustees elected Frank Marshall to replace him.[91]

A New Era: Texas Christian University

The university's leadership struggles forced the board of trustees to realize the importance of not only having a president, but a particular kind of president. Glenn Miller explains the trend of the "strong presidency" emerging in the early twentieth century:

> The new president was, whatever else he might have been, a person able to convince others that his particular vision of the future was

> the one the church and its schools needed to follow. . . . In that intellectual world, it was easy for the faculty to allow the president of the school considerable power over the school's future direction. There were simply many more important things than directing an institution or recruiting new teachers. The presidents, who had a vision of how things fit together, were ready and able to take over the task.[92]

The trustees recognized that the time had come to fill the office in order to continue the university's progress. The trustees voted to call Ely V. Zollars as its next president "at a salary of $2500 per year, with the understanding that he . . . receive $500 additional, provided the revenues of the school justify" doing so.[93]

Zollars came as the school entered a new era. The name of the school changed to Texas Christian University to reflect "the greatly enlarged purposes and work of the school."[94] Hall writes, "The adoption of the new name, Texas Christian University, was, without doubt, a part of the consciousness of the new era. The new name intimated the institutional rather than the family characteristic of the school."[95] Zollars, a graduate of Bethany College who previously served as president of Hiram College, entered this more institutional and less familial context.[96] Zollars wrote of his vision for Christian education in a 1902 letter to the *Christian Courier*:

> Texas Christian University will find the foundation of her strength and the source of her prosperity in the service she renders to the church of Christ. Her education must be pre-eminently Christian. . . . Her mission is to send out Christian young men and wom en to perform their part, in a strong way, in the business and professional world, and especially to educate and train a strong body of young men for the Christian ministry.[97]

Like many of his day, Zollars believed that the aims of Christian education intersected with the development of "the American nation, and eventually the world, in the light of a religious understanding of democracy."[98] As Conrad Cherry has documented so clearly, the promotion of an Anglo-Saxon Protestant establishment accompanied the rise of modern American universities and the development of Protestant university divinity schools in such a way that Christianity and western civilization seemed indistinguishable.[99] In his inaugural address, Zollars expressed this theme:

> What education should do for the individual? It should make him realize he is the thing the Lord God made and gave to have dominion over land and sea. He is the lord of all other animals. . . . The difference between savage and civilized nations is the difference in education. It may be truthfully said that Christianity is the highest and most beneficial form of civilization. But does not Christianity embody the highest form of education? To say Christianity is the mother of modern civilization is but another way of saying it is the parent of modern education. Christian education is the palladium of our national greatness. The true worth of a nation lets in the amount and kind of knowledge it possesses.[100]

The College of the Bible changed in important ways during Zollars's presidency. Biblical criticism's impact on the academic world and on the Disciples was clear.[101] When Zollars began his service at Texas Christian University, he also taught in the College of the Bible. In fact, the only faculty members listed in the catalog were Zollars and Dr. Frank Marshall.[102] Together they added several classes that solidified the College's conservative response to modernist thought. Zollars taught a class on higher criticism, the purpose of which was "to acquaint the student with the various phases of higher criticism, to point out the reliable results so far attained, and to fortify him against the fallacies and unreliable canons of criticism employed by the destructive school." Zollars also taught a course called the Divinity of Christ, which he described as "the great central doctrine of the Christian religion, and doubt on this point is an absolutely fatal weakness in the minister of the Gospel. It is the aim of this study to present the arguments for the Divinity of Christ in the fullest way."

Zollars introduced a class called First Principles, claiming, "The converging lines of preparation for the coming of Christ are traced, and the superiority of the Christian Dispensation is shown." Marshall taught a class titled Mission Fields, which examined "the various heathen religions, and study of the fields."[103] Then, in 1904, Zollars added a class called Credibility and Inspiration "to set forth the grounds on which the credibility of the Scriptures rests and to establish the claim for inspiration put forth by the Scriptures themselves and held by all evangelical Christians." True to the course title, Zollars chose J.W. McGarvey's *Credibility and Inspiration* as the textbook for the class.[104] More curriculum changes came in 1905 with the revision to the longstanding Christian Evidences course. Citing "the onslaughts upon Christianity by its enemies," the 1905 catalog included a lengthy defense of the importance of the course for the curriculum:

> The inspiration of the scriptures, the divinity of Christ, and consequently, the divine character of the Christian system are being assailed today as fiercely as they have at any previous period. It behooves the Christian man to examine the foundations of his faith and to be able to give a reason for the hope that is within him. Students educated in a Christian College should certainly be rooted and grounded in Christian Evidences that they may go forth to their work panoplied for the inevitable conflict. The aim of this study is to present the leading arguments that have been relied upon to defend the citadel of Christian faith.[105]

Interestingly, the class in New Testament theology used *The Christian System* by Alexander Campbell as its primary textbook.[106] This was the first time since the school began in 1873 that a catalog listed any of Campbell's works or the works of any other key figure of the first generation Disciples.

With these curriculum changes came an intentional focus on training greater numbers of ministers. An entry in the yearbook for the College of the Bible argued, "The great problem is that of ministerial supply and the rapidly multiplying churches will look more and more to the College for their preachers."[107] To help meet these challenges, in 1904 the university formed a ministerial association for student preachers and those preparing to be preachers. The association organized a bureau of ministerial supply to help secure resident work for students and serve "as a medium between the churchless collegian and the unshepherded church."[108]

If the training of theologically conservative pastors dominated Zollars work in the College of the Bible, his work on behalf of the university as a whole focused on the modernization of the campus environment. One of his first moves "was to improve the sanitary provisions of the plant and tone up the buildings in several ways." He also initiated plans to build a gymnasium as well as other building projects. By 1904, "$40,000 had been spent on plant improvement."[109]

In spite of the progress and modernization Zollars brought to the campus physical plant (or perhaps because of it), he found himself embroiled in controversy during the session of 1904–1905. A rift eventually emerged between Zollars and the faculty over discrepancies in salaries,[110] and another erupted between Zollars and the trustees over Zollars's management of the school's fiscal resources. According to Zollars's biographer Ronald E. Osborn, "The board now requested that the University be operated under a budget, with all income going into the regular treasury and with specific authorization for expenditures." Zollars refused to comply with the new policy and resigned in June 1906.[111]

Zollars' resignation opened the door for Dr. Clinton Lockhart, who had already accepted the trustees' offer to come to Texas Christian University as dean of the College of the Bible. Shortly after Zollars resigned, the trustees appointed Lockhart acting president of the university in addition to his role as dean of the Bible College.[112] While Zollars's presidency committed itself to the modernization of the campus and the preservation of conservative teachings in the Bible College, Lockhart's presidency committed itself to the modernization of the curriculum, especially in the College of the Bible. Boring notes the significant backdrop for Lockhart's presidency:

> It is at this point in Disciples history that the divergence was beginning to develop between the churchly tradition developed within the Disciples' own schools, which were extensions of the church and propaganda centers for the inculcation of Disciples tradition, and the major universities where a nonchurchly academic tradition of biblical interpretation was beginning to develop.[113]

Much like Addison Clark's background helped establish the school within the Disciples tradition of the nineteenth century, Clinton Lockhart's background helped place the school in the Disciples tradition of the early twentieth century. Lockhart entered the College of the Bible at Lexington, Kentucky, in 1878, studying under J.W. McGarvey, Isaac Grubbs, and Charles Louis Loos.[114] He concurrently enrolled in Kentucky University, where he completed much of his work in absentia while he served as pastor for various churches.[115] He graduated from the College of the Bible in Lexington in 1885 with a certificate of completion, and in the spring of 1886, he received his AB degree from Kentucky University. He continued studying at the university and "completed all except one course in mathematics for the master's degree by the time he started to Yale in September of 1887," where he received his AM degree in 1888.[116] From 1890 to 1893, he continued his education at Yale University, where he studied under William Rainey Harper, professor of Semitic languages, who later became the first president of the University of Chicago.

William Rainey Harper's brother, Robert Harper, professor of geology and archaeology, influenced Lockhart most profoundly. Lockhart's interest in languages, stimulated by Robert Harper's work in the Far East, provided the basis for an appreciation of contemporary approaches to the study of the Bible. Before earning his PhD, Clinton Lockhart went to Ann Arbor, Michigan, in the fall of 1893 to fill a Bible Chair at the University of Michigan.[117] Here Lockhart struck up a friendship with the "prominent liberal" Herbert L. Willett, who taught in the Bible department.[118] When Lockhart's work ended at Ann Arbor, he returned to Yale and finished his PhD in 1894. From 1894–1895, he served as president of Columbia College, and in 1895, he accepted the presidency of Christian University in Canton, Missouri. After five years, he resigned to take the chair of Biblical Language and Literature at Drake University in Des Moines, Iowa, where he remained until 1905.[119] Lockhart's sympathies toward modern biblical criticism appear clearly in his role as an original member, along with Herbert Willett and Edward Scribner Ames, of the Campbell Institute, a group established in 1896 "to reconcile academic and religious values and loyalties. Through its meetings and its journal, the Institute expressed support for the social gospel, biblical criticism, and Christian unity."[120] Lockhart's research interests and circle of friends brought him into the broad world of higher education, a world he brought to Texas Christian University in the form of teaching and policies.

Lockhart immediately moved into the role of a strong president by introducing significant policy changes. He instituted a raise in teachers' salaries and annual increases after each year's service. He also transferred responsibility for addressing student discipline cases from the office of the president to a committee, feeling that "the President's duties should be executive, and that the dignity of the office was above dealing with unruly students."[121] Lockhart saved his most important changes for the College of the Bible. The catalog entry during his first year as president reflected his approach to the relationship between the academy and the church:

> The advancing requirement in the education of preachers to keep pace with popular scholarship has called for a curriculum quite the

> equal of any among the Disciples. This demand has resulted in a complete reorganization of the Bible College. The election of three new professors and the use of three very prominent members of the former faculty have made it possible to offer as complete a course of study as that in the standard Biblical seminaries, and in some respects more thorough than any other in the Christian brotherhood. . . . The new course of study leads to the degree Bachelor of Divinity, which, since it requires three full years above the Bachelor of Arts, and two years more than the Master of Arts, registers a high grade of scholarship. . . . The aim is to prepare the student for an honorable place among the religious thinkers of his time, and to lead in the chief activities of the church.[122]

Lockhart's initiation of the bachelor of divinity degree represented a new educational advancement for Disciples colleges. The College of the Bible at Lexington did not offer the degree until 1914.[123] Bethany College delayed implementing the degree at their newly established School of Religion until 1917.[124]

The faculty for the College of the Bible at Texas Christian University expanded to six professors, including Dr. Lockhart, and two others who had studied at the University of Chicago, Ellsworth Faris and Dr. James Eskridge.[125] The college also employed Miss Olive Leaman McClintic as professor of public reading and speaking in the College of the Bible.[126] Miss Mary Clyde Reeves later assumed this position in 1907.[127] Subtle changes in the yearbook descriptions of the College of the Bible indicate the advancements Lockhart sought, a direction he located within the heart of the Disciples tradition:

> The church under whose auspices this University is conducted, is at the very front in its appreciation of an educated ministry, and provides liberally for the accomplishment of this worthy purpose. . . . The spirit of the institution is free and scholarly, while it is candid and faithful. The faculty hold it as a privilege to lay under tribute the best scholarship of the age, and at the same time to reserve the right of calling in question every theory that is inconsistent with a devout faith and with the evident facts of history and science.[128]

Texas Christian University seemed, at least for a time, to flourish un-

Waco campus, post fire (1910).

der Lockhart's leadership. The enrollment increased over 65 percent, and the debt, which had been over $60,000 when he came in 1906, had decreased nearly 50 percent by 1910.[129] Unfortunately, catastrophe came on March 22, 1910, when a fire destroyed the university's main building. The insurance money was not enough to pay the debts against the property. Several cities offered to help by relocating the university. The trustees selected the offer from Fort Worth. Hall notes the extent of this financial arrangement:

> The contract with Fort Worth provided for a campus of fifty acres, $200,000 in money with assurance of connections with city utilities and streetcar. The "money" was to come from two sources. One hundred thousand dollars was to be raised by the Board of Trade and the Christian Churches of Fort Worth by July 1, 1910. The net realization of this effort was $75,000. The other $100,000 was to come, and did come, from the sale of lots through the Fairmount Land Company.[130]

The relocation required several temporary facilities while the new campus underwent construction. The university leased the "Ingram Flats" at $5,000 for the year. These two-story buildings were at the corner of Weatherford and

Goode Hall (first Brite residence hall).

Commerce streets near the county courthouse. The "Commerce Street building contained class rooms, chapel, music rooms on the first floor, and boys' rooms on the second. The Weatherford Street side housed the offices, print shop, dining room, and Business College on the ground floor and girls' rooms on the second. On nearby streets were homes for teachers, one additional home for girls and several for boys."[131] The university opened its new campus in the fall of 1911.[132] Dr. G.A. Lewellen raised $28,000 to build Goode Hall, a dormitory to house ministerial students that opened that spring.[133]

The crises at Texas Christian University occasioned by the fire worsened as Clinton Lockhart and Professor Ellsworth Faris fell under attack from those who possessed a more conservative view of biblical interpretation. As we have already seen, the issue of higher criticism had already made its way into American religious culture and Texas Christian University.[134] Historian Conrad Cherry explains some of the resistance from the church:

> Both the scientist and the biblical critic were portrayed as holding, in effect, that religious truth belonged to the domain of the highly educated expert. . . . Protestant laypeople . . . were inclined to defy any specialist who insisted that higher learning was a precondition to a proper understanding of the Bible, of God's creation, and of other things religious. Democratic folk have not been predisposed to turn their sacred worldview over to the

educated elite.[135]

This assessment certainly fit within the Disciples tradition of biblical interpretation of the nineteenth century. The new biblical studies flourished within leading schools such as Yale University, Harvard University, Union Theological Seminary, and the University of Chicago, the same schools where many Disciples ministers were beginning to receive advanced degrees.[136] Heresy trials soon followed at several schools, including Andover Theological Seminary, Boston University, and Union Theological Seminary.[137] Though Disciples educational institutions had not yet encountered this, many prominent figures, such as John W. McGarvey, vocalized their opinions against the new biblical studies and lashed out at those who supported this work. Texas Disciples had already taken a stand on the issue in 1898 at the seventh annual session of the Texas Christian Lectureship series when they voted unanimously to support a resolution to "recognize the work of Brother J.W. McGarvey on Biblical criticism in defense of our Bible against a class of distinctive critics."[138]

In spite of this resolution, some Texas Disciples voiced support for higher criticism. In 1902, before becoming a member of the faculty at TCU and the College of the Bible, Ellsworth Faris wrote an article for the *Christian Courier* titled, "Is Higher Criticism Infidelity?" in an attempt to respond to McGarvey's writings in the *Christian Standard*:

> It is allowable to criticize the books, that is study them to learn more about them. . . . The questions of criticism are purely intellectual questions. They do not affect the essential truths of my religion. . . . I had often been told and had often read that the foundations of faith were being destroyed by the critics. But they can't destroy them. We are not saved by believing on Moses, Jonah, and Paul or by believing any facts about the date or authorship of any book.[139]

McGarvey said of Faris's work, "Though evidently intended to be impartial, it has the bearing of an apology for criticism of the injurious kind." Faris's article espoused a view of christocentric liberalism and although he made an appeal to the intellectual tradition of the first generation Disciples like Alexander Campbell, McGarvey labeled Faris a "higher critic."[140]

The conflict at TCU during Lockhart's administration initially began over a paper Dr. H.G. Fleming (a medical doctor) read at a meeting of preachers held in Dallas in the spring of 1908.[141] Fleming complained in an editorial in the *Christian Standard* that "not one of the TCU professors spoke a word of approval" and that Lockhart criticized the paper as "a very extreme view of the conservative."[142] Chalmers McPherson, who came to TCU in 1907 as the endowment secretary, responded with a letter defending President Lockhart saying, "The article left the impression that Dr. Clinton Lockhart was one who was possibly a dangerous heretic as pertaining to Bible teachings. As a friend to Dr. Fleming, a strong admirer of Dr. Lockhart and a firm believer in his loyalty to Christ and the Bible . . . I was very much pained to see the publication."[143]

While McPherson defended Lockhart publicly, he did not make similar attempts on behalf of any of the other professors mentioned in the article, including Ellsworth Faris. The Fleming matter did get a response from Faris's father, G.A. Faris. In November of 1908, the elder Faris sent a letter to Chalmers McPherson suggesting that McPherson played a role in inciting the attacks:

> You no doubt remember the very strenuous effort on the part of Dr. Fleming to injure Ellsworth and myself last summer a year ago. . . . I was aware at the time that M.M. Davis, A.P. Terrell, and yourself were giving him encouragement. . . . It seems he read your letters and commented on them to every family in Forney, which is connected with our church, and with some who are not, and that he arrayed you against me with all the power he could command.[144]

The controversy deepened in 1909 during the Texas Christian Lectureship hosted by Texas Christian University. Lockhart gave a series of lectures in which he questioned the Davidic authorship of several Psalms and "emphasized the necessity of remembering that the psalms are poetry and not history, and that they should be read and studied with this thought in mind."[145] The discussion that ensued over the next several months prompted Lockhart to write a letter to the *Christian Standard* defending the soundness of his theology: "I speak freely regarding known facts and their bearing on Old Testament problems, as every man is entitled to do; but I do not use or even know any facts inconsistent with loyalty to faith."[146] Chalmers McPherson again defended Lockhart and the university in an article in the *Christian Standard* by arguing that higher criticism, or at least its "destructive" elements, did not exist at TCU.[147]

While McPherson did his best to defend the school publicly, he found the issue hampering his ability to raise money. Both Chalmers McPherson and G.A. Lewellen had been corresponding with L.C. Brite, a rancher from Marfa, about donating money to the school. The issue of higher criticism emerged as a barrier between the school and Brite's money. The rancher spelled out, rather bluntly, his concerns in a letter to McPherson in 1909. Claiming that a "degree of polite infidelity commonly known as 'higher criticism' has crept into and manifested itself in some of the faculty of the institution," Brite told McPherson he was "no longer proud" of the school, but had, in fact, become "suspicious" of the faculty:

> It is useless to deny that Ellsworth Faris belongs to this "cism" and the fact that the Board in control quietly allows Faris to hold a position there seems to indicate that they are either in sympathy with the faith (or lack of faith) or that they are grossly negligent of their duty. I cannot tolerate this so-called "higher criticism." To my mind, there is no middle ground for the Bible—that it is either the greatest burning truth ever published, else it is the vilest lie, and I desire that whatever contribution I may be able to make shall be given to foster Christianity rather than infidelity. I prefer to support those who believe Moses and the prophets rather than to cast pearl before swine. And whenever your Board sees fit to go over the faculty from head to heel, from tip to toe, and promptly dismiss all such as are tainted with infidelity and declare themselves to hereafter defend the institution against such, then, God helping me, you can put me down for $500 per annum, for the support of the institution. But until this is done, it is useless for you to waste stamps in writing, or car fare in coming to interview me.[148]

Brite's use of the term "infidelity" is particularly important for the way the term departed from the historic Disciples tradition that "prohibited the labels 'orthodox' and 'heretical' from being widely used." At the same time, the term "infidel" gained prominence among some third generation Disciples like J.W. McGarvey, who readily used the term against his opponents.[149]

Brite's mention of Ellsworth Faris in his letter prompted a series of correspondence over the next two months between Faris and Chalmers McPherson. In the first letter of the series McPherson requested Faris respond to several questions about his beliefs and teachings. "I am sure," he wrote, "you will be glad to answer these questions:"

> What is your belief and what do you teach concerning the following points? 1. Moses as a Lawgiver, inspired by the Lord. 2. The reliability of the records of the Pentateuch which purport to be historical. 3. The messages and inspiration of those men of the Old Testament periods who claimed to give to men the Word of the Lord, as prophets of God. 4. The virgin birth of Jesus. 5. The divinity of Jesus of Nazareth. 6. Whether or not the teachings of Jesus Christ, as given to us in the New Testament, are the ultimate authority for the Church of Christ and for the Disciples of Christ. 7. The resurrection of the body of Jesus of Nazareth from the grave. 8. The teachings published by that class of men usually designated as "destructive critics." These questions are asked only that I may give to those who inquire of me, authoritative replies.[150]

Faris replied and answered all eight questions.[151] McPherson wrote again to let Faris know he planned to send copies of the questions and answers to the *Christian Courier*, the *Christian Standard*, and the *Christian Evangelist* for publication, as well as to L.C. Brite. McPherson had a concern about one of Faris's responses in which he suggested that not everything in the Bible should be taken as history.[152] McPherson went so far as to suggest that Faris change his answer, but he refused.[153] When the eight questions and responses appeared in the *Christian Courier*, which was edited and published by G.A. Faris on December 9, 1909, an editorial comment critical of McPherson accompanied them. This raised concerns among the trustees and prompted Chalmers McPherson to send another letter to Faris with a list of twenty-one questions to answer.[154] Ellsworth Faris refused.[155] Chalmers McPherson also wrote a letter to the *Christian Courier* requesting that the elder Faris "retract what has been said in as public a way as it was published."[156] G.A. Faris answered back with a scathing chastisement of McPherson's actions as they related to his position as endowment secretary at TCU. His five-page letter also suggested ulterior motives for McPherson's actions against Ellsworth. "You were employed to raise money," he told him, "not to take the place of the board of trustees." He also told McPherson that he should have "sent copies of the Brite letter to the different members of the board."[157]

> At the end of your first ten months there was a meeting of the trustees to whom you made your report. . . . Your report showed that it took a fraction less than 60 percent of all the money you raised to pay your salary and expenses. This was a most discouraging showing, so much so it was never given to the public. . . . During the next ten months your success was not even so good, for you failed to get enough money to pay your own salary and expenses, and wrote to the treasurer for money, though it was explicitly stated at the very beginning that there should be no draft on the school for your work. . . . Not until you got the Brite letter, did you say a word, and even then, you did not follow your instructions to turn such matters over to the board for their action, but at once commissioned yourself to act.[158]

In addition to the problems associated with Faris and his work, Clinton Lockhart delivered a sermon and lecture dealing with the book of Jonah at First Baptist Church, Dallas, in the fall of 1910 that drew the attention of the *Dallas Morning News* in an article entitled "Lockhart Criticizes Present Bible Study." Lockhart called for "better methods of study, more scientific, literary, and sensible." Baptist sources would not let this go, and other newspaper articles soon appeared. The next month, Tarrant County Baptist workers passed a resolution in response to Lockhart that affirmed their faith "in the Bible as a book wholly inspired." A few weeks later, Dr. B.H. Carroll of Southwestern Baptist Theological Seminary spoke at First Baptist and publicly attacked Lockhart and his approach to the book of Jonah. "The preacher or professor," he said, "who does not believe in the full inspiration of the Bible should resign his position at once and get over with his own crowd. It is a crime for a so-called Christian school to attack the inspiration of the Scriptures."[159] The public nature of these debates made many at TCU a bit uncomfortable.

Perhaps all this controversy had an adverse effect on many of the trustees' opinions of Lockhart's ability to govern the school, for when Lockhart asked for a leave of absence to take a year and travel abroad with his wife, the trustees refused.[160] In response, Lockhart resigned as president.[161] The resignation from the presidency came less than one month after the last article appeared in the *Dallas Morning News*. The trustees also granted Ellsworth Faris a year's leave of absence.[162] Faris would not return to TCU, electing instead to take a position teaching at the University of Chicago. Lockhart ultimately returned to teach in the College of the Bible.

Lockhart's resignation and Faris's departure not only opened questions about who might fill their roles, but they also did little to allay concerns that modernism had infiltrated TCU. Trustee J.J. Hart corresponded with Colby Hall, who served as a field worker for the school, to persuade Hall to consider obtaining more theological education in order to become dean of the College of the Bible.[163] Hall declined to pursue this option but recommended Dr. G.A. Lewellen for the position.[164] At the same time trustee J.C. Mason sent a circular letter to individuals across the state asking whether the trustees should appoint Chalmers McPherson as chair of the English Bible and Homiletics.[165] Over a dozen letters of approval came back. Some of the responses indicated the tensions Disciples felt in relation to biblical scholarship, particularly as it played out during Lockhart's tenure at the university. In his support of Chalmers McPherson, for instance, Homer Magee wrote, "One thing is certain, no one has ever had to guess as to his [McPherson's] attitude on the question of destructive criticism."[166] J.S. Stockard said, "We need just *this* man [McPherson] in this place [the Bible College] to bring our Bible department to where our brethren cannot question the methods of Bible teaching in our TCU."[167]

Several letters echoed these sentiments of shaken confidence in the institution because of the controversy surrounding higher criticism. Many advocated a return to a more conservative approach to biblical interpretation. One person, Colby Hall, did raise concerns about Chalmers McPherson teaching at the university. In a letter to TCU trustee T.E. Tomlinson, who was also Halls's father-in-law, Hall wrote, "I will express my frank opinion that he is not suited for a teacher. I mean his character of mentality, and his habits of thought, as well as his lack of school preparation tend to weaken him as a teacher. . . . His becoming a teacher would be disappointing both to himself and the school."[168] When the trustees officially met, they took no action concerning the creation of this position or the appointment of Chalmers McPherson to the faculty, yet the impetus for allowing pastors and lay members of the church to have a voice in faculty selection had begun.

When Texas Christian University opened for the 1911–1912 year, Dr. G.A. Lewellen became dean of the College of the Bible. The catalog now advertised the College of the Bible differently than it had during Lockhart's administration, retreating from the scholarly emphasis Lockhart had placed on ministerial education:

> This College therefore invites worthy people to prepare for worthy tasks in life, and seeks to kindle an unquenchable desire for useful-

> ness in a world that sorely needs the best endeavor of Christian manhood and womanhood. It further seeks to enthrone the Christ in faithful hearts, to adorn the gifts of mind with the graces of culture, to awaken as the deepest longing of the soul, a yearning to lead other souls into the light of truth, and to help in humble measure to attune the thought of the time to the thought of the timeless Teacher of men.[169]

The trustees also initiated the search process for a new president. The fact that some Texas Disciples expressed a lack of confidence in the leadership at Texas Christian University brought added attention to the search. A letter to Trustee Tomlinson expressed the concern: "I believe the resignation of Dr. Lockhart will restore faith in the unbelieving, and I trust the man who has been or may be secured will be a man in whom the brotherhood may have the fullest confidence and faith."[170] Another letter to the board of trustees offered the following advice: "Please allow me to suggest, modestly, that in selecting someone to preside over Texas Christian University do not 'go up North' to find the man."[171] Once again, some controversy involving Chalmers McPherson surfaced. In a letter to the trustee president, T.E. Tomlinson, concerning the search process, G.A. Faris raised concerns about McPherson's meddling in the work of the search committee. Even though Faris served on the search committee, McPherson, who was not on the committee, took charge of tasks, along with "a group of four or five to do the work."

> The board of Trustees as a whole are charged with the management of the school, but at present this has to be done by proxy. I feel indignant that the board should be subjected to the pettifogging tricks of men writing all over the country asking other men to write letters to the board in order to bring pressure to bear to accomplish certain things, when these same men have not shown the board the courtesy to come before them and make their requests known. We will have to change some of our methods if we expect to make progress.[172]

Chalmers McPherson acknowledged the validity of Faris's claims later in an article sent to the *Christian Courier*. He wrote, "At the request of three of the four members of the committee—brethren [C.W.] Gibson, [T.E.] Tomlinson, and [Dr. Bacon] Saunders—I undertook the work of a 'still hunt' for a President. . . . A most diligent search was quietly made for the proper man."[173] A record of "Statements of Brethren Concerning Possible Material" that McPherson had put together from the letter-writing campaign showed he sought input about potential candidates primarily from J.W. McGarvey, I.N. McCash, and Russell Errett, who commented on candidates' leadership abilities and proclivities toward biblical criticism.[174]

After Vernon Stauffer rejected the university's offer in order to continue his education at Columbia University and Union Theological Seminary, the trustees called Frederick Kershner of Milligan College as the next president of Texas Christian University.[175] Kershner graduated from Transylvania University in 1899, having taken the course of study in the school's College of the Bible. He entered Princeton University, receiving a master of arts degree besides completing most of the work of the doctorate of philosophy.[176] The *Christian Standard* offered the following congratulatory comment: "The brethren of Texas can rest assured that in their new representative they have a man sound in the faith, thoroughly trained, and absolutely devoted to his calling. We predict that . . . he will be as true to them as he is to the Bible, and to his own ideas of a teaching ministry."[177]

In November of 1911, Kershner sent an open letter to the *Christian Courier* outlining his plans for the educational atmosphere at Texas Christian University:

> Texas Christian University will stand very definitely for three things: First. It will stand squarely, unhesitatingly and unequivocally upon the Bible as the Word of God, and upon Jesus Christ as our Divine Lord and Savior. Second. It will strive toward the highest educational ideals, the most thorough and broad intellectual culture, and the most exacting standards of scholarship. Third. The business affairs of the University will be conducted on such a basis as will invite the most careful scrutiny, both of the churches and of the general public.[178]

With a renewed confidence in the conservative theological direction of the university under Kershner's leadership, the Texas Disciples responded, especially L.C. Brite. At the trustees meeting held October 26, 1911, the trustees voted to accept the "L.C. Brite contract for endowment of the English Bible Chair of Texas Christian University . . . on the terms stipulated in the contract . . . and the proceeds and interest of $25,000 in promissory notes be hereby accepted for investment according to direction of said donor."[179] The terms of the gift are particularly important for gauging the theological direction of the College of the Bible:

> That said Chair shall never be knowingly permitted by said donee corporation or its managing board of whatsoever name designated or to be designated, to be occupied by anyone as teacher or lecturer in said Chair who denies (or refuses or omits or declines to profess and as an occupant of said Chair to teach in a literal sense and meaning) the supernatural birth of Jesus, His Divinity or His actual resurrection (on the third day after His death, according to the mode of computation of time by the ancient Hebrews; counting the day of the death and the day of the resurrection).[180]

L.C. Brite wanted to insure that a conservative biblical interpretation would be a part of the ministerial education at the College of the Bible and took his stand against higher criticism with his money.[181] The terms associated with Brite's gift raised significant concerns from some. G.A. Faris sent a letter to Trustee President Tomlinson expressing his fears about the conditions attached to this money:

> [L.C.] Brite makes it impossible for the University to be free to teach the truth. . . . He knows cows, but he lacks lots of knowing how to run a Bible college. We need money, and I am anxious to see the Bible chair endowed, but I am not willing to subscribe to a falsehood, nor to sell out freedom to get it. . . . I am not afraid that infidelity will creep into our school, for the tendency of the times shows that materialism is on the wane, and the faith in Christ's divinity grows stronger than ever as the days go by. . . . There is no wisdom in placing men of decided limitations in a position of such power, or allowing them to make their dollars say what is and what is not Christian. . . . Knowledge has not reached its final goal, and to put hobbles on investigation is but to delay the day of its triumph. . . . If we now reverse this and make hard and fast rules of interpretation, forbidding inquiry, we put clogs on the wheels of progress . . . and do the cause of truth and God incalculable harm.[182]

Brite College of the Bible students and faculty (1914).

As Faris feared, changes to the curriculum followed Brite's gift. The faculty members and their teaching areas reflected an emphasis on practical ministry and moral formation rather than scholarly academic work. The yearbook for 1913–1914 noted, "To send men and women of staunch Christian character into every walk and profession of life, as leaders for the true and good is the peculiar aim of the Christian College. There is an inner motive, more specific, which actuates many of the supporters of Texas Christian University. It is the purpose of furnishing to the service of the church a supply of trained ministers of the gospel."[183] Kershner, with his honorary doctorate listed after his name, served as a professor, and Colby D. Hall joined the faculty as professor of English Bible and corresponding secretary.[184]

A monumental change and a new era for the College of the Bible at Texas Christian University came in 1914 when the trustees accepted L.C. Brite's proposal to charter and fund the Bible College.[185] The idea for a separate building had already been on the minds of some for a few years prior to Brite's donation. The Ministerial Association of the College of the Bible at TCU, for instance, circulated a petition in 1910 for a separate building.[186] However, the administration sought a more distinct institution, influenced in part by another Disciples institution, the College of the Bible in Lexington, Kentucky, which established a separate charter from Kentucky University in 1878. Colby Hall noted in a letter to trustee T.E. Tomlinson in 1911:

> The time has come to make more of this department as a distinct school. I would not have it as separate as it is at Lexington, with different government entirely, and separate legal organization, but I would like to see it more than just a department of the University. It should have someone to build it up who would not be burdened with the affairs of the whole school, and someone at its head to stand with some strength for it, distinct from the President.[187]

L.C. Brite's gift in 1914 allowed for something closer to the Lexington model. Brite's gift proposed that the Bible College erect a new facility and separately incorporate itself from TCU.[188] Chalmers McPherson wrote an article for the *Christian Courier* outlining the theological positions of the school:

> The charter states that the College stands for and maintains the following great truths: (a) That God is a personal God, and there is no other God, and He is our Creator and Preserver and Redeemer; that He has revealed Himself to the world through Jesus the Christ—the Christ of the Inspired volumes called the New and the Old Testaments, (b) That Jesus the Christ is the Son of the Living God, the only begotten Son of God, born of the virgin Mary; that He died for the sins of the world and that His crucified body was raised from the dead as declared in the Scriptures, and that through Him the resurrection from the dead should now be preached, (c) That the Holy Spirit is present in the Church and His office is to cultivate, illuminate and nurture the Church, and through the preaching of the Gospel of Christ to convert the world of sin and proclaim salvation from sin, as is offered in the Gospel, (d) That all of God's people should unite on the one Foundation of Christ's absolute Lordship and Divine Sonship, having one Lord, one Faith, one baptism (the form of baptism being immersion in water into the name of the Father, the Son, and the Holy Spirit); that the Bible furnishes an all-sufficient revelation of the Divine will and a perfect and final rule of faith and practice; that Peter's confession to-wit: "Jesus is the Christ, the Son of the Living God," should be the universal creed of the Church; and that the ordinances of the Gospel should be observed as they were in the days of the apostles. . . . All teachers, professors, officers and trustees shall upon their employment, appointment or election as such, be required to state in writing that they accept and

> will advocate each and every proposition embodied in said paragraphs (a), (b), (c), and (d) of Article II.[189]

McPherson used this article in print to accept the terms of the charter for his employment as a faculty member.[190]

The nature of the charter as a kind of creedal statement, and the stipulation that all members of the community agree to the theological standards contained in the charter, raised significant alarm from many Disciples. J.C. Mason wrote about the "Confessions of Faith" in an August 1914 letter to the *Christian Courier*, saying, "We will need to change our front as to declaiming against creeds. . . . Custom and cash have wonderful power."[191] In an article in the same publication later that year, A.E. Ewell wrote:

> They have subscribed to a creed as full fledged as any in Christendom. I for one would rather the Bible were never taught in TCU than that a creed should be thrust on that institution. . . . The Presbyterian Church has been in a turmoil over their creed for some time. Just as much has Union Theological Seminary. . . . Brite Bible College is as much a sectarian institution as these.[192]

In a July 1914 issue of the *Christian Standard*, Chalmers McPherson responded to the controversy surrounding the adoption of a creed and defended the terms of Brite's gift requiring agreement of "trustees, officers, and teachers" to a doctrinal standard:

> This is done, doubtless, to avoid the paradox situation of a school standing for one thing and teaching another. There is not the least declaration concerning Christian fellowship, nothing which attempts to limit the beliefs or opinions of any person, nothing which attempts to restrain the fullest investigation of any subject, nothing which interferes with individual liberty or thought. But the trustees do declare that the school which they are to control is to stand for something which is definite and which they deem vital in the Christian religion. If men wish to teach that which is along other lines, all these gentlemen ask of them is that they teach it under another roof and at the expense of some other person or institution. Only this and nothing more.[193]

In September of that year, TCU President Frederick Kershner also responded to the challenge of a creed by indicating only faculty had to accept these views, and that no creed, other than the one identified by Peter's confession of faith, was given. He hinted at his interpretation of the motivation behind the charter when he wrote, "Parents who want to be sure that their children will be taught the Bible and not the speculations of some German rationalist . . . will find Brite College of the Bible the school they are looking for."[194]

Later that month, an editorial in the *Christian Evangelist* challenged these responses in defense of the charter, even using Kershner's previous views as a basis for characterizing the charter as a serious threat to the tradition of Disciples identity:

> The fathers of the Restoration Movement and the leading men since had only words of condemnation for human creeds that claim authority over conscience. . . . Within a few months, the trustees of one school have drawn up a series of doctrinal statements that must be signed by the officers and teachers of that institution; and from these statements there must be no departure, even in opinion, except at the peril of the one holding a different opinion. These statements are a creed and nothing but a creed. . . . The attention of the founder and the trustees is invited further to an article written by the president of the new institution [Kershner] in which . . . the president says, "Creeds are often procrustean beds for the torture of theological thinkers. They never conserve orthodoxy or preserve Christian unity. They are divisive rather than unitive.". . . If the president approves the course of the trustees, that only goes to show that even the best of men are not always logical in their reasonings. . . . We shall not consent to place human creeds in the deeds to church property, or in college charters.[195]

This editorial highlighted the impetus for Brite to give money to establish a separate institution in order to protect the Bible College from academic influences that theologically conservative Disciples deemed unacceptable. The establishment of a creed in the charter of the Bible College, while not the norm for Disciples schools, reflected the response of Disciples schools, such as Milligan College, Johnson Bible College, Minnesota Bible College, and Kentucky Christian College, to preserve their conservative academic environments from the encroachment of liberalism in academic thought.[196] However, President Kershner tried to soften the perception that the college created a separate institution for the preservation of particular theological beliefs, writing, "Bro. Brite's gift is of further significance because it blesses the way for the successful carrying out of the University plan of separate colleges, modeled after the Oxford system, which has been adopted as the ultimate ideal of the institution."[197]

The separation from Texas Christian University by means of incorporation did allow the Brite College of the Bible to exert more control over its own academic direction. The battle over control of the Disciples identity during the turbulent third generation ceased for the moment at Texas Christian University and the College of the Bible. A conservative biblical interpretation became the norm thanks in part to the money of L.C. Brite. However, the move created significant tensions between academy and church. As Miller writes of theological education at the time, "The most difficult question before a seminary in a democratic denomination was whether its primary task was to reflect the best opinion in the church or to reflect the best of its own scholarship."[198] Brite College of the Bible took a path similar to Andover Theological Seminary, whose "founders . . . wanted to establish a school that clearly taught a certain understanding of the Christian faith, and they wanted only teachers who accepted this purpose to be part of the faculty."[199] Hall expressed the same sentiment about Brite's gift in his *History of Texas Christian University*:

> It was given because he believed in the purpose of the College. That is shown in his extreme care to see that the right kind of teaching should prevail. He had a faith which he wanted propagated; he tried to set up safeguards to see that no other teachings would ever be presented. He was therefore very careful in the selection of the groups that would control: the Trustees and the Faculty; he exercised caution in a third safeguard: the Charter.[200]

The conservative side of the Disciples tradition prevailed in the teachings at Brite College of the Bible thanks to the financial contributions of L.C. Brite. For those in the Stone-Campbell Movement who valued a conservative approach to the Bible, the "Book" appeared preserved at institutions like Brite. To others such as G.A. and Ellsworth Faris, who assumed a more modernist perspective, the school seemed to be abandoning the freedom of academic inquiry and destroying the very book it hoped to preserve.

2

A Professional Curriculum: Educating Preacher Boys, 1914–1939[1]

GREG HENNEMAN

On February 9, 1915, the Reverend Carey E. Morgan dedicated the Brite College of the Bible with the following words: "The preacher must know the age in which he lives, because while the gospel is always the same, the church is a part of the age and is profoundly influenced by it."[2] Although he might have encountered debate regarding his claim about the "sameness" of the gospel, Rev. Morgan's assertion of the dynamic relationship between changing times and the church proved truer than even he could have imagined. Unforeseeable events such as the United States' involvement in the First World War, turmoil within the church between modernists and fundamentalists in the 1920s, and the Great Depression affected the church over the next three decades. These events profoundly influenced theological education, including the school housed in the new yellow pressed-brick building, bearing the name Brite College of the Bible.

A process of professionalization wove through many of the changes within society, culture, church, and academy in the quarter century that followed Brite's incorporation. Clergy and faculty increasingly adopted a sense of themselves as professionals, people who developed a coherent body of knowledge and specific set of skills related to their occupations through education and formal structures of oversight. When Brite was first incorporated, most churches, particularly in the rural expanses of Texas, were more than content to hire a pastor with a high school education, possibly some college, and the assurance of having received "a call." Such an education placed the pastor among the highest educated in most communities. Over the next two decades, society began to expect greater levels of "specialization and technical competence" from people in a number of occupations, including medicine, law, and ministry.[3]

Americans credited education with playing a critical role in the economy and society by equipping budding professionals to face the problems of their age.[4] At the same time, many leaders in theological education sought to modernize the seminaries by introducing the most recent advances in academic research and reorganizing the seminary curriculum to include new fields of study. The combined interests of a society that sought a more professionally trained clergy and an increasingly more academic environment affected every facet of theological education at Brite, from the ethos of the institution to the types of programs offered to the educational background of faculty. Brite's progress in achieving these ends waxed and waned according to various internal and external forces, including finances, tension between traditional and critical biblical interpretation, and broader changes within academia. Nevertheless, from 1914 to 1939 Brite grew from a typical Bible college that provided undergraduate religious education into a self-described professional theological seminary.

Opening Brite College of the Bible

With a move initially intended to prevent the forces of modernization from influencing the training of ministers, Brite College of the Bible incorporated as a distinct institution with a separate charter from Texas Christian University. As a separate corporation, Brite held its own property, administered by its own board of trustees. The first group of trustees included Dr. Bacon Saunders (president), L.D. Anderson (secretary), James Harrion (treasurer), L.C. Brite, Milliard Patterson, Van Zandt Jarvis, C.W. Gibson, Jonathan W. Kearns, and Eugene Holmes. Three of these trustees (Anderson, Kearns, and Holmes) served as pastors. Dr. Bacon Saunders, who served as the president of the board of trustees until his death in 1925, worked as one of the most well-known physicians in Fort Worth. The school's benefactor, Lucas C. Brite, succeeded Saunders as president. Of the original nine Brite trustees, six also served as Texas Christian University trustees.[5]

The annual Disciples of Christ Texas State Convention held the sole authority to appoint and reelect the Brite trustees.[6] This system illustrated the influence that the church exercised over Brite at the time of its incorporation. Interestingly, some of the trustees that the convention appointed held more liberal or progressive views than many within the university or

Bible College—particularly the college's benefactor, Lucas C. Brite—might have preferred.[7] In spite of this, Brite played a critical role in shaping the character and curriculum of the Bible College. He not only provided the financial capital necessary for building a new facility for the college (he paid $37,500 of the $41,000 it cost to construct the facility, with the university absorbing the difference in the cost),[8] but he involved himself in the selection of professors and, through his attorney Millard Patterson, oversaw the creation and establishment of the charter, which served as Brite's defining document for its first fifty years. The charter outlined the purpose of the college and provided for the aforementioned board of trustees. It also outlined a four-part doctrinal statement that all trustees, faculty, and students had to sign.

The *Christian Evangelist*, which published the statement, questioned: "We wonder why it is necessary to make this declaration. Does it suggest that these brethren are to sign certain statements or declarations of principles before they are eligible to office?"[9] History would prove that the answer to this question, albeit uncharacteristic of the Disciples, was yes. As the previous chapter indicated, the establishment of a doctrinal statement among the typically anticreedal Disciples of Christ became a source of conflict. Although the Brite charter and bylaws called for trustees, professors, and administrators to sign the articles of faith before service, the trustees did not complete this action until 1926, likely under the assumption that all original members ascribed to them.

Establishing a Professional Curriculum

Brite College of the Bible exhibited a concern for equipping preachers with the tools necessary to proclaim the Scripture within the context of the modern world, not so much to accommodate to the changing world but to counter the challenges posed by modernity. The introductory statement of the 1914 Texas Christian University catalog made this clear when it emphasized Brite's mission to equip a minister to be "conversant with the needs and demands of his own age." According to the introductory statement, students did not gain knowledge of philosophy and church history for their own sake, but to understand "the history of the twentieth century and the problems of thought and life which are perplexing men now on the scene of action."[10]

In order to create a new generation of preachers who could display reverence for the Bible and concern for people, Brite College of the Bible initially offered two programs. The Classical Course, which culminated in the bachelor of divinity (BD) degree, served as the traditional path for the young college student who intended to pursue lifelong service as a pastor. The BD degree required the bachelor of arts degree from a "creditable college" as a prerequisite. Students could apply as many as thirty credit hours from a bachelor of arts program toward the 144 credits required for the bachelor of divinity. As a result, a student could potentially graduate with a bachelor of divinity in six years of college instead of seven. This system was the standard for many divinity schools, including nearby Southern Methodist University.[11]

The school designed its second program, the English Course, for students who either came to the ministry later in life or did not have the time or resources to devote to the full program, or for those whose vocational interests did not require as thorough a preparation as the Classical Course. Thus, Brite offered the English Course not only for second career preachers, but also for men and women who desired preparation for a wide range of church ministries, particularly those especially important to Disciples: religious education and missions. While, in most cases, the English Course required a high school diploma, the school made some exceptions by requiring students to rectify some academic deficiencies through the Texas Christian University Academy. After the closure of the academy in 1921, the Bible College utilized advanced ministerial students as tutors for students who desired to enter the English Course.[12] Graduates of the English Course received a three-year degree, the Brite College English ministerial degree, based on a wide range of coursework from history and hermeneutics to doctrine and literature.[13]

Initially three people taught and administered the Classical and English programs. Frederick D. Kershner, president of Texas Christian University; Clinton Lockhart, the former Columbia College and Texas Christian University president; and Colby D. Hall, a former student at Add-Ran University who received a bachelor of arts from Kentucky University and a master of arts from Columbia University. Hall, one of the most beloved faculty members on campus, later served as dean of both the Bible College and university. In 1928, Hall quietly turned down Transylvania University's offer to become its next president, and the TCU board offered Hall its presidency when E.M. Waits retired, but he declined citing his advanced age.[14]

In 1916, the Bible College added two new programs that furthered the school's early orientation toward church training: the Missionary Course and the Church Workers' Course. The Missionary Course met the growing demand for mission work among Disciples and provided one year of Bible coursework for those intending to serve in the mission field. However, the coursework did not include language training or specific study in foreign missions. In fact,

Brite expected that students who received its missions diploma would pursue further training at a school such as the College of Missions in Indianapolis, Indiana.[15] The Church Workers' Course served as a one-year program that provided a broad exposure to history, doctrine, interpretation, and religious education for men and women who desired to serve as volunteers in the local church. It did not require any prior college work and resulted in the awarding of a certificate. Laypersons who did not want to pursue the full certificate could attend any of Brite's courses by paying a fee, though the school did not award academic credit to these students or grant them full access to university facilities.[16]

In addition to the preparation earned through their formal coursework, students also served in preaching appointments in Fort Worth and surrounding cities. This service, typical among divinity schools, offered a three-fold benefit, giving students practical experience, providing a service to the local churches, and helping students and faculty earn extra income.[17] Providing an opportunity for students to reflect on the relationship between educational context and practical experience, Colby Hall taught a course titled Ministerial Seminar that sought to offer guidance and direction for the young pastor "wrestling with the problems of the pulpit and the pastorate." The course helped Brite meld theological education with service to the church. The work of integrating theory and practice that occurred while student pastors reflected on their experiences in the classroom served the growing desire among churches and theological educators for technically competent pastors.[18]

A Christian Ethos

The organizational structure and relationship of Brite College of the Bible with Texas Christian University created a unique situation. Brite was neither a freestanding Bible college nor directly under the control of a larger university. Thus, in 1920, when Robert L. Kelly studied the question of which of these two normal arrangements worked best, Brite fell into neither camp.[19] Rather, Brite operated as an independent corporation that worked in concert with the greater university. The relationship between the schools allowed for an exchange of work, resources, and ideas while permitting a separate purpose and vision. Brite students had the benefit of taking courses in the university, while university students had the benefit of taking Bible and elective courses taught by Bible College faculty.[20]

However, this unique organizational structure did not remove the problem that Kelly saw inherent within theological education: the influence of a church body. Kelly saw theological education's connection to denominations, and factions within denominations, as hampering the movement toward "ministerial formation or theological scholarship."[21] Unlike law and medicine, which trained according to academically designed standards, the professionalization of theological education as a whole was hampered by the control of denominational bodies that, because of different polities, traditions, and theological commitments, could not agree on a shared set of standards for theological education or the licensing of pastors. These same tensions within the Disciples tradition, while never manifesting to the point of fracture, existed throughout Brite's early years between those described as restorationists (L.C. Brite, Frederick Kershner, Chalmers McPherson) and others leaning toward critical scholarship (Clinton Lockhart, William Morro, William Roosa).

As Brite struggled in its response to modernity, the school and the university assumed an ethos typical of the triumphalist Protestantism of the day. In 1909, Stephen J. Corey addressed the Centennial Convention of the Disciples of Christ in a manner common for the day: "We are under orders. Christ's program is one of conquest. Men, he has said it—he has expressed his ultimatum. His bold call should make the very blood leap in our veins and challenge us to do his sacred bidding."[22] In support of the Disciples' vision and in line with the ethos of the time, the foreword to the 1915 Texas Christian University catalog expressed the purpose of the school as "vigorously and energetically Christian":

> Assuming the highest type of character to be embodied in the Christ of Galilee, the institution endeavors by precept and example to hold up His life before its students for realization and embodiment in their own careers. It holds that the supreme need of the present age is a positive Christian manhood and womanhood.[23]

As this description suggests, students attending Texas Christian University received a distinctly Christian education, intended to equip them for the work of the "present age." From 1914 until 1925, all undergraduate students in arts or sciences had to take a minimum of fifteen credit hours in English Bible and could take as many as thirty-six hours of electives taught by Brite faculty. Likewise, master of arts students could take as many as twenty credit hours from Brite toward their degrees.[24]

The university also hoped to influence the Christian life of students through social activities such as the YMCA and YWCA. The stated purpose of the YMCA was to "promote spiritual growth, fellowship, and strenuous Christian living among men."[25] Corey noted that the principal aim of the YMCA was not to "sharpen men's wits with night classes [or] to strengthen their biceps with dumbbells" but to win men to Christ.[26] As Glenn T. Miller points out, the emphasis of these organizations promoted the ideal of "Christian manhood or masculinity."[27]

Texas Christian University also attempted to enforce a code of behavior and discipline to regulate student activities in the fashion of Alexander Campbell's ideal that "education and the formation of moral character are identical expressions."[28] The university prohibited younger students from visiting "the allurements of the city" of Fort Worth without giving just cause and receiving written permission. Loitering in hallways or owning a vehicle was strictly controlled, while smoking justified the withdrawal of financial aid. Under President Waits's leadership, Texas Christian University also supported the temperance movement.[29] It was not until 1937 that chapel became optional for seniors, but still mandatory for freshmen, sophomores, and juniors. However, this change occurred not so much because of changing times, but because the student body had outgrown chapel facilities.[30]

Similar to the wider university, the Bible College sponsored organizations and activities that promoted a distinctly Christian life. Student activities at Brite included the monthly social gathering of the Ministerial Association (later renamed the Brite College of the Bible Association) and the weekly gathering of the Homiletic Guild, which met to discuss issues of practical church work.[31] In 1927, Professor Frank E. Billington led the founding of the Timothy Club, which primarily focused on developing students' skills in preaching.[32] The College of the Bible integrated these associations into the central life of the school. In fact, a failure to participate in the full range of activities, including class attendance, chapel service, and ministerial association meetings, served as grounds for dismissal.[33]

All of this showed the emphasis that TCU and Brite placed on personal piety and conservative Christianity. The schools joined the emerging professional standards for education with, in their eyes, an equally significant commitment to forming professionals with particular personal qualities.

The Influence of Preachers

In the fall of 1915, Brite appointed Chalmers McPherson to the position of professor of New Testament Christianity. McPherson had served as a university lecturer in 1911, in addition to his role as trustee, but received appointment through his friendship with Lucas Brite as a full professor. Alongside his courses in New Testament, McPherson taught a course titled the History of the Restoration Movement, which connected church history with the Stone-Campbell Movement. As a well-known and experienced pastor, McPherson also taught a class called the Practical Work of the Christian Minister, which included topics such as sermon preparation, pastoral care, and missions.[34]

Leadership within TCU changed in 1915 when Frederick Kershner left the university to serve as the editor-in-chief of the *Christian Evangelist*. Kershner's work at the *Evangelist* was short-lived, and in 1917 he left for its rival publication, the *Christian Standard*, through which he trumpeted the restoration movement. To fill the void of university president, the board of trustees selected Edward McShane Waits (most commonly referred to as E.M. Waits) as its new president in 1916. Waits served as the pastor of Magnolia Avenue Christian Church in Fort Worth, having previously served as a pastor in El Paso and in Kentucky. He graduated in 1896 with a bachelor of arts degree from Transylvania University's College of the Bible; however, unlike the university's past two presidents, Waits had no graduate training.[35] Colby Hall, who served as dean of the university from 1920 to 1943 and traveled and worked closely with Waits, described him as "a pulpit speaker of forceful language, a devotee of beauty, and a personality gifted in making friends."[36] While Waits served as president for over twenty-five years and led the school through incredible growth and unexpected challenges, he remained first and foremost a church man.

Despite his paucity of experience in higher education when he assumed the presidency of TCU, Waits's continued much of the work of his predecessors. As president, he outlined a mission of developing "Christian character, Christian scholarship and Christian culture."[37] In 1927, Waits stated, "The Christian College is necessary as a stimulus to the State University; the Christian College is necessary to preserve the church; the Christian College is necessary to the preservation of society."[38] In fact, throughout the 1930s, the front cover of the Texas Christian University catalog declared in bold letters: "AN IDEAL EDUCATION," followed by Luke 2:52, "And Jesus advanced in wisdom and stature and in favor with God and man." In numerous speeches and writings, Waits often used the verse as an illustration of the full expression of a college education in that "Jesus advanced in wisdom (the education of the mind) and in stature (physical education) and in favor with God (religious education) and in favor with man (social or education for service)." Waits, like Kershner before him, did not view an "ideal education" as one based on critical scholarship, but on the formation of moral character.[39]

World War I

In August of 1914, the guns of Europe erupted, dividing the continent. As reflected in the broader American culture, Texas Christian University and Brite College of the Bible adopted a stance of isolation. Separated by an ocean from the carnage of trench warfare, the students and faculty viewed the conflict as Europe's war. However, even before the United States' entry into the war in 1917, the editorial pages of the university newspaper, the *Skiff*, trumpeted the superiority of Western democracy over the kaiser. Around campus this sentiment manifested itself in the fact that, although the university continued to offer German in its foreign language department, no one enrolled.[40]

Attitudes at the university quickly moved from passive interest to nationalist zeal in the spring of 1917. Once the United States officially entered the war, editors of the *Skiff* adorned the paper with flags and praised the names of the young men who gave up their studies to enlist in the military. The medical college recruited medics, and the chapel held patriotic services with President Waits in attendance. Waits espoused Christian education as the fundamental response to the war as 145 young men left the university to join the war effort.[41]

In May of 1918, the Student Army Training Corps was formed at the university, and in October 1918, the entire campus became a military post. With the militarization of the campus, 320 volunteers endured thirteen hours of drill, marching, digging trenches, and training per week. Even the byline of the *Skiff* recognized the change in the university's purpose: "An Army Camp and College Paper Combined."[42] Inconvenience most likely served as the university's greatest sacrifice for the war as a surge of young men stayed in Clark Hall for military training and used the entire basement of Goode Hall as a dining room.[43] No TCU or Brite trustees, faculty, or students publicly questioned the school's support of the war.

Likewise, for the most part the Disciples of Christ leaders and churches supported the American war effort. Ironically, TCU's former president, Frederick Kershner, was one of the few prominent Disciples to oppose the war. At the onset of war, Kershner addressed a gathering at the YMCA and stated, "Nationalism is wrong, that militarism is folly, and that the highest kind of heroism is not dependent on war."[44] Although Kershner's words did not differ sharply from the American view of the war in its first years, the majority opinion in the nation had shifted to favor nationalism and patriotism by 1917.

Yet, through his editorial role at the *Christian Evangelist*, Kershner continued to oppose the war based on his opposition to the prominent belief "that only the Allies had sufficient reason to ask for and receive God's favor."[45] Kershner offered one of the few voices among Disciples calling for critical thought on the war.

Once the war ended, Brite and TCU refocused their efforts. The 1919 *Alumni Bulletin* published the following vision: "The Great War has closed, and we are now faced with the task of building a new world out of the wreck of the world that was. . . . This is the hour of the Christian college. The small Christian college is the hope of America."[46] These words provided the immediate post-war vision of Texas Christian University. The *Bulletin* went on to describe what the university hoped to form in the hearts and minds of students: "to make of them kingdom-building men and women . . . [to create students of] ideals instead of ideas."[47] In a nationalistic sentiment characteristic of the day, the *Bulletin* summarized, "The supreme contribution that the Christian college makes is Christian character, based upon the ethics of the Bible."[48]

More than Preaching

On the eve of the First World War, the Disciples of Christ launched the Men and Millions campaign in 1913.[49] The leadership at Texas Christian University and Brite helped the nationwide campaign, which lasted until 1918, to recruit eight thousand young men and women who pledged themselves to Christian service. Additionally, the campaign raised over $7 million in financial pledges, of which over $6 million was collected.[50]

The work accomplished in the Men and Millions campaign demonstrated the interest of Brite, TCU, and Disciples alike not only in training pastors, but also in creating missionaries who would share the gospel message at home and in foreign lands. Mission work had long held a place of central importance at Brite, where guest missionaries frequented chapel services and several faculty members served in leadership positions on mission boards.[51] The Brite graduates who went on to serve around the world in the continents of Africa, Asia, and Central and South America provided the clearest example of the connection between Brite and missions.[52] Additionally, many Brite trustees and faculty served terms as president of the Texas Christian Missionary Society.[53]

In 1921, Brite College of the Bible began to offer another program that prepared people for vocations other than as pastors: the Church Secretary Course. Largely designed for women who would serve as a church secretary or pastor's assistant, this two-year program included courses in religious education and practical church work. Before graduating, the student also had to show proficiency in English composition, writing, typing, and shorthand. Graduates received a certificate upon completion and a recommendation for a church position.[54]

While these two programs met the needs of the church and increased Brite's enrollment, they provided little evidence to suggest Brite was moving in step with the broader trends in theological education that focused on strengthening academic standards. The school designed these programs more for high school graduates looking for a general theological survey than for a college graduate seeking advanced, graduate-level education.

The expectations of the church and the underpreparation of students also proved a common stumbling block for Brite's ability to keep pace with the emerging standards in theological education. The majority of students who initially came to the college did not come with the needed background. In the beginning, as many as fifty percent of Brite students lacked a high school degree. Moreover, the mostly rural churches of Texas, not unlike many areas of the United States in the early twentieth century, did not value graduate education for their pastors.[55] In the eyes of many churches, if a young man could finish a bachelor of arts degree with a high number of Bible courses, this more than satisfied the church's needs. Although throughout this period Brite offered the bachelor of divinity degree, it was not until the 1930s that Brite awarded this degree with any regularity. Because churches and denominations did not require graduate education, aspiring pastors were unlikely to spend the time and money necessary to receive the best education.[56]

In contrast to the church-related programs of secretarial work and missions, a more professionally oriented program emphasizing religious education as a discipline began in the 1920s. Around this time, religious education appeared as a new emphasis at Brite, in theological education, and among Texas Disciples. Although an emphasis on education was inherent to the nature of the Disciples, the move toward religious education as a professional discipline began with the establishment of the Religious Education Association in 1903 and increased with the growing demand for specialized professionals in the early twentieth century.[57] Brite's description of a graduate in it's 1920–1921 catalog attests to the high profile given to religious education: "[The graduate] is on a level with the Superintendent of Public Schools and with the pastors."[58] Under the leadership of S.W. Hutton, Southwestern Superintendent, the American Christian Missionary Society raised over $28,000 to fund the program. With the endorsement of President Waits and the approval of the Brite board of trustees, Frank E. Billington, a pastor from Ellensburg, Washington, was hired to fill a chair in Christian education.[59] Hall described Billington as a man of a "sweet Christian spirit [who] blessed the campus the remainder of his career."[60] While Billington may have brought a good spirit to the faculty, his hiring is another example of Brite's tendency to select faculty more for their church affiliation than their professional skills, as Billington lacked a doctorate in education.

Brite's more churchly orientation existed alongside a more scientific and academic degree plan that began to take shape in the early years of the twentieth century. By 1925, Brite more clearly demarcated the line between its three undergraduate and non-degree programs—the bachelor of arts with a major in Bible, the Church Secretary Course, and the English Bible Course—and its two graduate programs—the bachelor of divinity and master in religious education.

Brite's modest efforts to modernize its curriculum did not sit well with the founding benefactor, Lucas Brite. In the early 1920s Mr. Brite tried to recruit Frederick Kershner to return to Fort Worth as a member of the Brite faculty in order to stem the tide of modernization. He wrote to Kershner, "Don't forget that you are more responsible than any one else for the donation that I made in establishing the Bible College and it is up to you to come to the rescue at this critical time."[61] However, by this time, Kershner declined based on the direction of the school, feeling that his presence was unwanted: "It would be useless for me to go to Texas if these folks are to be in control of the school."[62]

Finances

Finances played a crucial role in the changes occurring at Brite in the quarter century after its incorporation. In the post-war era, TCU dealt with financial hardships that forced it to question its identity as an institution. Following the end of the 1918 school year, the medical college, which had operated for six years, closed due to high costs.[63] The law school, which had opened in 1915, closed in 1920 because of the difficulty in meeting state requirements.[64] Although Brite did not make money for the university, its role in providing undergraduate religion courses to all students and TCU's greater vision of Christian identity provided security for Brite.

Without the large donations and denominational support given to other universities and Bible colleges, TCU undertook numerous campaigns to raise funds. These included the Men and Millions campaign of 1914 to 1918, the

Fort Worth campaign of 1916, the United Campaign of 1919, and the indebtedness campaign of 1922 to 1923.[65] Additionally, TCU continuously solicited churches throughout the Southwest to provide any support possible, asking them to view Texas Christian University as part of their mission. However, TCU struggled to raise funds commensurate with other local schools such as Southern Methodist University, which received contributions of $1 million in just one year. Without financial backing, the university and Bible College could not offer the best facilities or attract the highest quality professors.[66] Brite's financial dependence on TCU left the Bible College with little choice but to hire local pastors for teaching positions since the school could not initially pay salaries competitive with the most prestigious seminaries.

Despite a series of seemingly endless campaigns, several private donations, and significant enrollment growth, the financial problem compounded in the 1920s.[67] In 1921 alone, the university had a bottom-line loss over $22,000, with only $7,000 coming in from outside sources. As a result, the business manager titled his annual report, "The Crisis." By 1922, as the demands on the school increased with higher enrollment, the debt grew to $300,000, and the Southern Association of Colleges mandated that the university have a $500,000 endowment.[68]

In 1923, President Waits challenged the university to pay off all of its debt, build an endowment of $500,000, secure membership in the Southern Association of Colleges, build a boulevard connecting the university with Fort Worth, and acquire a $200,000 endowment from the Disciples of Christ Education Board. One trustee, Andrew Sherley, raised the stakes by recommending the university raise $1 million for the endowment. The university hoped to reach these goals in the spirit of the celebration of the Fiftieth Anniversary Golden Jubilee Celebration of Texas Christian University.[69]

The optimism of meeting these financial needs rose with financial contributions made possible by growth in the Texas oil and cattle business. Harry Rogers of San Antonio led the way by writing a check of $25,000, which was matched by four others. Dave Reed and Ross Sterling, the future governor of Texas, each gave $100,000. During the Great Depression, Ross Sterling lost his fortune and later commented, "The only money I have left is what I gave away."[70]

With the payment of all of TCU's debts, the General Education Board of New York promised a financial gift of $166,666.67 if the university could raise its endowment to $500,000. In 1923, TCU's leadership saw this contribution as the ultimate path to financial health. These funds would later provide the much-needed strength to withstand the trying times of the Great Depression.

A much greater gift fell into the lap of the university in December 1923 when Mary Couts Burnett donated $150,000 to build a new library and pledged another $3 million upon her death.[71] Curiously, Mrs. Burnett had no prior affiliation with the university and was not a member of the Christian Church. Her husband, Burk Burnett, had acquired millions of dollars through cattle, oil, and gambling and said during his lifetime that he would never give any money to a church or a school. Burk and Mary had a strained relationship which deteriorated to the point that Burk had her deemed legally insane, based on alleged hallucinations, and confined to a mental institution. On the day of Burk's death, Mary escaped from her imprisonment and through the work of her personal physician, Dr. Charles Harris, the founder of Harris Methodist Hospital in Fort Worth and benefactor for the Harris College of Nursing, gained her freedom and legally established her sanity. In a later chance meeting with Colby Hall, Harris described Mary as "one of the most intelligent women I know."[72]

The impact of Mary Couts Burnett's gift, which brought a net gain of over $3 million to TCU, is difficult to overstate. Before the trust, the university struggled with a debt that hampered its growth. After the gift, President Waits believed that TCU could become one of the largest colleges in the United States. While this vision did not come to fruition, the Burnett Trust provided TCU and Brite with solvency and security through the Great Depression.

One of the most significant gifts to Brite came in 1935 when property belonging to Millard Patterson was willed to Brite following his death. Patterson had served as a Brite trustee and personal lawyer of Mr. Lucas Brite. In his estate, he left business property in El Paso, Texas, valued at approximately $60,000. As per the will, Brite rented the property with the profit "to be held in trust for the benefit of the Brite College of the Bible."[73] Patterson also made the provision that as the trustees saw fit they could sell the property and place that money into trust.[74] Over the long term, this property provided a steady increase in endowment funds for Brite.[75]

The Morro Affair

In 1926, Brite took a large step toward increasing the quality of its faculty with the hiring of someone described by Colby D. Hall as "one of the most distinguished scholars ever produced by the Disciples," Dr. William C. Morro.[76] Morro held a bachelor of divinity from Yale, a PhD from Harvard, had served as the dean of the College of the Bible in Lexington, and taught at Butler and the College of Missions in Indianapolis, Indiana. Despite Morro's impressive resume, his career at Brite almost ended before it began.[77] In 1924, Frederick Kershner clandestinely forwarded to L.C. Brite a confidential letter from the president indicating that Waits was considering hiring Morro.[78] Brite replied that he knew nothing of Waits's interest, and both men agreed that such a hiring would be detrimental to maintaining the school's conservative ethos.[79]

Waits, though personally conservative, had fewer concerns about Morro's theology. He also did not find it necessary to consult the Bible College's most powerful trustee and benefactor, L.C. Brite. Waits probably did know of Kershner's ongoing relationship with Brite, but Brite clearly held a poor opinion of the president, declaring Waits was "either wrong in faith else he is weak in his convictions."[80] Although Kershner characterized Waits as weak, Waits showed a certain cleverness in bringing Morro to the faculty despite L.C. Brite's attempt to use the statement of faith in the articles of incorporation to block him.[81]

At his interview with the Brite board of trustees, on June 11, 1926, Morro received the statement of faith, which the Brite charter required all professors, trustees, and administrators to sign. On June 12, Morro responded in a letter to the secretary of the Brite board of trustees, L.D. Anderson, that he did not have any conflict with the wording of the charter. He stated that if he were to write such a statement, "I would change the wording here and there (though not necessarily the sense), and in a number of points would make the emphasis different, but this would probably be true of any other human declaration or statement."[82] While Morro intended these words to demonstrate his conformity with the statement and hoped to avoid signing a creed, his assurances failed to sway Lucas Brite, who had been opposed to his hiring from the beginning.

Brite refused to compromise on the charter he had so carefully crafted for the sake of a modernist professor. He responded to Anderson, "Unless he can sign the agreement as provided for in the bylaws of said institution, then I am unalterably opposed to employing he, or any other, who entertain such views."[83] Brite went on to state, "I am not ready to adopt a precedent that will virtually destroy the safeguard intended to protect the rising generation from wolves in sheep clothing."[84]

Several trustees and Colby Hall then tried to convince Brite of Morro's sincere faith. In fact, Chalmers McPherson, a close friend of Brite's and an influential figure in the controversy surrounding Ellsworth Faris earlier in the century, thought Morro's action acceptable saying "that the letter rather than his signature filled all of the requirements of the charter."[85] McPherson even wrote Brite to reassure him that in Morro there was "nothing to fear."[86] Likewise, Brite trustee John Kerns wrote his own letter to Brite supporting Morro.[87]

Despite appealing to Brite's friendship and shared faith, Kerns's and McPherson's letters did not persuade him. Brite stated that he did not personally have anything against Dr. Morro, but he made clear that as president of the trustees his "first and most important duty is to our God in protecting the patrons and student body from the ravages of infidelity and false teaching, or the so-called 'modernism.'"[88] Thus, Brite stood his ground and stated that if Morro truly believed in the words of the charter, he could sign it. Otherwise, he would not become a member of the Brite faculty.

This stalemate had the potential to divide the institution. The issue of creeds and a failure to agree or comply with them served as a source for numerous heresy trials across academia in the late nineteenth and early twentieth centuries. At nearby Southern Methodist University, such controversies resulted in the resignation of professors John A. Rice in 1921 and Mims T. Workman in 1925. Additionally, Professor Harvie Branscomb, who criticized the firing of Workman in the media, was fired by President Charles Selecman with the words, "I have just read your gratuitous letter in the morning News and want to say that the sooner you leave this campus the better."[89]

With several Brite faculty and trustees backing Morro, division seemed imminent, particularly in light of the existing undercurrent of strife between the traditional and more modernist camps at Brite. Reflecting the tensions, Lucas Brite wrote to Kershner that if "something should happen to Bro. McPherson, there would be nothing left in the whole TCU institution that could be depended on to promulgate our plea."[90]

Morro's own experience at Butler University, where he struggled to gain the support of church leaders who exercised direct control of the university, informed his perspective. Clearly, Morro wanted to avoid encountering the same situation he faced at Butler in which the church controlled the institution.[91] Nevertheless, on July 1, 1926, Morro diffused the situation in a letter to L.D. Anderson in which he signed a copy of the statement of faith. Morro might have made his decision in the spirit of Alexander Campbell's notion of Christian unity being more important than political agreement.[92] However, Morro added to the statement the following caveat: "I accept and advocate the above teachings. This is not to be construed as a creedal statement or as a test of fellowship. If my convictions should change as to oppose these teachings, I would voluntarily withdraw from my position in the college." Morro referred directly to Alexander Campbell's statement of human creeds being the "bones of controversy, the seeds of discord, the cause as well as the effect of division." Therefore, Morro came to sign the words of the charter by viewing them as a "means of expression" and not "an authoritative creed or test of fellowship."[93] Yet, these conditions still did not satisfy Mr. Brite, and in the end, Dr. Morro signed the statement with the following addition:

> I assent to and approve of the above as agreeing in substance with my own faith, with that which I have taught in the past and with that which I expect to teach in the future. I make this endorsement with the understanding that the intention of the charter is to define the aim and policy of the college and not to place obstacles in the way of search for the truth.[94]

The issue of signing the articles of faith arose again in 1936 as the trustees sought to replace the recently deceased A.C. Parker with Charles Mohle. Mohle received his bachelor of divinity from Brite and went on to complete a PhD at Yale. The familiarity with this well-respected, home-grown scholar created a natural fit. However, Mohle refused to sign the articles of faith, and the Brite trustees refused to budge on their position. Instead, Brite hired Thurman Morgan, a pastor from Hillsboro, Texas, who had not yet completed his bachelor of divinity work. The hire continued the trend of Brite hiring a pastor without a PhD for a faculty position.[95]

The Morro affair also brought to light another issue, which up until that time had not publicly surfaced at Brite or Texas Christian University: open membership. The issue centered on whether people could become members of the Christian Church without having been baptized by immersion. The divisive topic appeared most clearly in the work of the United Christian Missionary Society. Missionaries who accepted nonimmersed members were derided as progressive and modernists. This controversy resulted in the approval of the Sweeney Resolution of 1922, which stated that only "immersed, penitent" people could gain church membership. Historian Mark G. Toulouse describes the resolution of the open membership debate as driven largely by pragmatism, with decisions made based on the need for financial support of missions over intentional theological considerations.[96]

In a letter to Lucas Brite, Chalmers McPherson made passing reference to the issue when he read Morro's statement concerning his theology as "clearly rul[ing] out all advocacy of open membership."[97] In this, McPherson remained true to his traditional, restorationist heritage. Although he did not make his statement public or use the issue of open membership to create division, his letter suggests that Brite could have made open membership a litmus test for the hiring of new faculty.

The tensions illustrated in the Morro affair demonstrated the enduring division between groups within the church and academy. Most notably, this event showed the implicit threat to academic freedom that lurked behind the actions of those opposed to critical biblical scholarship.

A New Structure in Brite

In 1928, following the arrival of Morro, Brite College of the Bible realigned all of its courses under five departments: F.E. Billington served as the head of the Department of the Christian Ministry, Colby Hall headed the Department of History of Religions and Missions, William Morro served as the head of the Department of New Testament, Clinton Lockhart headed the Department of Old Testament, and H. Lynn Pickerill served as the head of the Department of Religious Education. Pickerill initially joined the faculty in 1925 as a temporary professor while the trustees hoped to acquire the services of H.S. Hilley, president of the Atlantic Christian College. When the hiring of Hilley fell through, Pickerill remained on the faculty.[98] Although Pickerill brought a scientific understanding to the classroom that won him the favor of many people on campus, the financial implications of the Great Depression overcame the desires of the school to keep him. In 1933, Pickerill pled the case for the continuation of his position, whether he was part of it or not, but the trustees did not have the money to support his plea.[99] As a result, the school eliminated Pickerill's position, and he left Brite for the University of Michigan.[100]

Throughout the economically booming years of the 1920s, the catalog of courses nearly doubled in size, with new courses in specialized areas such as Christian Worship, Egyptian History, and Arabic language. Other courses drew from the fields of philosophy, psychology, and sociology. This emphasis on the social sciences and sociology had become normal for divinity schools.[101] In fact, in 1929, Brite began to require that all of its students take General Psychology 121 from Texas Christian University.[102]

In addition to the new structure, Professor William Morro introduced new courses that provided a more critical and academic view of Scripture than typical in previous years. Two of these courses included New Testament Problems, which offered "a more mature and complete understanding of the

Brite College of the Bible Academic and Administration Building (1915–1953).

New Testament by studying some of its problems either historical, critical, or spiritual," and The Christian Religion with Its Israelitish Background, which explored the "customs, rites, beliefs, forms, and ideals" that influenced the "religion of Jesus Christ."[103]

As the decade of the 1920s came to a close, Brite had grown into a much different institution from its earlier roots. The school placed a greater emphasis on the bachelor of divinity and master of religious education degrees, responding to the cultural shift toward specialization and professionalization that increased the requirements for pastoral leadership.[104] As such, with forces both internal and external, Brite grew into a more professional school of theology, which prepared men and an increasing number of women for a wide range of ministries.[105]

Unfortunately for Brite and TCU, just as the financial capital of the 1920s provided a means for growth, the Great Depression brought a halt to the era of prosperity. By 1932, faculty salaries had been cut by 43 percent and, in the following year, the TCU board of trustees approved a loan of $70,000 against the Burnett Trust to pay the reduced salaries as the university's income ran $140,000 below budget.[106] By 1937, Brite only paid $3,130.50 of its $8,581.70 payroll, with the difference covered by Texas Christian University.[107]

Even before the Depression, Texas Christian University contributed the funding essential for Brite's operation. In 1928 alone, the university contributed $18,661.27 to the Bible College. Much of this came in the form of indirect contributions such as the remittance of tuition for ministerial students ($8,691.75) and rebates on room and board ($5,500). In this same year, the university also transferred $4,469.52 in cash from its treasury directly into the Brite treasury, based on the expected contributions from church offerings. Actual offerings for the year only amounted to $1,440.00.[108] Without TCU's financial support, Brite might have faced closure. Colby Hall listed twenty-three Texas schools that opened between 1865 and 1922 that were affiliated with either the Churches of Christ or the Christian Church. By 1938, only one of those twenty-three Disciples colleges remained open—Texas Christian University.[109]

The Depression not only affected the pockets of faculty, but it quickly manifested itself in the classroom. Within five years, the university's enrollment fell from over 1,687 to 907 while the number of ministerial students dropped from 111 to 59. In a 1933 article in the *Christian Evangelist*, Colby Hall wrote, "The financial stringency has reduced the enrollment a little bit too much. It has reduced the income very seriously. Salaries have had to be reduced, but so far the size of the faculty has held up."[110]

Historian Robert T. Handy notes that the United States also went through a religious depression beginning in 1925. Handy suggests that this religious depression originated from disenchantment with the institution of the church and its idealistic support of the First World War. As such, this religious depression resulted in a decreased interest in missions, foreign service, and church membership. The economic depression weakened a church already hit by its own religious depression. Handy quotes Robert T. Miller, who lists the combined effects of this religious and economic depression: "Memberships dropped, budgets were slashed, benevolent and missionary enterprises set adrift, ministers fired, and chapels closed. All of this can be demonstrated statistically."[111]

Although these assessments accurately represented the general condition of American Protestantism in the second and third decades of the twentieth century, they did not capture the situation everywhere. Texas did not experience a similar decline in membership. From 1920 to 1939, church membership among Disciples nearly doubled in Texas from 51,621 to 96,971. While the number of churches gradually declined, this can be attributed more to the urbanization of society than a decrease in church participation.[112]

If Texas Disciples did not experience the normal symptoms of the religious depression, they did have a corresponding drop in support of missions and benevolent giving. The aforementioned open membership dispute rather than post-war apathy accounted for much of the decrease. In 1923, Texas Disciples sent $340,075 from their churches to the denomination's mission and benevolent organizations. Following events such as the *Christian Standard's* response to John Brown's report of open membership in the mission fields and the *Standard's* publication of periodicals such as the *Spotlight*, which called those actions into question, this number quickly dropped.[113] By 1927, support declined to $209,087 and by 1933 to $89,872. Although the economy recovered much of its pre-Depression strength by the end of the 1930s, giving to missions and benevolences by Texas Disciples only amounted to $141,896 in 1939. In this same year, Disciples giving at the national level had returned to its mid-1920s levels. However, in Texas the effects of the open membership debate appeared irreversible.[114]

Continued Work

Despite the dramatic economic and social impact of the Depression, the work of Texas Christian University and Brite College of the Bible proceeded. The university continued to emphasize an intellectual and moral education whereas Brite moved forward in its mission of training men and women for ministry. While Brite held fast to its primary work of training pastors, it reevaluated its role in supporting and training for missions.

The waning of Disciples support for missions at the end of the 1920s left the Disciples' United Christian Missionary Society in debt.[115] At the same time, some concern in church and academy emerged over the traditional hope of a triumphant Protestant civilization that had dominated Protestant culture at the time of Brite's incorporation.[116] For example, the 1934 Indiana Convention of Disciples called for a new perspective on missions that sent the smaller numbers of women and men entering the mission field to "go humbly, realizing our own inconsistencies, and seeing the need of our own redemption; not as a superior race, but as Christian bretheren, with the common need of a Savior."[117] Support for Brite's mission program fell, resulting in the school putting greater emphasis on the bachelor of divinity and master of religious education programs.

Throughout the 1930s, the Brite College of the Bible also continued to standardize its practices with other seminaries and professionalize its approach to theological education. In 1931, Brite distinctly separated undergraduate work from graduate theological studies. Brite specifically outlined the six-year program for an undergraduate student entering college who sought to graduate with a bachelor of divinity or master of religious education degree. Under this program, students completed the majority of the freshman and sophomore years in courses such as history, psychology, English, and sociology. In the freshman year, the pre-ministerial student took six hours of Bible, followed in the sophomore years by six hours of religious education and six hours of Greek. Under this plan, the student received the "cultural foundation" necessary for a "successful mastery of the later Bible courses." Upon completion of the first two years of undergraduate work, a student could then matriculate as a "Junior Seminary" student who would spend the majority of the next four years of school taking courses at Brite, though some class work, such as sociology and philosophy, would be taken at the university.[118] Illustrating the increased importance of the social sciences in seminary work, the ideal undergraduate pre-ministerial student entered Brite with a minimum of eighteen hours in sociology and psychology.[119] After completing the undergraduate requirements, the student had to accumulate ninety hours from Brite in order to receive the bachelor of divinity (thirty hours of which could be transferred from undergraduate work).[120]

In 1931, for the first time since its inception, Brite began to offer a wide array of English exegesis courses focused on Hebrew Scripture. These courses were designed not only to teach the content of books of the Bible, but more importantly to provide instruction on the "correct methods of interpreting Hebrew literature" in ways that adhered more closely to critical methods in biblical studies.[121]

The Great Depression reduced the number of programs and variety of courses at Brite College of the Bible. By the middle of the decade, Brite only offered the bachelor of divinity and the master of religious education degrees. While the Great Depression had a negative impact in terms of financial strength, it forced the college to focus all of its resources on those areas that defined it most clearly as a professional, theological institution.

University Relationships

From 1914 to 1939, Brite College of the Bible enjoyed a largely mutually beneficial, cordial, and cooperative relationship with Texas Christian University. The university saw the preparation of ministers as part of its overall mission and supported that vision with financial contributions. The fact that many of the same trustees served on the boards of the university and Brite further supported the positive relations. Of the sixteen trustees who served Brite from 1914–1939, six also served as university trustees. Brite's trustees also served in key leadership positions: L.D. Anderson, the secretary of the Brite board, served as president of the university board, and L.C. Brite, the president of the Brite board, served as a member of the university board. As president of TCU and Brite, the university president occupied a dual office that later became a source of conflict. However, in this era there seems to have been little reason to raise serious question about the arrangement.

Differences over the implementation of a pension plan became one of the few areas in which the Brite and TCU Boards departed in the 1930s. Chalmers McPherson was the first of the original cadre of Brite professors to pass away. McPherson's lack of benefits for his family at the time of his death led the Brite trustees to explore the prospect of adopting the Disciples Pension Fund.[122] However, since TCU paid the majority of faculty salaries, Brite could not implement the plan without the help of the university. The university could not adopt a pension system for the Brite faculty without offering the same to its professors. Therefore, although the Brite trustees had approved a pension plan in 1931, the university trustees disapproved the plan under the financial confines of the Depression saying, "We fear so large a budget as would be necessary to carry it, would not be in favor at the present time."[123]

New Life

Beginning in the mid-1930s, the economic impact of the Great Depression slowly waned, and the university reversed its deficits, which exceeded $46,000 in 1934, to realize a surplus in excess of $10,000 in 1936.[124] However, churches still struggled to support the university, with only twenty-five churches making financial contributions totaling $3,150 in 1936. In the midst of the economic hardships, the Brite College of the Bible continued to fulfill its threefold mission of teaching classes to general undergraduate students of Texas Christian University, guiding ministerial students through the undergraduate process, and providing graduate-level professional and theological education that culminated in the awarding of the bachelor of divinity and master of religious education degrees.[125]

Since the number of students entering undergraduate education fell in the early and middle 1930s, and Brite relied heavily on TCU students continuing on at the school to pursue a BD, a lagging effect took place into the later 1930s in seminary enrollment. In fact, the reduction became so dramatic that in the 1936–1937 school year, Brite counted eleven faculty members (including ten-

The ministerial quadplexes allowed Brite students with families to live on campus.

ured faculty, instructors, and fellows) and only twenty seminary-level students. By 1938, Texas Christian University had an enrollment of 1,875 students, surpassing its numbers on the eve of the Depression. Meanwhile, the increase in Brite came much more slowly, with only seventy-two total students, of whom twenty-two were considered seminary students.[126]

Despite the small ratio of faculty to students, Brite hired a new full-time faculty member, Dr. William V. Roosa, in 1937. Roosa served as Associate Professor of Old Testament and received his PhD from the University of Chicago. The school hired Roosa not because of an increasing demand for Old Testament courses, but because of the age and imminent retirement of Clinton Lockhart.[127] Reflecting a growing movement toward specialization within the faculty, the following year Brite hired its first full-time professor in the area of Christian ethics, Dr. Cortel K. Holsapple.[128]

Over its first three decades as an independent corporation, Brite generally mingled its money with that of the greater university. At the time, this did not present a problem for the faculty or trustees of Brite since professors taught both general undergraduate and ministerial students. In fact, for most of the first twenty-five years, Brite paid the salaries of two full professors while the university paid the salaries of the two others. As acknowledged in the 1939 American Association of Theological Schools report, endowments and contributions given for ministerial students ended up in the Texas Christian University coffers, and the title and land of Goode Hall and the ministerial quadruplexes, built beginning in 1936, remained with the university.[129] However, the permeable boundary between Brite's and TCU's money was less the result of an intentional move on the part of Texas Christian University leaders or trustees to control Brite than the similarity of mission and purpose that gave rise to the relationship in the first place. Lines of division did not begin to appear until Brite limited its focus to graduate education in 1939.[130]

Not Just Boys

From the outset, both Texas Christian University and the Brite College of the Bible sought to serve as coeducational institutions. In 1916, following an address in the chapel, the university established a women's suffrage league with Mrs. Lena Gardner serving as president.[131] Though President Waits did not support suffrage himself, he allowed the group to operate on campus.[132]

As early as 1921, the Brite catalog explicitly stated that the school sought "to train men *and women* who will devote their lives to the preaching or teaching of the Gospel of Christ, as a vocation [emphasis added]." Yet, Brite College acknowledged that the world outside of the academy might not be as willing to accept women in church leadership roles. From the late 1920s, and through the 1930s, the Brite catalog carried the following caveat: "Women who have such a career in mind should be aware that employment will scarcely be found in it without mental ability and personality rating far above average."[133]

Since churches rarely opened the pulpit to women, Brite supported the training of women in areas that provided greater opportunity for them, particularly in missions.[134] Numerous women trained at Brite who went on to serve as missionaries. Among the most notable, Katherine Schutze graduated from Brite with a bachelor of arts in 1927, went on to receive a master of arts from Yale in Chinese Religion and Government, and studied at Marburg University in Germany.[135] Since no church would hire her, Brite College held an ordination service for her before she left Fort Worth for eventual service in China.[136] Schutze later taught at Drake University and Lexington College of the Bible and served as an advocate for the ordination of women. Other women who completed work at Brite and went on to the mission field included Esther Bonham, who received her bachelor of arts and served in India; Vida Elliot, who received a bachelor of arts, went on to obtain a PhD at the University of Minnesota, and served on the faculty of a school in India; and Ruth Musgrave, who received her BA in 1916 and served in Africa.[137]

Throughout the 1920s and 1930s, women represented a significant percentage of Brite students, though female enrollment suffered tremendously during the Great Depression. In the late 1920s and early 1930s, women accounted for as many as a third of the seminary students. In 1934, six of the twenty-two graduate seminary students were women. However, the number of female students dropped to four in 1936. By 1938, women disappeared from the roles altogether. Women's enrollment did not recover its earlier percentage of the overall enrollment until the 1970s.[138]

As the enrollment numbers suggest, Brite's and TCU's vision for training women did not always proceed smoothly. In December 1921, for instance, President Waits engaged in a debate with H.E. Stout, the president of Texas Woman's College in Fort Worth. Waits's presentation made negative comments about women's colleges in general and single-sex colleges overall. In response, Stout ran to the podium and tried to punch Waits. Even after the event, the two presidents traded sharp words. Waits stated his belief that "women are getting too independent when they are educated separately without men," and Stout responded, "We stand for women's rights and we can hand out the lefts too."[139]

In 1932, Brite faculty also entertained the notion of offering courses to African Americans. Professor Pickerill had contacts with the African American community through the "Colored YMCA." Pickerill raised the issue at a faculty meeting, and the group responded that he "make further inquiry regarding the demand and the educational background of those desiring courses."[140] However, the head of the YMCA, Secretary Fowler, informed Pickerill that while the YMCA appreciated the offer, black church leaders had the ability to take seminary courses through the Baptist church. Fowler suggested that taking courses through Texas Christian University's Arts and Sciences departments represented a more intriguing opportunity, an offer Pickerill was not able to extend.[141]

Conclusion

In 1939, Brite College of the Bible celebrated its Silver Anniversary as an independent corporation. As part of its anniversary, Brite boasted that it had educated more than five hundred men and women who went on to serve in various forms of ministerial service, with over three hundred serving as Disciples of Christ and more than one hundred from other denominations. Many students went on to serve as foreign missionaries and twelve students who studied at Brite came from other countries.[142] One estimate stated that Brite alumni filled as many as 50 percent of the Disciples' pulpits in Texas by 1940.[143]

In 1939, the college also published its first printed catalog separate from the university. The subtitle of the catalog read: "The Theological Seminary of Texas Christian University." This subtitle illustrates the growth of the school from a traditional, conservative Bible college to an academic theological seminary. This development occurred through the efforts of faculty and trustees who responded to changes in theological education, the financial growth of the 1920s, and even the limitations of the Great Depression.

In his analysis of the Brite College of the Bible from 1914 to 1939, Dr. Joseph R. Jeter Jr. describes the school as "solid, conservative, and unspectacular."[144] Jeter bases this on the fact that Lucas C. Brite and Colby Hall "were both of the classical conservative bent frequently found in Middle Period Disciples in Texas."[145] Jeter notes that Brite and Hall were not fundamentalists in the Church of Christ sense of the term, but were "classical Campbellian."[146]

Although Jeter is correct that Brite and Hall (as well as McPherson and Kershner) brought a classical conservatism to Brite, theirs were not the only voices. Even prior to the incorporation of Brite in 1914, Clinton Lockhart introduced critical methods of biblical interpretation to the classroom. Lockhart once stated, "The plan of the University is not to promote traditional theories, some of which are more imaginary than true. Its plan is to make a larger collection of facts than those upon which popular theories are based."[147] While Lockhart may have contributed a minority voice in the first decades of Brite College of the Bible, William C. Morro joined him in offering a more liberal and modern view. In his history of theological controversy within the Disciples movement, Stephen J. Corey views Morro as a transitional figure of modern training who led Disciples schools toward "a new pedagogy."[148]

In the 1930s, several full-time faculty, assistants, and instructors trained at the University of Chicago built upon the legacy of Lockhart and Morro. These Chicago-trained men (a term used in derision by former president Frederick Kershner) included professors S.W. Hutton and William Roosa, as well as Perry Gresham, University Christian Church pastor and part-time Brite lecturer.[149] The Chicago influence resulted in an increased application of the methods of higher criticism.[150] While Brite may have begun to show interest in the principles of contemporary scholarship and criticism later than many other seminaries, it certainly offered hints of moving in that direction by the 1930s.[151] Nonetheless, the tension arising from the introduction of modern scholarship remained as evident at Brite as it did at many other seminaries across the nation.[152]

By 1939, the Brite College of the Bible had also adopted many of the features of professionalism. One of the questions posed by the Brown-May Report of 1935 was whether theological education should precede or parallel the general movement in academia and the workplace for professionalization. The report concluded that seminaries nationwide had engaged in a process of fundamental change for over twenty-five years that made major changes unnecessary. Rather, seminaries needed to "continue and accelerate" the changes already taking place.[153] This analysis certainly applied to Brite. The school had undergone dramatic change over the past quarter century, but that change needed to "continue and accelerate" to meet the growing needs of the academy and the church.

Brite's development benefited from the region's financial and demographic resources, drawing from a rapidly expanding population in Fort Worth, which increased from 73,000 people in 1910 to 177,000 by 1940.[154] The economic boom of the 1920s, especially in Texas through the success of oil and cattle businesses, provided the financial capital necessary for the growth of the Brite faculty, the hiring of highly trained academic professors, the offering of diverse programs, and the creation of specialized courses. In contrast, in the 1930s, the number of courses dropped significantly due to the effects of the Depression. However, this reduction in courses and programs forced Brite to focus on the two programs that would allow it to become a true graduate theological school: the bachelor of divinity and the master of religious education.[155]

A growing market interest in graduate-level education also benefitted Brite's evolution. In 1914, most churches did not demand a pastor with a graduate education. In 1919, only 123 students, in seven Texas colleges, did graduate-level work. By 1928, that number had grown to 909 students across ten Texas colleges.[156] In keeping with these trends, Brite began to lay the groundwork from 1914 to 1939 to move from educating students with the minimum requirements for employment in a church on the western frontier to a professional graduate theological seminary preparing for accreditation through the American Association of Theological Schools.[157] As stated by Colby Hall at the end of the spring 1939 semester, "Next year will mark the beginning of the full theological status of the Brite College."[158]

3

Accreditation and Change: From Brite College of the Bible to Brite Divinity School, 1939–1963

Blaine Hamilton and Dyan M. Dietz

The years between 1939 and 1963 brought impressive change to American education, and for society as a whole. World War II, the Holocaust, the rise of the Cold War, and the spread of nuclear weapons raised deep ethical and theological dilemmas that seemed to destroy much of the basis for the Western liberal tradition, which emphasized society's limitless progress and human capacity for good. At the same time, the United States realized some of its greatest achievements. The civil rights movement provided hope to millions of Americans that the country might be moving toward racial justice. Likewise, the GI Bill, *Brown v. Board of Education*, and other legislation and court rulings granted access to people who otherwise would have been excluded from higher education.

This chapter will focus on Brite's responses to several changes within society and academy. It will also explore the clashing visions for how Brite engaged these changes within the context of Texas Christian University. As most of the figures involved in Brite's incorporation in 1914 faded from the scene, including Lucas Brite, Chalmers McPherson, Clinton Lockhart, and Colby Hall, a new movement arose within the leadership of TCU and Brite in the 1940s to reintegrate Brite more firmly within the governance structure of TCU. Such hopes fell on hard times in the 1950s as Brite chafed under the control of TCU's M.E. Sadler. By 1963, Brite came full circle by renewing its charter as an independent corporation, though a corporation that granted greater control to the university as it cast aside its identity as a Bible college in favor of the more culturally prized and educationally relevant category of divinity school.

The Importance of Accreditation

Brite's path toward accreditation with the American Association of Theological Schools in the early 1940s encapsulated many of the details surrounding Brite's response to changes within theological education. The American Association of Theological Schools (first AATS, then later, ATS) began as an informal meeting of Baptist professors from Newton, Harvard, and other New England seminaries in the early 1900s. The meetings escalated into a Conference of Theological Seminaries concerned with the state of American theological education in the wake of World War I. W. Douglas Mackenzie of Hartford Seminary organized the group's first meeting in 1920. He focused the meeting's agenda on the common concerns of seminaries, particularly fees, pre-seminary curriculum, financing, and administration.

The conference also attempted to gauge the pulse of theological education by sponsoring Robert Kelly's survey of American seminaries in 1924. However, Kelly's report shook the confidence of conference members. Glenn T. Miller summarizes Kelly's findings in his history of the Association of Theological Schools: "There were too many theological schools, operating with too low standards and too few resources, to produce the type of religious leaders that Kelly, a typical Protestant liberal, believed the churches needed."[1] Like law and medicine, theological education, Kelly argued, needed to focus on the preparation of highly literate and skilled professionals. As a result, Kelly proposed that many of the seminaries consolidate to form larger, more efficient, ecumenical, university-related educational institutions with higher standards for entrance and completion.

The conference offered a mixed response to Kelly's work and called for another study in the 1930s, this time by William Adams Brown and Mark May. Brown and May hoped their study, unlike Kelly's, would allow for diversity in approach to theological education while offering alternative means for correcting the inadequacies of the seminary system. Brown and May's study, completed in 1934, paved the way for the conference to become an accrediting agency that established and enforced clear standards for theological education. To keep pace with its new identity, the conference changed its name to the American Association of Theological Schools (AATS) in 1936.[2]

The first record of any communication between AATS and Brite College of the Bible occurred in 1936. Colby Hall, dean of Brite, received a letter from Lewis J. Sherrill, executive secretary of AATS, describing the association's proposed guidelines for a pre-seminary curriculum.[3] Leaders in theological education hoped that by proposing guidelines for students entering seminary, they could dissuade schools from enrolling ill-equipped students. The perception was that quality education was compromised by the fact that many theological schools at the time, including Brite, allowed students to count their senior year of college as their first year of the bachelor of divinity (BD) program, thereby reducing the BD to a two-year degree. Both the Kelly and Brown-May studies cited this overlapping of programs as a hindrance to the development of graduate theological education in the seminaries.

Hall expressed his gratitude for the contact with Sherrill, though he confessed, "The Brite College of the Bible is a theological seminary in the making but not yet made up to the standards described by the Association.... We should like to keep the contact, the helpfulness and receive the literature of the Association in the hope that in a few years we may reach these standards."[4]

Sherrill, recognizing that every institution was valuable to the burgeoning association, replied to Dean Hall by encouraging the growth and development of the seminary:

> It is a pleasure to know the plans and hopes you have for the future development of the Brite College of the Bible. . . . It has been of much interest to know the plans of some of the other institutions of your communion, who have been in a position similar to your own. . . . The College of the Bible at Lexington, Kentucky, in connection with Transylvania, has just voted, through its Board of Directors, to base their work on the three year plan for theological work on top of four years of college, thus ending their use of the telescopic plan.[5]

Sherrill no doubt used the reference to Brite's peer institutions to spur Dean Hall towards action. Hall was already familiar with accreditation and its role in strengthening collegiate academics. As academic dean of the university, Hall served on several committees responsible for overseeing the academic integrity of other regional colleges. Hall served as chairman of the Commission on Standards and later as president of the Association of Texas Colleges and vice president of the Southern Association of Colleges and Secondary Schools.[6] Through this activity, Hall became familiar with the growing trend towards accreditation and cooperation among institutions of higher education. So, it was no surprise that the prospect of Brite's accreditation intrigued Hall.

On October 20, 1938, the *Christian Evangelist* published an editorial acknowledging the newly formed AATS. The editorial recognized Phillips University's application to AATS and the College of the Bible at Lexington, Kentucky, as the Disciples' only representatives in the association.[7] Hall wrote to Charles Lynn Pyatt, dean of the College of the Bible at Lexington congratulating him on the accomplishment.[8] In response, Pyatt told Hall that AATS needed continuing positive publicity in order to overcome the fears against a new accrediting agency.[9] In a follow-up letter, Pyatt encouraged Hall to move forward with accreditation: "I am sure you realize that I am more than delighted that Brite College of the Bible is looking toward accreditation. I have never believed that one institution by itself could educate a whole brotherhood to the acceptance of high standards for ministerial training."[10]

Recognizing the credibility that Brite could gain through AATS accreditation and feeling the pressure of other Disciples seminaries moving towards accreditation, Hall decided to marshal the support of Brite's faculty and trustees for recognition with AATS. On November 21, 1938, the faculty held a discussion of the "Report of the Committee on the Standardizing of the AATS." According to the report, Brite needed to focus on teaching only graduate level courses, adopt the three-year BD curriculum, add one more full-time graduate-level professor, and another full-time undergraduate professor to accommodate the undergraduates at TCU since the Brite faculty would no longer teach undergraduate courses.[11] After a few weeks of discussion, the faculty met on December 19, 1938, and voted to present the three-year BD curriculum to the trustees and move forward with membership in AATS in preparation for accreditation.[12] In February of 1939, the Brite board of trustees confirmed the requests of the Brite faculty.

Dean Hall followed this action by submitting the appropriate schedules and forms supporting Brite's accreditation with AATS. Unfortunately, the organization did not respond favorably. E.H. Roberts, the new executive secretary for AATS, wrote to Dean Hall in November with the disappointing news:

> I feel quite certain that if a visit were made to your institution at this time and your application for accreditation were brought before the Commission in December, the Commission would be disposed to suggest a postponement of action, in view of the fact that it was

> not until September 1939 that Brite instituted the three year course for the B.D. degree and the curriculum in its present form. I am confident, therefore, that it would be greatly to your advantage for you to postpone your application for the present. I want to congratulate you on the splendid steps you have taken at Brite, and to assure you that the Commission wants to do everything it can that would benefit your institution.[13]

The AATS did count Brite a member school, but insisted it could not consider Brite for accreditation since their three-year curriculum had only just begun. Hall, frustrated and disappointed, replied to Roberts, "We were conscious of our weak spot in having had the new standards operating so short a time. . . . Our hope for recognition was based on the observation that we are free from many of the criticisms charged against other approved schools in the 'notations.' So we must confess to a genuine disappointment." However, in the same letter Hall asked for further clarification concerning the points of weakness in Brite's program. He claimed, "If we can have the benefit of the mature and expert suggestions from the members of this committee, we will have a line to work on for our improvement. This will not only be helpful to us as a faculty, but it may be of influence in gaining the support of our Board of Trustees for any matters of improvement."[14] Hall was determined to move forward in the development of Brite College of the Bible.

A month later, Dean Hall received another letter from Roberts that mentioned a forthcoming trip to the Dallas/Fort Worth area to visit with local faculties at Southern Methodist University (SMU).[15] Hall sensed an opportunity to showcase Brite and quickly responded, offering to bring Roberts by car to Fort Worth so that he could see the facilities of Brite College of the Bible.[16] In the faculty meeting on January 15, Hall described this visit as "one of acquaintance rather than inspection."[17] To further support Brite's accreditation efforts, Hall petitioned the board of trustees to pay for William Morro and himself to travel to Lexington and attend the 1940 meeting of AATS at the College of the Bible.[18] While there, the AATS appointed Hall to the Committee on Extension Theological Education, effective February of 1941, before Brite was even officially accredited with AATS.[19]

Finally, on January 5, 1942, Roberts notified Hall that the AATS officially accredited Brite College of the Bible. Roberts wrote that "the members of the Commission were impressed with the hard struggle that you have made to raise the standard of your institution." The commissioners made a single notation to Brite's listing as an accredited institution: "Inadequate library and library support."[20] Hall had already recognized the flaw in the library resources at Brite. Since TCU and Brite held all their books in common, Brite found it difficult to list the theological volumes it owned in the library. In 1939, Hall requested that the TCU trustees allow Brite to purchase its own books that would then be housed in the Mary Couts Burnett library at TCU. Hall hoped this arrangement would enable Brite to list more books in its collection for the AATS applications, though ultimately the list failed to persuade the commissioners.[21]

Despite the note related to library resources, Brite celebrated its accreditation. Hall responded to Roberts's letter: "You may be sure that we are highly gratified that the committee saw fit to give accreditation to our institution. Our faculty believes very sincerely in high standards, and in cordial cooperation with other institutions and faculties in our field. So we are very much encouraged by this recognition."[22] Hall reported the good news to the faculty in their meeting on January 19, 1942. He pointed out the reference to inadequate library resources, and the faculty committed to offering additional lists of books for the library to acquire.

The accreditation of Brite College of the Bible with AATS represented one of the school's central achievements. As we will see, the move towards accreditation affected the curriculum, the degree program, the faculty, the library resources, and more. Accreditation also symbolized Brite's hope to become an esteemed institution in theological education. Brite joined the ranks of its fellow Disciples schools—the College of the Bible, Butler University, and Phillips University—as well as other prominent institutions of theological education, including Yale, Princeton, Union, Chicago, and others. Brite was certainly still a small institution focused on regional issues and its Disciples heritage, but now it was also in direct communication with major theological educators from across the nation. This reality, along with the growing importance of the ecumenical, civil rights, and women's rights movements, influenced Brite to diversify its faculty and student body. Brite's evolving identity also led to growing tensions between the school and TCU over issues of economics and advancement.

Curriculum

Brite's accreditation played a critical role in the school's refinement of its curriculum. The College of the Bible offered the bachelor of divinity (BD) before its incorporation in 1914 (Clinton Lockhart introduced the degree in 1906 during his tenure as president). However, very few students had graduated with the degree by 1939. In his *History of Texas Christian University*, Colby Hall recognized, "The time was not ripe for this level of education on the cattle frontier. . . . [Disciples] churches were not demanding, or even expecting, graduate degrees of their preachers. The expectation of the students was not up to this level. To raise it so, was a responsibility of the faculty and administration of the University."[23] According to figures published in the 1939 Brite College of the Bible catalog, only twenty-five students had graduated with the BD by 1939.[24] Most students believed their bachelor of arts provided enough preparation for the ministry. In fact, BA students took courses from the same professors as the graduate students until the degrees were divided in 1939.

As we have already seen, the Brite faculty, after consulting the requirements for AATS accreditation, officially recommended the revised three-year BD plan to the Brite board of trustees in 1938. The faculty directed the Curriculum Committee (Dean Colby Hall, Dr. William Roosa, and Dr. William Morro) to work out the specifics of the curriculum changes. The faculty allowed current seniors to continue to apply their senior year towards the BD program. After 1940, however, all entering BD students enrolled according to the new three-year plan.[25] Almost immediately, enrollment in Brite College doubled.

Accreditation by AATS also influenced the way Brite organized the departments represented in the curriculum. Whereas in 1938 Brite maintained at least seven departments (Old Testament, New Testament, History of Religions and Missions, Doctrine, Christian Ministries, Field and Religious Education, and Speech), in 1939 they followed the lead of AATS and consolidated the curriculum into four departments (the Biblical Field, Historical Field, Doctrinal Field, and Practical Field).[26] While AATS claimed it was not concerned with defining "the proper theological encyclopedia" for seminary students, the application for accreditation divided the list of courses into the four fields mentioned above.[27] Most of the courses offered at Brite in the early 1940s, however, remained the same, just under different departmental headings. Until the outbreak of World War II and the introduction of new faculty in the mid-1940s, most of the substantial structure of Brite's coursework remained intact.

The United States' entrance into World War II in December 1941 profoundly influenced the work of Brite's faculty, as it did all aspects of American life. Texas Christian University immediately involved itself in the war effort by agreeing to offer its campus as a training ground for both US Air Force and Navy servicemen and women. While many other Disciples colleges and universities suffered, "these [armed forces] programs brought sustained enrollment increases to TCU during the war years."[28]

Along with the programs at TCU, Brite committed itself to train chaplains for the V-12 Navy College Training Program. Dean Hall first introduced the faculty to the plan for chaplaincy training on September 20, 1943. Hall provided few details about the plan, but presumed that "probably ten or twelve men [would] enter Brite College of the Bible for this training."[29] At the faculty's next meeting on October 18, Hall reported that a representative from the navy, Chaplain Faulk, had visited the campus and that both Brite and the College of the Bible in Lexington had been chosen as the two Disciples seminaries to participate in the program. On February 1, 1944, Brite contracted its services with the US Navy for the training of these chaplaincy candidates. The contract required that Brite "[accelerate] the program of study in order that students may complete six terms of instruction in two calendar years."[30]

Brite enthusiastically embraced the chaplaincy program. Hall described the program as "one fruitage of [accreditation with AATS]" because of the organization's influence in the recognition of seminary training programs for chaplains.[31] Brite even circulated letters describing the navy V-12 chaplain program and encouraging college sophomores to take the required tests and participate in the pre-chaplaincy program. The letter ended with "A Message from Brite College of the Bible":

> We are very glad to do our part for the Disciples of Christ and for the navy, since we are selected as one of the Seminaries to conduct this V-12 program. Our dealings with the Navy are exceedingly pleasant. There is no financial profit to Brite College.
>
> We shall be glad to receive students who have graduated from any of our colleges, and we invite correspondence by the officers of these colleges, as they counsel with their students. We shall in no wise solicit students from the college before their graduation. It is well, though, to begin correspondence during the senior year.[32]

In March of 1944, Brite began its navy chaplaincy program with two students, and also temporarily adopted the trimester system in order to accommodate the navy's request for an accelerated program. The 1944 *Brite College of the Bible Caller* explained, "During the emergency war conditions no provision is made for vacations, except for one week between trimesters, a total of three weeks each year. The Government assumes that men deferred or classified out of military service for preparation for the ministry will utilize every bit of time, and get into their pastorates or the chaplaincy as promptly as practicable."[33]

Brite also altered its admissions requirements in order to help undergraduate students who hoped to attend seminary avoid being drafted. In accordance with AATS standards, Brite required a completed BA degree for matriculation. However, on April 17, 1944, the faculty discussed a proposal received from the Federal Council of Churches and AATS concerning students and the draft. The proposal recommended that theological seminaries "indicate their readiness to accept for admission properly qualified men who shall have completed three academic years of college work, and that they so inform the colleges in order that pre-theological students may be properly certified to their draft boards." The proposal did not allow students to bypass their last year of coursework for the BA, but they could get an exemption from the draft board in order to enter a seminary program immediately after graduation. The proposal from the Federal Council of Churches and AATS was clear that "these recommendations are designed only to meet a war time emergency and would cease to be effective at the conclusion of the emergency."[34] The faculty voted to accept the proposal and recognize the pre-theological status of several students. On April 21, 1944, Dean Hall wrote a letter to Jerome Moore, dean of the Add-Ran College of Arts and Sciences at TCU, and S.W. Hutton, the TCU registrar, acknowledging ten undergraduate students who qualified for admission to Brite and whose names should be sent to their draft boards.[35]

The end of World War II brought other changes to the curriculum, particularly the introduction of Clinical Pastoral Education. In 1925, Richard Cabot's essay, "A Plea for a Clinical Year in the Course of Theological Study," popularized the idea of a year of internship for seminary students. Cabot claimed, "When we urge a theological student to get 'clinical experience' outside his lecture rooms and his chapel, to visit the sick, the insane, the prisons and the almshouses, it is not because we want him to get away from his theology but because we want him to practice his theology where it is most needed."[36] Cabot inspired numerous seminaries to develop relationships with independent clinical training centers that could offer their students valuable experience.

Brite instituted its clinical training program in 1948. The *Brite College of the Bible Caller* described the program:

> A limited number of students is received every year by the Council for Clinical Training for clinical internships in the general hospitals, mental hospitals, and reformatories in which it maintains training centers. The purpose of this training is to assist theological students to become better clergymen through first-hand, supervised experience with persons in distress. . . . Brite College of the Bible is listed among the institutions from which the Council will receive students. Scholarship aid will be granted to assist students in securing this training.[37]

Students participated in internships at local hospitals and other facilities, learning how to minister to those with medical and spiritual needs. Later, Brite expanded the program and included clinical training as a requirement for participating in the BD program.

New Leadership

Brite's responses to changes within society and academy during these years were profoundly influenced by the passing of longtime faculty and administrators and the emergence of new leadership. Beginning with only four full-time faculty members in 1940 in order to accommodate the AATS requirements, Brite ended the first half of the century with eight full-time faculty and numerous part-time and adjunct instructors supplementing the program with ministerial experience.

This expansion in the faculty occurred within the context of the absence of several very familiar faces. In 1943, the faculty learned of the passing of William Morro, Professor of New Testament, and the resignation of esteemed professor and former president Clinton Lockhart. Lockhart originally scheduled his retirement for 1941, but due to the conflict of World War II and the declining enrollment at TCU, the TCU board of trustees asked Lockhart to stay on for a short while. President Sadler and the trustees wanted to avoid hiring a new faculty member while also paying Lockhart's retirement package.[38]

Trying to fill the void left by Morro and Lockhart, Brite welcomed two new scholars to its faculty. In 1945, W. A. Welsh joined the faculty as Professor of New Testament, staying for only a short five years. In 1947, William L. Reed arrived as Professor of Old Testament. The faculty had already reorganized the Bible curriculum in 1944 from general courses and exegesis courses to background and interpretation courses. For the most part, Reed and Welsh preserved the curriculum they inherited.

Glenn C. Routt, a new faculty member appointed in theology, arrived in 1948. D. Ray Lindley, who succeeded Colby Hall as dean, had recognized the paucity of course offerings in theology, arguing, "It is essential that we be able to provide adequate offerings in this field no later than the fall of 1949."[39] Until this time, Brite had never maintained a permanent faculty member in Christian doctrine or theology. Routt apparently proved his worth because in the fall of 1949 he was appointed as head of the Department of Christian Doctrine. Dean Lindley claimed:

> The return of Professor Glenn C. Routt to our faculty with the fall of 1949 solves what has long been one of our keenest problems. For the first time in the history of the School, we have a first-rate theologian giving offerings which make possible a major in the field of Theology and Doctrine. . . . For the first time in the history of the school, we feel that we are now in a position to provide a strong program of work in all the major fields integral to a theological education.[40]

Along with the regularly offered course, A History of Christian Doctrine, Routt widely expanded course offerings to students by offering courses such as Theological Patterns in Protestantism, The Christian Doctrine of Man, An Introduction to Christian Ethics, Contemporary Religious Thought, and The Structure of Christian Theology.[41]

Among the most significant changes in leadership at Brite occurred in September of 1941 when Brite's original benefactor, Lucas Charles Brite, died. Brite served on the Brite board of trustees since its inception and also served on the board of trustees for TCU. After Brite's death, both the Brite board of trustees and TCU board of trustees nominated his wife, Eddie McMinn Brite, as his successor. Mrs. Brite accepted the nomination and served as a trustee until her death in 1964. In honor of her service to both Brite and TCU, Eddie Brite received an honorary doctorate from TCU in 1948.[42]

One of Lucas Brite's last, and ultimately most significant, acts as a TCU/Brite trustee occurred when he met with M.E. Sadler at the Disciples state convention in 1941, convincing him to accept the presidency of TCU. According to Noel Keith, "Mr. Brite talked three hours with Dr. Sadler. They talked of the kind of program which could be launched, how it could be done, what it would cost, and the support Mr. Brite thought he could rally for the enterprise."[43] Lucas Brite would never know the impact of Sadler's leadership upon the development and expansion of TCU at the cost of Brite College of the Bible.

A New President

As it searched for someone to replace President Waits, TCU's board of trustees offered a clear picture of the kind of leader they hoped to secure. A group of five search committee members drew up a list of "desirable qualifications" for TCU's new president.[44] The qualities contained in the list included Christian character, scholarship, and administrative experience. The search committee eagerly sought someone who was active in the Christian Church (Disciples), who could command the confidence and following of Texas churches, win esteem and cooperation of faculty, possess or acquire favor of alumni, and serve as an effective platform speaker. "Other things being equal," they argued, they preferred someone from Texas.[45] From this description, the search committee developed a list of twelve prospects, all male, and all Disciples.[46] Naturally, Colby Hall, who had served as a dean of the university and as dean of Brite College of the Bible since its charter, emerged as one of the top candidates. L.D. Anderson scrawled at the bottom of his copy of the board of trustees' list of "Desirable Qualifications" the words "Dean Hall!"[47] But Hall declined the invitation to apply due to his age.

L.D. Anderson, who chaired the committee, received letters on behalf of the candidates, including one from the students of Brite College of the Bible endorsing Dr. Kelly O'Neall because of his "genuine interest in both the University and Brite College."[48] Although there were many endorsements for the various candidates, the respect M.E. Sadler held within the "brotherhood," and the belief people had in his loyalty to that same brotherhood, won him the job. Roy C. Snodgrass, who later worked under Sadler as dean of Brite College of the Bible, sent the committee his recommendation. He wrote, "I should like to see Mac Sadler have the honor of this position. I think he possesses every qualification—experience, scholastic standing, organizational ability and respect of the brethern [*sic*]."[49] Elmer Henson, who would also serve as dean of Brite under Sadler, wrote, "Dr. Sadler is ideal for the place, and there is no question of his loyalty to the Disciples and the traditions for which we stand. Everywhere I go I find him held in high regard and loved by our brotherhood."[50] Interestingly, Sadler had been invited by President Waits to teach sociology at TCU almost twenty years earlier, but had declined the invitation.[51]

In a report to the board of trustees of Texas Christian University, dated April 19, 1941, the presidential search committee wrote its recommendation of M.E. Sadler as their candidate:

> By reason of the fact that, in the judgment of your committee, Dr. M. E. Sadler is preeminently fitted for this place of leadership among us: because he has received the highest scholastic training in this special field; because of his successful experience both as administrator and instructor; because of the conviction expressed by many members of the Faculty, including several heads of Departments that he would receive the unanimous and enthusiastic cooperation of the entire group; because of the desire of large numbers of the student body, including Brite College of the Bible, for his selection; because of the all-but unanimous desire of our pastors and congregations in Texas for his selection; we, your committee, present the name of M. E. Sadler, with our recommendation that he be made President of Texas Christian University. Believing that none of us would wish Dr. Sadler to come to the University at a financial sacrifice we recommend that his salary be placed at seven thousand dollars per year.[52]

Despite the report's contention that "large numbers of the student body, including Brite College of the Bible" were in support of the nomination of M.E. Sadler, the committee only received one letter of support from the students, and that letter recommended Kelly O'Neall.[53] In addition, James M. Moudy later commented that Sadler so impressed the trustees that they "chose him as the president when some of the faculty wanted Perry Gresham—very much wanted Gresham." Moudy added that "there was voiced opposition when he came as president, so much so that he didn't even set up for himself an inauguration. As he described it, he just went into the office, hung up his hat and went to work."[54] Regardless of any opposition that may have come from faculty or students, the majority of Disciples pastors stood behind Sadler's nomination.

Sadler brought a particularly strong interest in integrating Brite into the life of TCU rather than perpetuating L.C. Brite's vision of the college as a separate corporation. For their part, many on Brite's board of trustees, including the chair Elmer Henson, agreed with Sadler that it would be in the best interest of Brite College of the Bible to become a "divinity school" of Texas

Christian University. Henson helped lead the effort to change the relationship between the two institutions by forming a committee to evaluate the "needs of Brite," and to assess the best way these needs could be met.[55] As chair of this committee, Henson chose Oliver Harrison and Brite faculty member D. Ray Lindley to serve with him.[56]

Dean Hall, however, opposed the realignment of TCU with Brite. Henson acknowledged as much in his invitation to Lindley to serve on the committee: "At the board meeting the other day, the question of re-thinking the whole problem of Brite and its relationship to TCU was brought up." He added, "This is no attempt to go around the Dean, but he seems very reticent to do anything that would disturb the present condition. I do think that something must be done; and while we must move very carefully, this is absolutely essential as I see it."[57] That same day, Henson wrote Oliver Harrison about the possible changes in Brite's governance and the importance of having Lindley on the committee. "In regard to asking Lindley to serve on the committee," Henson wrote, "I believe Ray is the man; especially since the Dean is in favor of making no changes, or doing anything about the present set-up."[58]

Two months later, an opportunity to replace Hall presented itself through a monetary gift from H.H. Phillips, who had initiated the Living Endowment program at TCU four years earlier.[59] On December 23, Sadler wrote to Phillips in response to Phillips's effort to expand the ministerial education program at Brite and TCU by offering to donate $25,000 to the program with the stipulation that the Living Endowment program focus solely on ministerial education. Phillips also wanted D. Ray Lindley to oversee the program as vice president of TCU.[60] The original conversation between Sadler and Phillips included at least some understanding that Brite would eventually become a part of Texas Christian University.[61] Sadler responded to Phillips, "Dean Hall, Professor Lindley and several of our key board members have discussed this significant proposal of yours and see no reason why it cannot be carried out." He added, "Dean Hall, Professor Lindley and I feel that the most appropriate title for Professor Lindley would be, 'Dean of the Bible College.' Texas Christian University has had vice-presidents in the past who did not get along very well and this particular title is not frequently used in colleges and universities such as ours."[62]

Concerning Phillips's desire to have the Living Endowment reserved for ministerial students, Sadler wrote, "We have found that the total program of ministerial education appeals tremendously to our church people. In this program we have to take the student when he comes as a freshman from the high school and carry him all of the way through his pre-seminary and seminary training, covering a period of seven years." He concluded by saying, "All money secured through this special Living Endowment program would be devoted exclusively to ministerial education."[63] Sadler did not, however, limit his understanding of "ministerial education" to areas of specific ministerial training, but included every department within the university, both graduate and undergraduate. Phillips did not share this understanding. "To outline the plan, as I understand it," Phillips wrote, "this money will be used to finance a money raising campaign for the Brite College of the Bible."[64]

Because Brite had always taught both graduate and undergraduate ministerial students, Phillips did not see the four years of undergraduate education prior to seminary training as being separate from Brite's work. In response to Sadler's comments on the program covering a period of seven years, Phillips wrote, "It is understood, however, that every dollar of the amount raised will be used at Brite College, exclusively, and it will be expected to raise this amount from the members of Christian churches, using a plea for the education of ministers for the Christian Church."[65] Phillips closed his letter by saying, "If this program as outlined meets with your entire approval and understanding, simply deposit the checks."[66] Sadler deposited the checks the next day and sent two simple receipts to Phillips, one saying, "On December 31, 1946, we received from the Phillips Drilling Company, San Antonio, Texas, (by Mr. H.H. Phillips) check no. 3314 for $6250 (six thousand two hundred and fifty dollars), to be used in a special promotional campaign for ministerial education at Texas Christian University," and another noting the same for check no. 5257, for $5,000.[67]

Shortly before the checks were deposited, Elmer Henson called a meeting of the Brite board of trustees to explain that "Mr. H.H. Phillips of San Antonio offers to donate $25,000 to finance a Living Endowment for ministerial education in T.C.U. (graduate and undergraduate) with the understanding that Mr. Lindley be the Director of the campaign, while he continues as Professor. Mr. Phillips wants to pay half of the amount in 1946, hence the haste."[68] Henson went on to suggest that if the board were to recommend Lindley to take the place of Hall in June of 1947, Phillips would see his way clear to donate the remainder of the money.[69]

At that same meeting of the board, Hall offered his resignation with the suggestion that "it would be wise, if practicable to have my successor as Associate Dean so as to get accustomed to the routine of the office."[70] The following day, Sadler sent a telegram to Phillips informing him that Lindley had been elected dean of Brite.[71] In response, Phillips sent the remainder of the $12,500 pledged for 1946.

The Prospect of New Relations with TCU

The Brite trustees first recognized D. Ray Lindley in 1940 while he was still a graduate student at Yale. He had been serving a Disciples church in San Antonio, but Brite agreed to hire him for the 1941–1942 academic year in order "to allow him to resign his church in San Antonio in good grace, explaining to them the purpose in preparing to teach."[72] So, in 1941 Lindley was elected as Assistant Professor of Christian Ministries.[73] In his first year as professor, Lindley helped expand Brite's course offerings in the Practical Field with courses titled The Pastoral Ministry, The Local Church and the World Program, The Church in Its Community, and Contemporary Preaching.[74] Lindley received a leave of absence during the 1942–1943 academic year in order to complete his degree at Yale but quickly returned to his teaching responsibilities at Brite.[75]

At the time, Brite was accredited by the American Association of Theological Schools, along with Austin Presbyterian Theological Seminary, Perkins School of Theology, and the College of the Bible at Phillips University.[76] Enrollment in Brite College was high, and increased steadily through the latter half of the 1940s. As national movements for "expansion and consolidation" continued to grow within the church, interest in ministerial education within Disciples of Christ churches grew as well.[77] According to E. Brooks Holifield, at this time "various rating scales placed the ministry among the most desirable and respected occupations." In fact, a national poll in 1947 ranked the prestige of ministry thirteenth out of eighty-eight occupations.[78]

This rising prestige of ministry, along with a growing need for missionaries in war-ravaged areas and a renewed interest in postwar liberalism among Disciples, created the ideal environment for growth in American seminaries.[79] This interest presented opportunities for growth in both enrollment and resources. As interest in Brite grew among Disciples churches, it became even more important to Sadler that Brite become "an integral part of TCU." And with Lindley in the dean's chair, and Elmer Henson chairing the board of trustees, the time seemed ripe for an official change in the relationship between Brite and TCU.

In a letter from Sadler to Lindley, just prior to Lindley's entrance into the dean's office, Sadler wrote:

> As we approach the time when you are to assume the administrative

> work in our Brite College of the Bible there are two or three matters which I want to mention. Several significant developments have come in the life of the University during the past few years. Among these developments has been the organization of the work of the University into eight administrative colleges. The Brite College has become a distinct administrative unit along with the seven others. Our effort has been to keep all of these administrative units working together with the finest possible spirit of harmony and cooperation. In order to maintain this spirit each unit has to define its scope of responsibility rather definitely.[80]

The idea of Brite as a divinity school of Texas Christian University, and one whose "scope of responsibility" did not include the undergraduate religion students, was becoming a high priority to Sadler, and he worked to rally the support of Brite trustees. That May, Granville Walker, the minister at University Christian Church in Fort Worth and a Brite graduate, wrote Elmer Henson, "From time to we have talked about the advisability of making Brite College an integral part of T.C.U. The more I talk with President Sadler about the future of Brite College the more I am convinced that until such a move is made we are going to be crippled in our resources and in our ability to expand the program."[81] The idea that Brite would be "crippled" in its resources did not come from the statistics the seminary produced at the time. In his report to the board of trustees of November 12, 1948, Lindley wrote, "The largest number of Bachelor of Divinity degrees in the school's history was conferred in 1947," and "the largest number of total graduate degrees in religion" were conferred in 1948.[82] In addition, Lindley commented that the new division of funds for TCU and Brite would be fifty-fifty for all money brought in for ministerial education, and that "the school has been able to operate during this entire fourteen month period without the necessity of transferring any income from Endowments to the General fund whatever."[83]

Financial considerations clearly influenced Sadler's motivations for encouraging greater unity between Brite and TCU. The treasuries of the two schools had long been intermingled.[84] However, Brite managed to retain some control over funds designated for the College of the Bible. For instance, until 1942 Brite published a short paragraph in its catalog for those interested in bequeathing money to the school. The catalog directed the donor to specify that their donation was specifically for Brite College of the Bible, and not TCU. Then, in 1942 this notation was removed from the catalog. Around this same time, President Sadler reported to the TCU board of trustees: "Since the work of the Brite College of the Bible has been considerably changed during the past few months, since many churches are increasing their offerings to the Brite College, and since there are some possibilities of misunderstanding, I suggest that a committee be appointed to work out and recommend to both of the Boards a working agreement between the two."[85] President Sadler also appealed to the Brite board of trustees for their support in the fundraising efforts as well as their participation in a committee to negotiate the appropriate distribution of funds between TCU and Brite.[86] In 1946, along with the appeal to churches and the Living Endowment, President Sadler proposed a $2 million fundraising effort between Brite and TCU for the furtherance of ministerial education. This drive would support both the graduate work at Brite as well as a new undergraduate Department of Religion that Sadler had recently created.[87]

The Brite board of trustees, concerned about the equitable distribution of funds, provided for a committee "to work with the President and the Dean in ascertaining the needs of the budget of Brite College and to specify what portion of the Living Endowment and the Church offerings, and the faculty needs, in order to improve ministerial education and the relations between T. C. U. and Brite College."[88] Initially this arrangement resulted in Brite receiving one-fifth of the church offerings and one-half of the Living Endowment funds. After the appointment of D. Ray Lindley as dean, the distribution of funds would be renegotiated to a more equitable fifty-fifty arrangement.[89] However, in a report to the Brite board of trustees in 1949, President Sadler "stressed the teaching of Religion in all departments of the University; and called attention to the fact that all gifts of Churches and of Living Endowments are devoted to the teaching of Religion. He called attention to the fact that the Brite Board must not expect more than this from the Board of Trustees of Texas Christian University."[90] With this logic TCU could solicit monies from churches and individuals for "religious education" or "ministerial training," but utilize those funds for any department within the university since all departments of the university participated in the teaching of religion. Unlike many other universities that saw divinity schools as a drain on their budgets, Sadler recognized the potential funds that could be raised for TCU through its alliance with Brite and connection to the Disciples congregations.[91]

To assist in his vision for integrating Brite into TCU, Sadler proposed that Brite be included within a larger school of religion, with Brite teaching graduate students and a separate department teaching undergraduates. With

Construction of religion complex (1953).

this proposal, Sadler put forward the creation of a more formally organized undergraduate department of religion. The November 1949 issue of the *Texas Christian University Bulletin* announced that "a School of Religion is beginning to take shape on TCU's horizon. . . . Said Dr. Sadler: 'All support given to the University by Christian Churches is diverted from the University's regular budget and used specifically for the training of Christian Church ministers and lay leaders.'"[92] Sadler envisioned housing the new school in a single complex. Sadler publicly mentioned the need for "a new building to meet the needs of both the graduate and the undergraduate groups in Religion" at the Cincinnati Convention of the Disciples in 1949. Dean Lindley, who brought the matter before Brite's faculty for their input, received relatively strong support, in part because of the growing inadequacy of Brite's existing building. The faculty highlighted the "general accepted need of three units, a Chapel, a graduate unit and an undergraduate unit."[93] The groundwork was then laid for the religion complex, which would be constructed in the early 1950s.

Sadler hoped Lindley would publicly support and reinforce his vision for Brite. Sadler sent a memo regarding an upcoming banquet in which he instructed Lindley to "sit at the head table and be ready to make a two or three minute talk urging continued and increased support for our total ministerial education program at Texas Christian University." He went on to add, "I do not know how long in advance you have the ideas ready for the *Christian Evangelist,* but as soon as these present ones run out, I wish you would speak with me about some possible changes which might be made."[94] Here, Sadler pointed to the fact that the ads Brite ran in the *Christian Evangelist* made little of the fact that it was a part of Texas Christian University.

Sadler also made a point of requesting a change in Brite's letterhead, which had "Brite College of the Bible" with "The Seminary of Texas Christian University" and "Fort Worth, Texas" below it in smaller type.[95] On March 24, 1950, Sadler wrote Lindley, "In preparing letterheads, programs, or anything of that nature, it would be appropriate to put 'Texas Christian University' at the top and then the particular school or affair would be listed under the general heading."[96] The recommendation was most likely a message for the incoming dean since Lindley was already in the process of leaving. Sadler ended his memo by saying, "Texas Christian University is the big enterprise."[97]

Lindley's last report to the Brite board of trustees as dean listed Brite's assets at $93,675.13, with the value of endowments at $264,511.82. He also noted 118 students enrolled during the 1949–1950 school year. Several problems regarding faculty were also reported, including the fact that with Welsh's resignation, Dr. Reed would be the longest serving full-time faculty member, having just completed his third year at Brite.[98]

By July 1, 1950, when Roy Snodgrass, an ordained Disciples pastor who had served as president of the 1948 International Convention of Disciples, replaced D. Ray Lindley as dean of Brite College of the Bible, the relationship between Brite and TCU had been muddied to the point that it was difficult to tell where the actual authority to run Brite College rested. TCU's trustees required Brite to present its annual audit to them,[99] and all funds coming into Brite College in the way of donations were being filtered through TCU. Trusting that TCU had Brite's best interest in mind, Brite's administrators and board of trustees abdicated much of the control of Brite to Sadler and the TCU board of trustees. Many churches and pastors, however, still saw Brite as a separate entity, which legally it was.[100]

Sadler persisted in his understanding of the relationship between TCU and Brite, and between the president and the dean. Both the ads for Brite in the *Christian Evangelist* and Brite's letterhead were resurrected as issues for the president during Snodgrass's deanship.[101] In a notation at the bottom of a letter from Snodgrass to Sadler, Snodgrass simply wrote, "P.S. I had not heard of there being new letterheads for Brite College."[102] The new letterhead was something Sadler presumed Dean Lindley had already ordered, placing "Texas

Christian University" over "Brite College of the Bible" rather than the letterhead that was currently being used by Brite that had Brite's name on top and in larger letters. Shortly after this notation appeared, documents with a new letterhead did appear, but this new letterhead still did not place TCU's name on top. Instead of saying "Texas Christian University," it added "Office of the Dean" in the left hand margin.[103] By 1954, however, Dean Snodgrass's stationery resembled that of the deans of the other colleges of TCU. The new stationery included the Texas Christian University letterhead with "Dean of Brite College of the Bible" written in the left hand margin.[104]

Snodgrass was not one to spend time in political battles; however, these were important issues to President Sadler, and the public perception of the relationship between Brite and TCU was becoming more influential than the legal relationship. Sadler saw Brite not as an autonomous institution residing on the campus of Texas Christian University, but as a department of the University. As a result, he also saw his role as president of Texas Christian University inextricably tied to control and oversight of Brite College of the Bible. Interesting, however, is the fact that even as late as 1955, in response to the TCU board's continuing endorsement of an equal allocation between Brite and TCU of funds from Disciples congregations and other churches intended to support ministry, a separate typewritten note appended to the board of trustee minutes recognized, "Item one [the allocation of half of church offerings to Brite and half to the TCU general fund] will have to be considered conditionally, since it relates to Brite College of the Bible; and whatever is determined by this Board would have to be voted on by the Brite College Board before it could become official." In this way, in spite of Sadler's efforts, many on the TCU board continued to recognize the autonomy officially attributed to Brite's own board.[105]

Diversity

Although Brite grew in numbers by the end of the 1940s, the demographics of this growing student body remained largely as they had for the previous three decades. Most of the students had been undergraduates at TCU or were Disciples transplants from other areas of the country. The majority of the student body was also male. In 1939, the Brite faculty and administration publicly discouraged women from attempting the BD degree or enrolling at Brite. The 1939–1940 catalog included the following paragraph:

> The wives of ministers are especially encouraged to carry their

> training as far as practicable. . . . Experience indicates that out of the large numbers of girls who find it in their hearts to prepare for full-time Christian service, only a small proportion ever complete the training or enter the service as a vocation. But the church can use many in fields of missionary work, religious education, pastors' secretaries and helpers. And those who do not enter the work professionally can serve as lay workers with great blessing to themselves and the church. Hence those who prove their purpose by completing the undergraduate work are welcomed into the privileges of the graduate work. They are not, however, encouraged to enter the preaching service.[106]

This paragraph remained in the catalog until 1943, then in 1944, a new paragraph in the catalog directed women interested in ministry to TCU as well as Brite. The catalog noted that "Religious Education courses are offered for both men and women in the Seminary. Also they are available in the Add-Ran College of Arts and Sciences. Special scholarships are available for women who qualify and who make a good record."[107] Religious education was a growing field on the American religious landscape and one which readily accepted women who would accept lower pay or work as volunteers when male candidates were unavailable. Historian Glenn Miller explains, "Religious education programs in seminaries were marketed to female students, and some schools added or strengthened religious education programs to have a place for women students they had barred from, or at least discouraged from taking, the bachelor of divinity program."[108] Only much later would Brite confront this issue again and invite women to participate fully in all of the degree programs in the seminary.

The issue of racial integration emerged in the early 1950s. In a letter to Snodgrass, dated September 25, 1950, Sadler wrote, "You will recall that I spoke with you some time ago and with other faculty members of Brite College concerning the question of non-segregation in our graduate work and more especially in our Seminary." He went on to request a recommendation from Snodgrass "within a week" concerning the matter. He ended the note by writing, "Perhaps the teachers in the Seminary are ready to give you their judgment."[109] Snodgrass replied:

> In the light of conference with Reed, Routt, Troxel Hall and Morgan (Munro is out of the city) it is my judgement [*sic*] that Brite

> College of the Bible, Texas Christian University could do no less in the direction of the Supreme Court interpretation of our Constitution than to follow the policy of non-segregation on the graduate level adopted by the State institutions of learning. The fact that Brite is a seminary training youth for life service in Christ's kingdom would, it seems to me, mitigate the force of the contention that we are within our rights to refuse Negroes on the basis that we belong to a private university.[110]

At the October 20 faculty meeting, Snodgrass reported that "at the last Deans' Council meeting the group approved non-segregation in Brite College of the Bible."[111] The meeting minutes state that "the group here today accepted this report gladly and gave approval of the plan."[112] Later that day at the Brite board of trustees meeting, Snodgrass included this information in his report. However, the minutes from the trustees meeting stated, "Dr. Sadler also referred to the problem of race segregation in Brite College although at his request no action was taken."[113] It is not clear why it was put on hold when Sadler had approached Snodgrass about this issue, requesting a response within the week. However, the correspondence at the time suggests that Snodgrass's understanding concerning this issue was that if and when a person of color applied to Brite, the matter would be handled appropriately.[114]

Brite College of the Bible students and faculty (1952).

Vada Felder, back row left, Commencement (1954).

In June 1952, Brite decided to integrate on its own when John Claiborne, an African American, enrolled at Brite Divinity School. Dean Snodgrass, in order to admit Claiborne, sought permission from the Brite board of trustees. When board chair Elmer Henson informed President Sadler of the move to integrate Brite, Sadler's response seemed inconsistent with his original stance, unless, of course, he had expected the faculty and board of Brite College to vote against desegregation in the first place. In a letter to Dean Snodgrass dated June 19, 1952, President Sadler wrote, "I now have a letter from Dr. Elmer Henson, the main message of which is 'Those who like that kind of thing; that is the kind of thing they like.'" Sadler went on to claim that the board had not been clear enough in its intentions, and added, "I cannot at this time give approval to the admission of Negro students into our Seminary."[115]

The next day, Snodgrass called a meeting of the faculty to explain the situation. The Brite faculty requested a private meeting with the president, which was scheduled for the next day.[116] By the time the meeting was over,

Brite College had the permission it required to go ahead and integrate the seminary in time for fall semester. For recording purposes, the Brite board of trustees called a special meeting on September 3, 1952, before classes began, to make sure that approval to integrate was in the minutes. The board voted unanimously.[117] Two weeks later at the faculty meeting, Dean Snodgrass announced that "Negro students with standard Bachelor degrees were to be admitted to Brite College of the Bible beginning this fall."[118]

Two full years prior to *Brown v. Board of Education*, Brite began admitting African American students into the school. Perkins School of Theology at SMU in Dallas, and Southwestern Baptist Theological Seminary in Fort Worth, also opened their doors to black students in 1952, though, like at Brite, serious discussions had taken place for at least two years immediately prior to admission.[119] Austin Presbyterian Theological Seminary had already admitted its first black student in 1950, making it "the first postsecondary school in Texas to voluntarily admit blacks."[120]

The first African American to enroll at Brite in 1952, John Claiborne, was also the first to receive a BD degree when he graduated in the spring of 1955. Claiborne entered the military chaplaincy after graduating. However, the first African American graduate of Brite, Vada Felder, who enrolled shortly after John Claiborne the same fall, received her Master of Religious Education (MRE) degree in 1954.

While riding on a train returning to Fort Worth from a church convention, Felder read the Fort Worth newspaper that published news of Brite's integration. It happened to be the last day for registration. According to her account, she headed home from the train station, picked up a copy of her undergraduate transcripts, and enrolled that day at Brite College of the Bible.[121]As she put it, she walked in with her transcript that afternoon and walked out with a full scholarship that paid all her tuition for the program.

After spending her final year as the secretary of the Brite student council, Felder graduated in the spring of 1954 with an MRE, the first African American to graduate from Brite, or from TCU. In the months before her death at age ninety-seven, she recalled that her days at Brite were very comfortable and extremely fulfilling. She developed close relationships with several faculty members, which served her well during her years as founding director of the United Christian Leadership School (1954–1975). In fact, she often invited the participation of Brite faculty at the school, which provided Christian continuing education for pastors and other leaders in Fort Worth and surrounding areas.

Felder's importance to the community of Fort Worth also includes her role in bringing Martin Luther King Jr. to the city. In 1959, during her attendance at various Baptist meetings, particularly in Nashville, Felder met the Reverend Dr. Martin Luther King Jr. and his wife, Coretta Scott King. In her conversations with King in the summer of 1959, she invited him to come to Fort Worth to deliver a lecture. King agreed to come and confirmed in writing, in a letter dated August 8, 1959, that Felder treasured the remainder of her life.

King arrived in Fort Worth on October 22 and delivered a lecture, entitled "A Great Time to Be Alive," to about four hundred people at the Majestic Theatre. King's address traced "the struggle to save the soul of America."[122] During the afternoon preceding the lecture, Vada Felder had arranged for a meeting between faculty at Brite and Dr. King at a reception hosted by Dr. Harold Lunger, Professor of Social Ethics, and his spouse, Alberta Lunger, at their home in Fort Worth. Faculty who were there have long regarded that afternoon as a highlight of their time spent at Brite. Since no hotel rooms were open to Dr. King in the city of Fort Worth in 1959, he returned after the lecture to the home of Vada Felder and her mother at 1331 Stewart Street, where he spent the night in their upstairs guest room.

Souring Relations

In September of 1955, Elmer Henson, who previously served as the chair of Brite's board, officially became dean of Brite, although his work in that area had actually begun several months earlier. In May of that year, before Roy Snodgrass had officially retired, Sadler wrote Henson complaining that Brite had waited until six days before its graduation program to invite him. He wrote, "It seems to me just a little bit out of order for others to plan a graduation program and incidentally inquire of the President of the organization whether or not he might like to be present." Near the end of the letter he added, "One of the definite efforts I have put forth since coming to TCU has been to get all of our units to feel that they are a part of one great University." He went on, "The Brite College of the Bible and the Harris College of Nursing are the two units which seemingly have the most difficulty in integrating with the rest of the University."[123] Harris College not only began admitting African Americans at the same time Brite did, but Harris, like Brite, was legally a separate institution.[124]

By that June, when Henson began his deanship, he had already made a great deal of progress in securing donations for Brite College and TCU. "I should like to take this means of reporting to you about the work I have been doing," Henson wrote to the president. He went on to inform Sadler that he had secured gifts of $100,000 and had strong prospects for further donations.[125] Sadler responded with a note of appreciation for his "good promotional work" and expressed his anticipation in Henson's coming to Fort Worth.[126] Sadler's anticipation, however, was short-lived.

On October 25, 1955, Henson received a communication from President Sadler that said:

> In building the Religion Center it was necessary for us to secure and use general funds for all of the buildings with the exception of Robert Carr Chapel. Since we were not able to secure very much in the way of funds from those who should be primarily interested in Brite College the decision was that Brite College had approximately a 40% equity in the building which it is now using. In order to satisfy the interest of those who had made general contribution but not to Brite College and whose money had to be used in erecting this building, we told them all of the general facilities in the building would be directed by the University. This applies to such facilities as Weatherly Hall, the parlor, etc. I am sure this can be worked out with complete satisfaction to all persons concerned.[127]

If Sadler thought this agreement would bring "complete satisfaction" to Henson, he greatly underestimated the new dean. Three weeks later, after researching the subject with Unified Promotion, the company that had run the promotional campaign to raise funds for the religion complex, Henson, as the dean of Brite and as "the person who served as Chairman of the Board of Trustees of Brite College and Chairman of the Committee that had responsibility for building the Religion Center," replied to Sadler.[128] Henson wrote, "I was greatly surprised to know that a decision had been reached allocating Brite College approximately 40 percent equity in the present building. This matter was never discussed in the committee neither was it discussed in the Brite Board or in the University Board meetings."[129] He went on to explain that the $122,301.46 allotted to Brite through the crusade, the $9,000 donated by George Kuykendall, the $45,000 that TCU had agreed to pay Brite College for the old Brite building, the $75,000 given by Maggie Deahl Weatherly, and $50,000 that would be taken from Brite's reserve fund would leave a debt of less than $15,000 toward the final cost of $316,164.40 for the new building.

He added that he had reviewed the figures carefully and was making the letter "a part of the records of Brite College for your protection and for mine," and to register his "objection to any such decision without the knowledge of the corporation involved." In addition to the issue of the 40 percent equity, Henson pointed out that Sadler's letter was "the first indication that promises were made that funds would be used in the Brite College building for general facilities to be directed by the University." He closed the letter, "It is impossible for us to do our work here in Brite College as it should [be] done with the above conditions existing."[130]

Sadler, in a three-page response, agreed to meet with Henson. He also foreshadowed his arguments by explaining that Henson's figures were incorrect. According to Sadler, Weatherly had given more than $100,000, rather than the $75,000 reported by Henson, which actually supported Henson's argument that Brite did not owe money on the new building. Also according to Sadler, TCU had not agreed to pay $45,000 for the old Brite building, and he said that "it would have been more likely to have given credit for $15,000 to $20,000." Sadler went on, "You leave out of account in your letter the most important factor involved in the situation. If you had gone through the promotional processes such as I have for the past fifteen years, you would know how real this point is." Sadler argued that the Brites had been given "more recognition and publicity" in proportion to what they had done "than any other people who lived in this area." Because of this, Sadler said that in erecting the religion building they "had to be rather liberal in assuring people that this would not be just a Brite project." And then he added:

> Since we started promoting the Religion Center there has never been any talk on the part of the T.C.U. Board or the Brite College of the Bible as to any corporation ownership. Whenever any persons have asked me about it I have told them that we would probably let Brite College continue to own the old building and there would not be any adjustment in corporation titles. I would vigorously oppose any change in corporation title to any property which would further promote the Brite name unless the Brite family should see its way clear to do vastly more than it has done so far.... I expect we shall have to have long periods of conversation with reference to the whole question of ownership. Mr. Carr gave all of his money to Texas Christian University, and he wanted a University Chapel.... The first time I ever heard anybody mention a chapel

> was when Mr. Carr and I spoke about it following one of our T.C.U. Trustees' meetings one day. I told him I would like to have a chapel across the street which would symbolize the University's interest in Religion....[131]

Henson responded with a wide-ranging critique of Sadler's letter. Henson reminded Sadler that indeed each of them had polled their respective boards about the sale of the old building and agreed that "the cost of the building would be used as a figure for such a basis," a figure that was in excess of $43,000. He also explained that "it was the Brite College Board that voted to build this building and not the TCU Board," and that Brite College had assumed a debt of $40,000 for the land upon which its previous building stood. In addition, he pointed out that he, in fact, was the one who had visited Robert Carr when the idea of a chapel first came up. Henson then took up the issue of TCU's control of Brite's finances more generally:

> Recently I received a copy of a letter to Mr. Melton in which you state that Brite College is an integral part of TCU. I am informed by Mr. White that when a specially designated gift comes in to Brite College that half of that amount will be taken out of some other fund to balance the gift for TCU must have half of everything that comes in. Furthermore, I have nothing to do with the administrative committee regarding Brite College though we do have our own funds. The disposition of such funds is made with the Dean of a College that has no relation whatever to Brite College sitting in. May I assure you that when I came to this office at your invitation I had no idea such condition existed or would exist.[132]

Finally, Henson complained that after he had resigned as chair of Brite's board of trustees almost a year before, Sadler had not called a meeting of the board, and he noted that "terms of office have expired and no attempt has been made to re-elect or re-place them. No one has been elected to take my place on the Board." He closed his letter commenting that he did not resign his pastorate to take a deanship "that just means one of the Colleges of TCU. If that is what you want you have the wrong man." And he added, "We can neither build a seminary nor a faculty on that basis."[133]

When Sadler responded, he assured Henson that he believed they could reach consensus on the issue. He also warned, "I am not interested in working out any program for Brite College of the Bible unless it can be an integral part of our total University. I think this can be done."[134] That same day, Sadler sent another letter to Henson that addressed Henson's concerns about Sadler's failure to schedule a Brite board meeting. In addition to claiming he had been too busy to call a board meeting, Sadler asserted that "nothing has come into my mind which made us feel that we ought to have a Board meeting." Making clear his desire to control the board's agenda, Sadler insisted on receiving a "very specific list of items that you would bring to the Board." He cautioned, "If we do not get chance to discuss them [the agenda items] beforehand, I would approve any items which seemed to be needed and would oppose in the Board meeting any items which it seemed to me might be opposed."[135]

Sadler also took the occasion to claim ignorance about Henson's concerns for the new Brite building:

> You brought out in your letter several facts about deeds to property which I do not know about at all just because I have never been interested enough in that type of thing to bother to inquire. Frankly, I am not very much interested in this whole business of who owns it just so long as we can keep the University as a whole and all of the eight colleges going along in good shape.[136]

Henson refused to accept Sadler's excuse, writing, "In the beginning may I remind you that though you disclaim any interest in 'who owns what' that in a letter to me on Oct. 25th you specifically stated that Brite College had a 40% equity in the present building." "I took it from that letter," Henson went on to write, "that it did make a difference as you stated that because of that the general facilities in the building would be directed by the University." Henson also noted:

> As to the reasons for a Board meeting may I remind you that the laws of Texas under which we operate unless otherwise specified in the by-laws require a corporation to hold an annual meeting for the purpose of electing officers, receiving the report of the auditor and approving a budget of funds collected and accrued. I presume also that we would have an additional report from our endowment committee as to the investment or proposed investment of at least $100,000.00 for which I signed a check to be withdrawn from the Board of Church Extension and about which I have heard nothing.

> I notice further that you say that if I do not talk matters through you will oppose in the Board meeting those things that need to be opposed. I have attempted all fall to talk some matters through and have waited for time which I have requested.[137]

Exasperated, Henson concluded his letter by informing Sadler that he intended to resign at the board meeting.

Although no record of further communication between the two concerning this letter has survived, several things changed almost immediately. A week later, in a letter dated January 30, Sadler wrote Jerome Moore, who was chair of TCU's space allocations committee, to revise his "original suggestion" because "the situation with reference to Brite College is unique and I believe you will need to leave the new Brite College building out of your University-wide planning."[138] Sadler also requested that Noel Keith, a Brite faculty member who had functioned as a building supervisor, turn his keys to the Brite building over to Dean Elmer Henson and to give Henson any suggestions that had been worked out "for the use or direction of the properties." Sadler added, "It seems to me that Dean Henson should assume the responsibilities of directing the Robert Carr Chapel and the total Brite College building, including the guest rooms, Weatherly Hall, and that part of the Cloister nearest to Brite College."[139]

Finally, on February 2 Sadler wrote to two different pastors that the responsibility, of lending Brite College money had been transferred to Dean Elmer Henson, and on the third of that month, he wrote Henson that "carbons of the letters which I have written to Dr. Keith and Mr. White are self-explanatory. It will be a tremendous relief if you will accept the responsibilities for handling any Brite College loans and also the responsibilities for directing your Building plus the Robert Carr Chapel."[140]

On October 31, 1957, the Brite board approved a resolution authorizing transfer of the old Brite College of the Bible building, and its property, in exchange for the new Brite building and grounds. The minutes of that meeting state that "this exchange of property came about as the result of a study and recommendations made by a committee.... The exchange was to be effected without any consideration other than the property involved." A motion to accept the proposal carried unanimously. The minutes also note that "Mr. Sadler" commended the chairman of the board and "commended Dean Henson for his excellent administrative leadership."[141] That month, Brite College of the Bible had its own dedication of the new building, celebrating its ownership and honoring Colby Hall for his years of service. Sadler commented that in many respects the celebration was "the best one of its kind" they had had on campus in several years.[142]

The following summer, Sadler announced that "income from the churches, which formerly was established on a 50-50 basis between the Graduate Seminary and the undergraduate religious training program, more recently had been reallocated as follows: ½ for the Graduate Seminary and ½ for the whole Christian emphasis program of the University." He added, "Brite College could hardly expect a more generous division of the funds than is being made by this allocation."[143] The minutes reflect that "as a result of Dr. Sadler's report," and "after some discussion," it was moved that Brite College of the Bible reaffirm its "conviction as to the historical position of the functional unity of Brite College with TCU." The motion was offered in the interest of "making it clear that there was no intent or tendency on the part of Brite College to become a separate institution from TCU."[144] The struggle to have functional unity, along with clarity in matters of governance, would continue to be a part of the relationship between this autonomous theological institution and the university in which it resided.

Sadler, now chancellor of the university, still insisted that Brite's best course would be to become a divinity school or college of Texas Christian University. In a letter to Lindley, who now served as president at TCU, in 1961, Sadler wrote, "It disturbs me very greatly for persons to speak of 'Texas Christian University and Brite College of the Bible.' . . . Texas Christian University is Brite College of the Bible."[145] After twenty years, Sadler still resisted the implications of Brite's separate incorporation from TCU, but the clarifications that had taken place under the deanship of Elmer Henson made it a moot point, at least for the time being.

In the spring of 1963, Brite College of the Bible renewed and amended its charter (the Articles of Incorporation), but the bylaws were not changed. The amended articles changed the name of the school from Brite College of the Bible to the Brite Divinity School.[146] Interestingly, the discussion of the board regarding the name change did not center on whether the name should or should not be changed, or whether the name of the Brite family should be attached to it, but on whether the name should be "Brite Divinity School" or "Brite Theological Seminary," reflecting the ongoing struggle within theological education of following the "divinity school" model characterized by integration into a larger university or the "seminary" model characterized by autonomy in governance.[147] The new charter also removed the fifty-year time limitation on the school's charter, making the charter "perpetual" and stipulating that upon final dissolution, all assets would go to Texas Christian University, "to be used only in the training and education in preparation for Christian ministry."[148]

With two exceptions, the other changes in the charter involved updating of language and titles and deleting unnecessary verbiage. In contrast to these more mundane changes, the charter made a clear break with Brite's past by removing the doctrinal statement and accompanying requirement that all faculty adhere to it upon threat of dismissal. Since the statement had not been enforced for several years, the board made the change with little comment. Nevertheless, the change signaled the end of one of the most controversial components of Brite's early history. Finally, the purpose statement in Article II included a new phrase, one foreign to the original Articles of Incorporation: "The purpose for which this corporation is formed is to conduct a graduate school of religion as one of the constituent units of Texas Christian University."[149] . . . This shift to one of the "constituent units" of TCU provided TCU administration with a measure of control they could exercise whenever they chose. But Brite's bylaws, as well as these articles, continued to recognize Brite's status as an independent corporation. This recognition technically protected Brite's ability to place its "particularity and distinctiveness" on display in prophetic ways when administration and faculty felt it necessary to do so.

4

Culture and Education: Social Awakening at Brite, 1964–1977

Greg Henneman

On May 4, 1964, Brite celebrated the golden anniversary of its separate incorporation as a theological seminary (1914). Over three hundred people gathered for a ballroom dinner and lectures. Two ministers, Dr. Granville Walker and Newton J. Robinson, provided the speeches. Dr. A.T. DeGroot, professor of church history, summed up the event in a May 1964 issue of the university newspaper, the *Skiff*: "Brite Divinity School enters its second half century loyal to its original intent, to provide an effective graduate training program for the ministers of the Christian Church (Disciples of Christ) and the cause of Christ in Texas and around the world."[1] Among the accomplishments celebrated at the anniversary was the sevenfold increase in student enrollment in the previous decade and the addition of three new departments: Missions, Christian Ethics, and Pastoral Care.[2] DeGroot's summary reveals the extent to which denominational identity shaped Brite's understanding of its mission.

In many ways the institution, renamed Brite Divinity School in 1963, shared many characteristics with the Brite College of the Bible, legally incorporated in 1914. Of most obvious note, the composition of the 1964 student body was almost entirely white and male. At the same time, Brite remained financially dependent on the greater support of Texas Christian University. For example, in 1965, Brite Divinity School had a net deficit of $165,420, which the greater university completely underwrote.[3] This annual support given by the university equated to approximately half of Brite's total operating expense. Former Brite professor Walter Naff remembers the dire state of Brite's finances:

"I remember going down to the dean's [Elmer Henson's] office needing some chalk—blackboard chalk. We didn't have any, we couldn't afford it, that was the mindset."[4] As a result of this financial situation, Brite was dependent on the university for its survival. Of course, fundraising in the university also depended on its connection to the church and the primary role Brite played in educating ministers. Chancellor McGruder Ellis (M.E.) Sadler kept a tight rein on finances within the university. In the years he exercised control over Brite, Sadler used the mantra of ministerial education to raise funds that went directly into the university's endowment, and only secondarily into the seminary's budget.

From 1964 to 1977, the Brite Divinity School changed in dramatic ways—more than in the previous fifty years combined. Although the ever-present concerns of financial solvency and academic development persisted from 1964 to 1977, changes in these areas were not particularly remarkable. Brite faculty and administration appeared content and comfortable to continue the mission of "preparing men and women for the varied ministries of the Church of Jesus Christ" through the financial and academic channels already in place.[5]

Rather than describing the minor changes that took place in governance, the focus here is on the dramatic social changes that took place in the late 1960s and early 1970s. Although North Central Texas was not a center of unrest and national change during this period, Brite was not immune to the social upheavals of the era. Reactions to these social changes shaped the institution and altered the school's composition, curriculum, and general ethos.

Following the Chancellor's Lead

Chancellor Sadler played a strong role in the development of both Texas Christian University and Brite Divinity School. During his twenty-five years of leadership, from 1941 to 1965, the university campus grew by nearly 250 acres, the student body increased from 1,700 to 9,000 students, the annual budget increased from $700,000 to $9,387,000, and university endowment multiplied nearly seven times from $4 million to $27 million. Sadler possessed the solid reputation of a dynamic preacher, one who was passionate about church-related higher education.[6]

While the strength of Sadler's leadership brought both financial and numerical growth, it came with the tight control of his singular vision. Under Sadler's leadership, Texas Christian University remained a strictly conservative school. Sadler believed Christianity (usually a particular form of it) had to be central in every part of academic education, whether a student studied business, chemistry, or the Bible.

In Sadler's view, every academic department had to emphasize Christian ideals. Thus, Brite Divinity School simply did what every department within the university was expected to do. For Sadler, Brite's relationship to TCU simply paralleled the relationship between TCU and the College of Arts and Sciences. Though it had clearly meant something to Dean Elmer Henson, the fact that Brite, since 1914, possessed its own incorporation, charter, board of trustees, budget, and endowment meant little to Sadler. He exercised complete operational control over the seminary. An image in the 1964 Brite Catalog expresses symbolically the two institutions' close relationship under Sadler. In the first year since Brite changed its name from Brite College of the Bible to Brite Divinity School, the cover of the catalog showed well-dressed, professional-looking Caucasian students not in front of Robert Carr Chapel, but walking in the shadow of the columns of Sadler Hall, the name given to the administration building built in the 1950s.[7]

According to Brite's 1963 catalog, "The student body is interracial, international, and ecumenical."[8] While this inclusive vision may have been an accurate statement of the hopes of the faculty, it did not reflect the reality found in the classroom. At the beginning of this period, over 95 percent of the Brite student population was male, with the few women who attended oriented toward master of religious education degrees. The Brite catalogs of the early-to-mid-1960s featured only the faces of white students, including the all-white, twenty-four member student organization the Singing Seminarians.[9]

Although the dominance of white male students could be dismissed as reflective of the times, for many years it was the implicit and explicit policy of Texas Christian University. In 1962, the student body of the Brite College of the Bible, supported by Dean Henson, wrote a petition calling for the desegregation of the university, that "all areas of university life be made available to all qualified persons regardless of race or color."[10] Although the petition arrived at Chancellor Sadler's desk, it did not make its way to the trustees' meeting. While Brite's student body broke the color line in the early 1950s, TCU continued to maintain a policy of strict segregation. The next month, Henson "petitioned the executive Committee of TCU to permit Negro students" who were enrolled in Brite College of the Bible to take classes in TCU in order to address their deficiencies and "properly prepare them for their work in the seminary."[11]

In November 1963, trustees voted to maintain the university's segregation, noting that allowing a limited number of Negro students to attend the

Evening College was its preferred course of action.[12] In fact, TCU used the fact that it had allowed black military students to attend the Evening College since World War II and that Brite had integrated in 1952 as a point of bragging that it had integrated two of its colleges before the 1954 Supreme Court *Brown v. Board of Education* ruling.[13]

Despite this 1963 vote, Sadler called a special meeting of the trustees on the issue of integration on January 23, 1964. Sadler moved to enroll students "without reference to race, creed, or nationality. . . ." Although Sadler's proposal came a decade after the landmark case of *Brown*, several trustees balked at the proposal. A few trustees offered a counter-motion that the university continue its policy of segregation while other trustees proposed the university take no action. In the end, Sadler's proposal passed with twenty-one in favor and four opposed.[14]

Following the proposal's passage, the trustees issued a self-congratulatory statement, crediting Chancellor Sadler, in the *Skiff*, with the "smooth handling" of integration. They also reassured those who might be nervous that "at most 12 Negro students had enrolled in the Evening College under the new ruling [and] at the close of spring registration . . . no Negroes had entered day school as undergraduates."[15] An indication of systemic racism that most were blind to at the time, trustees casually remarked that few black students could attend the university anyway. Black students, they surmised, would be unable to meet increased academic standard and raised tuition fees, and, besides, most black students preferred to attend Negro colleges. In sum, the trustees believed that "for the next half century there would be few Negroes who had the intellectual abilities and financial resources necessary to attend Texas Christian University."[16] The events of the next five years demonstrated beyond any measure of doubt the inaccuracy of this forecast.

While overt racism existed at Texas Christian University throughout the 1960s, exceptions were also evident. Individual students within the university occasionally engaged in activities calling for racial justice. One such example came in the work of a TCU senior, Joey Jeter, who found himself jailed for helping African Americans register to vote in Magnolia, Mississippi. In 1964, police arrested Jeter as he accompanied three people to the county courthouse. Police held him for forty-three hours, denied access to phone calls, and treated the four arrested persons harshly.[17] Jeter later finished his doctorate at Claremont Graduate University and joined the Brite faculty in 1984.

Though faculty members at Brite during the 1960s were likely more progressive than the ethos found within the general university culture, racism and

Christian centrism existed in both schools. The cartoons printed in Brite's weekly newsletter illustrate the point rather clearly. They usually reinforced the ideals of white, Christian power during the period when racial demonstrations occurred across the United States. For example, one cartoon, titled "Either Discipline or Disorder," is dominated by a powerful white judge, quoting from the book of Proverbs, who slams his gavel to the bench and points his finger at a diminutive dark figure labeled rioter. Another cartoon features the face of J. Edgar Hoover alongside a church and describes those who attend Christian congregations as the most substantial citizens in the country. To make matters worse, the *Skiff* published an article within which Hoover connected "the Negro Civil 'Rights' movement" to the growing influence of communism.[18] Note the editorial prerogative exercised by TCU students by placing 'Rights' in quotation marks. The Brite newsletter also carried a cartoon series called "Church Chuckles." One particular cartoon showed two white pastors watching a group of black Africans, each with a spear in one hand, club in the other, and bone through his hair, carrying an elephant. One of the white ministers says, "I'm using it for an illustration Sunday." This type of cartoon was typical of the kind found in the Brite newsletters from 1964 to 1968.

From the late 1960s and into the early 1970s, new imagery began to replace the overtly racist cartoons. In contrast to caricatured Africans, editors printed a photograph of a mix of all peoples with the poem, "Psalm for All Races," that begins, "My God is very God of all races, His saints and his people are of handsome hues. . . ."[19] Once dominant, male faces gave way to pictures of women like Stephanie Mills, who gained national attention for her 1969 valedictory speech at Mills College in which she stated her right not to bear children.

While Brite and TCU struggled to move toward racial and gender integration, the university continued its long standing relationship with Jarvis Christian College, an all African American school located in Hawkins, Texas. From 1964 to 1976, TCU maintained official and formal affiliations with Jarvis.[20] Support included financial assistance and the work of university faculty who traveled to East Texas to teach seminars and other special courses. In 1969, TCU helped Jarvis achieve regional accreditation and improve its facilities. However, this support illustrates the university's divided understanding of race. The university was willing to give from its resources to help a struggling school in East Texas, but it did not create an environment where black students would feel welcome on its own campus.[21] Perhaps some thought the support for Jarvis would provide an alternative for black students and, simultaneously, enable the university in Fort Worth to avoid racial problems. Writers associated with the Brite newsletter communicated the general sentiment of Jarvis students, following a November 1968 visit by students from Hawkins, when they quoted these students as saying, "You were great to us, but what I want to know is why don't you communicate with the blacks on your own campus."[22]

In 1963, Brite faculty supported an initiative by the United Christian Missionary Society (UCMS) to provide education for laypersons and part-time pastors.[23] Through the resulting Lay School of Theology, Brite faculty became involved in education for laypersons from Arkansas, Louisiana, New Mexico, Colorado, Oklahoma, and Texas. The school existed to give church leaders the "opportunity for a week of serious and concentrated study in order that they may give a more adequate witness to the Christian gospel." From July 14 through 19, 1963, Brite hosted its first school, which became an annual event. The first year featured lectures by professors Lunger, Routt, and Stewart. Unlike the dominantly male make-up of the Brite student body, half of the fifty seats available for the lay school were reserved for women. The move recognized that women hungered for theological education even though cultural and systematic impediments restricted graduate-level participation.[24]

In 1964, President Sadler's vision of a wholesome Christianity found on every part of the campus may have seemed unremarkable to those hearing this often-repeated theme in his speeches. At the time, Sadler, the trustees, the faculty, and the student body could not have had any idea just how seriously assumptions relating to the centrality of Judeo-Christian values would be challenged in the coming years. When, on March 14, 1965, over six hundred people participated in the first biracial protest in Fort Worth history, ignoring the massive civil rights movement became a bit more difficult. Among the protestors were religion professor Dr. George P. Fowler and University Christian Church Youth Director Eddie Taylor.[25] Other overt challenges to WASP-ish values were not far behind.[26]

A New Style of Leadership

At an April 1965 meeting of the Texas Christian University board of trustees, three months after suffering a heart attack, Chancellor Sadler requested retirement. He had been chancellor for twenty-four years. Noting that he arrived to the job with little fanfare, and that he sought to leave in the same way, he said, "No one could put as much of his life in a single program as I have put in TCU without being very deeply concerned about the ongoing life of this institution."[27] So, TCU elected Sadler to a position created specifically for him—executive chair of the board of trustees.

Dr. James M. Moudy served for five months as interim chancellor before both TCU and Brite trustees elected him to serve as the new chancellor. In the first formal event of its kind in nearly fifty years, TCU inaugurated Moudy on November 19, 1965.[28] In many ways, Moudy spoke a different language than his predecessor. Sadler consistently espoused a triumphalist view of Christianity. He defined Texas Christian University as a place responsible for "the survival of . . . democracy" and emphasized the imperative to foster spiritual growth among all students through education. In his inaugural address, "Education without Magic," Moudy offered a different understanding, warning against placing too many expectations on education. He stated that education had "become the nation's rabbit's foot, thought to cure all ills and to guard against all evils."[29] Instead of understanding the university as the place from which democracy and pious Christian identity would emerge victorious, Moudy sought to attract the best possible faculty and provide the highest level of academic achievement. Where Sadler sought to "make religion the focalizing center,"[30] the 1973 Priorities Committee affirmed the school's religious heritage while embracing classical and progressive educational models, innovative possibilities, and critical awareness.[31]

Relations between TCU and Brite changed not only because of differences in the vision and personality of the new chancellor, but because of the unique relationship Moudy had with Brite. He attended Brite beginning in 1946, serving as an assistant minister at University Christian Church, and he graduated with a bachelor of divinity degree in 1949.[32] As an undergraduate student at TCU, Moudy found inspiration in the instruction of his undergraduate Bible teacher, Granville Walker. Colby Hall also influenced Moudy by raising Moudy's interest in church history, and Moudy went on to receive his PhD in that area from Duke University. Not only did Hall inspire Moudy academically, but when it came time to make a career decision, Moudy flew from North Carolina to Fort Worth to seek Hall's advice.[33]

Hall advised Moudy to become a professor in church history. In fact, while Moudy studied at Duke, he entertained the hope of replacing Colby Hall at Brite. However, two years into his studies, Hall retired and Brite hired Dr. A.T. DeGroot as its professor of church history. At the time, Moudy recalled, "My balloon burst again. . . . This is the end of my life, what can I do, no other place."[34] Despite this initial reaction, through Moudy's connections with Jack

Suggs, New Testament scholar and later dean at Brite, and Ray Lindley, who became president of Atlantic Christian College, Moudy became a dean at Atlantic Christian College in 1953.

After Moudy spent a year at Atlantic Christian College, Lindley returned to Texas Christian University as executive vice president. Moudy reflected, "I had just gotten there . . . and then he deserted me."[35] The board of trustees at Atlantic Christian College offered Moudy the presidency, but he desired to return to Texas, and through Lindley's connection he came back to Texas Christian University in 1957 as dean of the graduate school, moving later into the position of vice chancellor for academic affairs and executive vice chancellor.

From these experiences, Moudy assumed the position of chancellor of Texas Christian University and Brite Divinity School. Based on his own studies as a Brite student, his friendship with professors Hall, Lindley, and Suggs, his own studies in church history, and his administrative background, Moudy approached his relationship with Brite in a manner much different than Sadler had done. Although Moudy pushed the trustees and professors at Brite to increase the quality and size of its faculty and to build its endowment, he did not micromanage daily operations.

Moudy indicated to the Brite board of trustees that "under his administration, Brite would have the top priority in the University, and asserted that no other mandate to the University is so great as that of being a genuine servant of the churches."[36] These words of support for Brite were more than a mere token of good will. In the period leading up to the mid-1960s, Brite grew substantially, recording the largest student body since its founding. By the middle of the 1960s, the Brite student population held steady around 150. The stability of Brite's enrollment stood in contrast to the greater tendency in theological education of declining enrollment. Over a five-year period in the 1960s, enrollment in Disciples schools dropped by 15 percent while Brite's held steady.[37]

In order to accommodate student growth and remain competitive in attracting the smaller number of students interested in theological education, Chancellor Moudy initiated a move to hire an assistant dean. The assistant dean would handle administrative tasks and recruitment, which would free Dean Henson to do more fundraising.[38] This concept came to fruition in 1966, when Brite hired William E. Tucker to help Dean Elmer Henson. Moudy's leadership consistently cultivated the quality of faculty and education at Brite. In a 1967 visit by the American Association of Theological Schools, the governing body described the chancellor's support as outstanding.[39]

In the middle 1960s, Brite expanded its faculty, and within two years, from 1965 to 1967, the institution hired six new faculty members who remained fixtures at the seminary for decades: William Baird, Hunter Beckelhymer, Marcus Bryant, Walter Naff, Robert Olsen, and William Tucker. Most of these professors possessed both impressive academic credentials and strong church affiliation. For example, before coming to Brite, Tucker served as chair of the Department of Religion and Philosophy at Atlantic Christian College and gained denominational renown for his book, *J.H. Garrison and the Disciples of Christ*.[40] Beckelhymer received his theological education from the University of Chicago and Christian Theological Seminary. During his career, Beckelhymer wrote or edited four books and served as the pastor of several churches. William Baird completed his graduate and doctoral work at Yale University and taught for over a decade at Lexington Theological Seminary before arriving at Brite. Baird became one of Brite's most prominent scholars, well-known in the academy for his scholarship and deeply appreciated by faculty and students for his work as a colleague and teacher.[41] Marcus Bryant came to Brite from his previous teaching position at Drake University, and before that as a pastor from Nebraska, to become Brite's second professor of Pastoral Theology and Counseling.

Each of these professors introduced new courses upon their arrival. William Baird taught a seminar on Rudolph Bultmann, and Marcus Bryant taught a new class on interpersonal relationships and communications, which remained a popular course for the next twenty-four years.[42] Existing faculty, including Dr. DeGroot, who published his twenty-fifth book, *Church Unity: An Annotated Outline of the Growth of the Ecumenical Movement*, in 1969, also developed new courses. DeGroot used the new book for his new course covering the ecumenical movement.[43] As Brite navigated its way through the troubled era of the late 1960s, these professors who held loyalties in church and academy provided direction.

Illustrating the changing understanding of students brought by this new group of professors, Marcus Bryant introduced the practice of administering psychological tests to students. Both Charles Kemp, who began teaching at Brite in 1957, and Bryant proposed that testing could benefit the faculty if the results contributed to a greater understanding of students, their abilities, and intellectual capabilities. Under this program, Bryant administered the Minnesota Multiphasic Personality Inventory (MMPI), interviewed each student, and interpreted the testing. Bryant believed the testing helped students understand their capacities and could lead them toward fulfilling their potential.[44]

Faculty abandoned the testing in the early 1990s, believing responsibility for psychological testing properly belonged in judicatories rather than in the academy.

Given that the quality of Brite's library had often been a point of concern, in 1965, Brite also hired its first full-time librarian, Robert A. Olsen Jr. Olsen, a Presbyterian, was the first full-time faculty member not associated with the Disciples. Although Olsen helped to build library resources, this one move did not adequately address years of neglect. In 1967, the American Association of Theological Schools noted that book circulation among Brite students was half that found in similar institutions. Efforts to increase the quality of the collection had been partially successful, but the AATS still found the library lacking in scholarly journals and monographs.[45] Over the years, the quality of the library collection improved as Olsen solicited participation of the faculty. Additionally, many people attributed the growth in the library to the support and backing of Dr. Suggs.[46]

In addition to members of the full-time faculty, in the late 1960s, Brite had a number of part-time lecturers who served in important positions. These included Rabbi Abraham J. Brachman, the first Jewish lecturer at Brite.[47] Furthermore, with an influx of Methodist students in 1969, Brite asked Gilbert Ferrell to teach Methodist Studies. Ferrell had worked in urban ministries with the Metropolitan Board of Missions.[48] Brite also brought in Gaston Foote, pastor of First United Methodist Church in Fort Worth, to teach as an adjunct in parish ministries.

In 1967, in the midst of this unprecedented expansion of the faculty, Brite replaced its bachelor of divinity program with the master of divinity. Work had begun on this change two years prior, as the American Association of Theological Schools initiated a standardized change in the degree nomenclature. Though the name and status of this degree would indicate a significant change, the degree requirements remained the same: ninety-one credit hours of overall work, with sixty-five of those hours prescribed in fields of biblical studies, history and missions, theology and ethics, and pastoral ministries. The move to a master of divinity program did not bring with it any significant difference in content or purpose.[49]

When Brite renamed the degree, however, the school did add a requirement in field education. Brite sought to emphasize field education as a means by which students could test theory and implement it in practice.[50] While students participated in field education, they did not receive any credit hours for the work.[51] When Walter Naff joined the faculty at Brite, the field education program was little more than an income source for students and a pulpit supply for churches. Naff recalled that in those first years of the program, directors assigned students to churches based on financial need. Gradually, Naff introduced elements of supervision and the formation of theological reflection groups in order to integrate practical ministry with reflection in a classroom setting. These additions to field education focused the entire experience on the principle of thinking theologically. During these years, each theological school defined field education as it saw fit as ATS did not provide defined standards for field education until 1996.[52]

When Brite implemented the master of divinity, faculty continued to make a distinction between those students who entered the seminary under the bachelor's or master's programs. Brite maintained this separation until 1973; however, following the general practice across theological education, Brite allowed those who graduated from the bachelor of divinity program to apply for master of divinity certificates.[53]

1968

In a 1988 edition of *Time* magazine, Lance Morrow described the year 1968 as "the knife blade that severed past from future."[54] While historians have regularly noted the historical significance of 1968, the administration and faculty of Brite Divinity School at the time had no idea where the tumultuous events would lead. In one year, assassins took the lives of both Robert Kennedy and the Reverend Martin Luther King Jr. Riots erupted in Chicago, outside the Democratic National Convention, and elsewhere. Student protests broke out across college campuses, responding to both the civil rights movement and the Vietnam War.

According to Morrow, 1968 "was a time of change, a struggle between generations, to some extent a war between the past and future, and even, for an entire society, a violent struggle to grow up."[55] Recalling the atmosphere of Brite during the late 1960s, Gilbert Ferrell described the awareness, discussions, and divisions of opinions at Brite covering the issues of race, war, and urban crisis as "the Damocles Sword that hung over our heads all the time."[56] In the summer following the assassination of Martin Luther King Jr., violence erupted in 125 cities across the United States.[57] In particular, riots took place on campuses of the country's most prestigious universities, including Harvard, Cornell, Dartmouth, Columbia, Stanford, Ohio State, and culminating in the violence at Kent State University in 1970. However, no one disturbed the peace found on university or seminary campuses in either Dallas or Fort

Worth.[58] In 1967, for example, the American Association of Theological Schools noted that the American Southwest had not experienced the alienation from cultural values that had become prominent in some other areas of the nation.[59] In Fort Worth, most Christians continued to enjoy an easy confidence that Christianity and American culture were completely compatible and shared similar values.

Even though things remained quiet on the home front, the chancellor and board of trustees of TCU prepared for potential unrest. In 1967, the dean of students, Howard G. Wible, wrote a letter to Sadler warning him about the formation of a Students for Democratic Society organization on campus.[60] In 1969, given concern about direct action in the wake of campus riots across the country, the board established procedures to be followed in the event of a campus disturbance and gave Chancellor Moudy the authority to deal with any "interferences in the normal educational processes" by taking any action he deemed appropriate.[61]

On the same day the trustees approved this measure, unrest showed up on the campus when students gathered to protest the expulsion of a student who owed the university $185. In the wake of this protest, students formed a Students Rights Organization, which sought to publish materials without administrative approval, allow twenty-one-and-older students to live off-campus and drink in dormitories, permit greater dorm visitation, and prevent search of dormitory rooms without warrants.[62] Across Texas Christian University, a heightened awareness and desire for participation resulted in greater student involvement in university governance. In 1969, in a move designed to give students a greater voice and to alleviate unrest, the university granted student representatives voting rights on twenty-six different committees.[63]

The day after students gathered to protest the expulsion of a student, flames engulfed the campus ROTC building. During the same weekend, fires were also set in the ROTC building on the North Texas State University campus.[64] The fire on the TCU campus caused approximately $6,000 in damage. The damage became more extensive when fifty students interfered with fire department efforts to extinguish the flames and cut one of the fire hoses, sending water forty feet into the air.[65] While the university sought to keep this matter quiet, TCU prevented several students from returning to school in the fall of 1969.[66]

In addition to students' outward expressions of unrest, Brite hosted speakers whose views were inconsistent with the university's perspectives. In

1966, reflecting the "theological uneasiness of the decade,"[67] students at TCU invited Dr. Thomas J.J. Altizer, known for his "death of God" theology, to speak in a televised debate, without first receiving Moudy's authorization. In 1967, Brite hosted Don Luce, whose work in Vietnam with the International Voluntary Services and the World Council of Churches led to his public opposition to the Vietnam War.[68] In February of 1968, Brite hosted the Vietnamese peace activist Thich Nhat Hahn, who offered a Buddhist proposal for peace.[69] In 1972, Brite hosted Dr. James Cone, who had gained notoriety for his 1969 book, *Black Theology and Black Power*.[70] While speakers such as Hahn and Cone had divergent views from most of the university's administration, Moudy supported their appearances because he understood a university to be "a place where ideas are taught, tested, and refined."[71]

Although TCU tolerated the appearance of these speakers at Brite, the limits to freedom of speech became clearer when Professor Glenn Routt and others invited Jane Fonda to come and speak on the issue of fishing rights for Nisqually Indians. Although Jane Fonda accepted the invitation, TCU refused to allow her on campus because of her activism during the Vietnam War. After hearing about the invitation, Moudy, who had once been Routt's student, called him into his office and told him that Fonda did not possess the qualifications to lecture on a university campus. In response, Routt retorted, "Jim, what does it take to be qualified to be a prophet?"[72] Although that response silenced the chancellor, Moudy continued to refuse to allow Fonda on campus. Instead, she spoke near campus at the TCU Theater (later known as the Frog Theater).

Throughout the late 1960s and early 1970s, seminary students across the nation participated in numerous protests.[73] While Fort Worth was not known as a hotbed of protest, on October 15, 1969, Brite was one of only two schools (along with Perkins School of Theology) in the Dallas–Fort Worth metroplex that closed in order to allow faculty and students to participate in National Vietnam Moratorium Day. This day called on people to abandon their normal day of work to lobby for peace.[74] The decision to close Brite's classes for an entire day did not meet with unanimous consent. Bill Tucker, the assistant dean at Brite, opposed the dismissal on the grounds it violated university policy. At the time, a division existed among the faculty, with some serving as members of a local chapter of the Clergy and Laity Concerned about Vietnam, chaired by Dr. Lunger, and others who believed that faculty should not take an official public position on such issues.[75] Nonetheless, the faculty dismissed classes so students could participate in the protest. On that day, Brite

Brite students (1970s).

held prayer services in the Robert Carr Chapel and student groups met for discussion. One of the major topics of discussion centered on the theological understanding of war and how such an understanding could be integrated with church leadership.[76]

Participation in the moratorium illustrated the gulf that existed between church and academy at this time. In 1969, according to national trends, the great majority of seminary professors supported withdrawal from Vietnam, while the majority of church members supported continued engagement.[77] The growing separation between church and academy manifested itself in financial support. From 1965 to 1966, Texas Disciples congregations and individuals gave over $200,000 to the university; by 1971 that amount fell to just over fifty thousand $50,000.[78]

As the late 1960s brought a greater social awareness and more diverse student body, the difference in classrooms across campus appeared in the photographs shown in the Texas Christian University catalog. In the early 1960s, photographs showed only Caucasian students, sitting in straight rows—men in crew cuts wearing button-down shirts and ties and women in full-length skirts. By the early 1970s, photographs showed classes gathered outdoors, casual clothing, long hair, and a diversity of faces. A photograph in the 1972 catalog featured a majority of black students at a student bonfire, while catalogs less than a decade earlier did not have one black face in two hundred pages. Less than a decade after the integration of Texas Christian University, the

1973 catalog featured black and white students riding tandem bicycles. These catalogs clearly communicated two different messages: in the early-to-mid-1960s, TCU did not welcome black students; in the early 1970s, the university worked hard to recruit them.[79]

Brite's faculty reflected a concern for changing social and cultural norms in their revised master of divinity comprehensive examination questions, approved in 1968. These questions included use of contemporary sources such as Heinz Zahrt's *The Historical Jesus* and an analysis of a quote by Mahatma Gandhi meant to provide a means for exploring the differences between the Hindu and Christian religions. Another question asked students to utilize H. Richard Niebuhr's *Christ and Culture* to analyze civil rights, the Vietnam War, and "the new sex morality."[80]

Changes in the social culture of Texas Christian University and Brite Divinity School were a response to the dramatic external forces that culminated in the events of 1968. The day following King's assassination in Memphis, Brite hosted a memorial service in the Robert Carr Chapel. Dr Lunger prayed using the following words:

> As the shadow of the cross falls upon our way this Passion Week, we gather together, Our Father, in shocked disbelief in the double shadow cast by the cruel death of another of the Servants thou hast sent to save thy people. Grant, O God, that his death, like his Master's, may not have been in vain. Grant that, like his Lord, Martin Luther King, Jr. may accomplish more in his death than the hardness of men's hearts permitted him to accomplish in his life.[81]

After the chapel service, the Brite Student Council convened an emergency meeting in which the student body clearly and unanimously articulated its stance on the civil rights movement. As part of this vision, students sent seven telegrams: to Mrs. King and her family expressing sympathy, to Governor John Connolly censuring his comments about Dr. King's death, to President Johnson applauding his statements about future legislation, and four telegrams to local senators and representatives. Using these final four telegrams, the Brite Student Council advocated four courses of action: "(1) We want social justice for all Americans, (2) We want legislation more constructively aimed at the causes of riots and less exclusively aimed at riot control, (3) We want the civil rights bill before the House passed immediately, (4) We want immediate legislation on the recommendations of the Riot Commission."[82]

In response to these telegrams, the Brite student body received a response from Representative Jim Wright. While Wright recognized the students' concerns, he disagreed with their politics. For example, Wright described the type of legislation supported by Brite students as "illusionary to the jobless ghetto dweller." Wright went on to note, "The need is far more basic, fundamentally economic, and cannot be achieved without the expenditure of money."[83] The Brite student response to the King assassination illustrates a point Glenn T. Miller has made about Dr. King's profound impact on theological education. Miller notes that King's background in theological education and his ability to speak the language of liberal theology "changed the way many theologians. . . . understood theology."[84] Students at Brite, like many others across theological education, found inspiration in King's bringing together of liberal theology and social action. Dr. Lunger and a few other faculty members at Brite also brought theology to bear in their reflections and activities concerned with social justice.

Although the Brite student body took an active social role, some of Brite's official leaders were, by nature, more passive. Although most viewed Dean Henson as a strong administrator and effective church builder, no one ever characterized him as an outgoing visionary. Routt recalled that Henson preferred to leave all decisions about curriculum and policy up to the faculty.[85] In fact, faculty meeting minutes clearly indicate that Dr. Jack Suggs often assumed leadership in the faculty. Bill Baird recalled that, in effect, Suggs served as the academic dean of Brite because Henson realized his own limitations when dealing with academic issues.[86]

The events of 1968 were not limited to those of social movements challenging societal norms and institutions. The year also marked a momentous period of change for religious institutions themselves. On September 27, 1968, in the Municipal Auditorium of Kansas City, Missouri, the 119th Assembly of the Convention of Christian Churches (Disciples of Christ) voted overwhelmingly to restructure the denomination. In doing so, Disciples actually officially recognized their own status as a denominational body, something they had historically been hesitant to do. The vote of the convention culminated eight years of study on restructure. Rev. Granville Walker, pastor of University Christian Church and secretary of the Brite board of trustees, had chaired the Commission on Restructure.[87]

The Kansas City vote reconstituted the International Convention of the Christian Churches (Disciples of Christ), transforming what had been a loose confederation of congregations into one body newly christened the

Christian Church (Disciples of Christ). Disciples, in this vote, actually reconsidered what it meant to be a church.[88] Such denominational changes were not limited to the Christian Church, but reflected a wider movement as churches sought to reorganize against the backdrop of an unsettled culture. The 1968 merger of the Evangelical United Brethren and Methodist Church resulted in the United Methodist Church and represented the same general trend.[89]

Growth in Programs, Response to Culture

The cultural challenges and changes that took place at Brite during the 1960s not only opened the door for the possibility of a more inclusive institution in the future, but also resulted in a changed curriculum. During this period, theological education began to shift from a primary orientation centered in the "hard sciences" of theology, history, and exegesis to include "practical" work such as clinical pastoral education, supervised field ministry, and pastoral care and counseling. Playing its role in this shift, Brite opened the Pastoral Care Center and began a doctor of ministry program. These changes in program and curriculum were more than a matter of catalog items; instead, they reflected a culture that increasingly defined ministry not by the intelligence or knowledge of ministers, but rather by how well ministers performed their ministry.

Changes in academic culture did not always have their intended result. In May 1970, in response to a greater cultural demand for ministerial professionalism and competency, Brite inaugurated its Doctor of Ministry Program.[90] The beginning of the program occurred after five years of intensive planning and discussions and was the first of its kind among institutions similar to Brite. For example, Perkins School of Theology did not implement its program until 1973.[91] The Brite program initially required twenty-four hours of work in practical areas (i.e., homiletics, pastoral care) and classical studies (i.e., biblical studies, theology) and a dissertation.[92] The simplicity of the program allowed many students to complete their DMin during the year following their graduation from the MDiv program. By the mid-1970s, Brite granted seventy-nine degrees in just four years. In 1976, under the direction of Dr. Harold L. Lunger, Brite began requiring students to possess two years of ministerial experience before applying for the program. Faculty also increased requirements to thirty-two hours of course work.[93] By 1976, even with more stringent requirements, Brite boasted the most highly attended program among Disciples schools.[94]

As Miller argues, increasing uneasiness associated with the DMin program not only originated from the minimal degree requirements established by ATS, but also from the era in which schools developed the program. The late 1960s constituted a time of theological unsettledness. In the midst of this theological uncertainty, the DMin program emerged.[95] While the surrounding culture sought a more highly skilled ministry, however, the increasing professionalization of that ministry often failed to lay a strong theological foundation. Robert G. Duffett argued that while the doctor of ministry degree was "one of theological education's most innovative programs in the last few decades, [it] lacks a clear identity and is not by a technical definition a professional doctorate."[96]

Given the cultural shifts of the late 1960s, Brite established a new department in 1970, the Department of Church in Society. Led by Dr. Richard A. Hoehn, courses in this program included titles such as Responses to the Urban Crisis, The City and the Church, and Social Scientific Styles. Although Hoehn also helped with the additional course load created by the doctor of ministry program, Brite faculty hired him to create the Church in Society Program.[97]

One of the distinctive characteristics of practical theology within the curriculum at Brite has been its focus on pastoral care. In the early 1960s, this included agreements with Harris Hospital, All Saints Hospital, and the United States Public Health Service Hospital in Fort Worth to provide clinical training for Brite students.[98] Starting in 1963, Charles F. Kemp served as the head of Brite's newly formed Department of Pastoral Psychology and Pastoral Care. Beginning in the middle 1960s, Brite required all of its master of divinity students to take one introduction and one seminar course in this program, while Kemp taught a number of more concentrated electives.[99]

Curriculum growth in pastoral care, however, was not unique to Brite, but followed a common thread in theological education. Theological schools generally reduced the dominance of the classical programs of theology, Bible, and history and increased attention paid to the "practical" programs of supervised ministry and pastoral care.[100] From 1954 to 1965, the number of theological schools offering graduate-level pastoral care increased from seven to forty-two.[101] The rationale accompanying these changes stressed the need to achieve better integration of theory and practice. The growth of these practical programs did not intend to negate the importance of traditional studies; rather, as Seward Hiltner put it, the practical work of ministry had the potential to construct and amplify theology.[102]

The growth of pastoral care as an academic area also arose from emerging expectations in society and from the mental health and psychological communities. The formation of the American Association of Pastoral Counselors, which held its first official meeting in April 1964, added to the mix.[103] From the nineteenth to the middle of the twentieth century, many communities were content to have a pastor who also served as a counselor, even though that pastor had minimal training in the area. By the 1950s, as expectations changed, teaching in the area of pastoral care required greater depth than the previous practice of having an experienced pastor share perspective and experience through a seminar or as part of a class on church leadership. Pamela Couture has noted the paradox that pastoral counseling experienced during the 1950s and 1960s. According to Couture, pastoral counseling had emerged from a long struggle to find respect, but avenues and methods to provide adequate education for this emerging discipline were not yet fully developed.[104]

While the inclusion of pastoral care became common throughout theological education, the field assumed a greater prominence at Brite, largely through the work of Dr. Charles Kemp. Kemp established Brite's Pastoral Care and Training Center, which opened in September 1968, in order to provide students with clinical experience and to complement the coursework in the area that had been available at Brite since 1957. Dr. Charles Sanders served as the first director of the center, which offered counseling to people throughout Fort Worth.[105] In 1973, the American Association of Pastoral Counselors accredited the center.[106]

A significant portion of the initial funding for the center came from an unlikely source—a lay student, Dr. Charles McKissick, an optometrist from McKinney, Texas. McKissick enrolled for a pastoral care class against Charles Kemp's recommendation. Following the class, he recommended that Brite open a center where its students could gain experience in providing care while offering a service to the local community. Kemp liked the idea, but indicated that Brite did not have the funding for such a facility. Within a short amount of time, McKissick provided $10,000 of his own money, and raised another $2,000, to serve as the seed money for the center.[107]

Kemp turned to the task of identifying the center's purpose, functions, and limitations. He chose the title "pastoral care" in order to provide broader possibilities for learning than the term "pastoral counseling" could have conveyed.[108] Dr. Kemp wrote letters to every institution offering clinical pastoral education, and he and Bryant personally visited similar centers, such as the ones at the Claremont and Boston Schools of Theology. Using his correspondence and the experiences of these visits, Kemp outlined a series of focal points to serve as the basis for founding the center: (1) it must be pastoral in nature; (2) adequate psychiatric consultation must be accessible; (3) an interdisciplinary advisory committee must be formed; and (4) a director's position must be created to handle administrative duties.[109]

Soon after its creation, the center connected with impoverished areas in Fort Worth. Beginning in 1970, Brite students provided counseling for people served by Fort Worth's Community Action Agency Center. The program provided Brite students with firsthand, supervised experience in counseling, while also providing a service for individuals and families with little income.[110] By 1973, in the first five years of its operation, Brite's Pastoral Care and Counseling Center provided advanced training in pastoral care to Brite students while serving more than 2,500 clients. In the 1972–1973 school year alone, 548 clients were seen in nearly three thousand counseling sessions.[111]

Moving Forward

In 1970, Chancellor Moudy began an annual State of the University day in order to promote openness and communication among the trustees, faculty, and student body. In his first address, Moudy reflected on the state of college education at the beginning of the decade. "Today in American universities," Moudy told his listeners, "there are numerous signs of crack-up, loss of community, dispute as to purpose, and either disdain or hopelessness regarding the maintenance of community."[112] In applying this observation to the specific conditions at TCU, Moudy described the faculty, students, trustees, and administration as above average. However, six months later, in contrast to the optimistic vision cast in his state of the University address, Moudy noted the prevalence of narcotics, marijuana, and LSD on the campus.[113]

The cultural changes and developments that began in the late 1960s continued into the new decade, yet they rarely proceeded linearly. Even though integration came later at TCU than at other peer schools, its lateness did not necessarily smooth its arrival. One Kerrville lawyer wrote the chancellor a heated letter when students at the university chose their first black homecoming queen in 1970.[114]

The pace of change within Brite remained slow as well. While the number of women in the classroom steadily increased, and Brite attempted to reach out to students from underrepresented racial and ethnic communities, genuine change in these areas came slowly. Part of the problem resided in the fact that the faculty and administration had difficulty overcoming their own cultural blind spots. For example, in an attempt to recognize the sacrifices wives made when husbands sought a master of divinity, many seminaries across

North America began the practice of awarding a certificate to those wives when husbands graduated. Most likely, seminaries purchased them from one of the church publishing companies. Like many other schools, Brite awarded these "PhT" certificates—the "PhT" standing for "Putting Hubby Through"—throughout the 1970s. While women were enrolling in the MDiv program, and the first woman graduate with a DMin, Virginia Jarman, graduated from Brite in 1973, wives continued to receive certificates from Brite's faculty and administration that implied the lives and careers of women were subservient to their husbands' careers. In a 1971 interview, Ginger Brittain, a female student serving in a rural church through Brite's Field Education program, noted, "A woman going into ministry right now has no role model. The woman has to build her own image and not copy the male image because we have our own potentials and contributions to bring to the ministry."[115] There were, of course, no women faculty members at Brite throughout the 1970s, though women occasionally taught as adjuncts.

Some cultural changes, of course, seemed to threaten the very life of the church. The decline in mainline church attendance, after all, began in the mid-1960s. A photograph in the Brite catalog from 1964 shows nearly every seat occupied in the Robert Carr Chapel. A decade later, while Brite enrollment had gone up, participation in chapel services had dramatically decreased. Even as early as 1968, Dean Henson recalled an experience in chapel when, out of the 154-member student body, only twenty-seven attended the weekly worship service. Henson recalled the high quality of the sermon preached by a senior student, but noted that an equal number of students were "doing nothing" in the student lounge and missed the service. In an article in the *Brite Divinity School Newsletter*, Henson wrote comments about the experience for the community: "Maybe the church member who absents himself regularly from the church we attempt to minister is right; at least as right as we are. To him worship doesn't make any difference."[116] One ATS document indicated that the drop in participation among mainline churches had not been as dramatic in the Dallas–Fort Worth area as in other areas of the country. This created an interesting challenge for Brite faculty: how to educate students in a post-1968 cultural atmosphere rife with religious skepticism when these students largely grew up in a mostly conservative and church-oriented Texas.

On March 16, 1971, Dean Elmer Henson made his final address to the Brite board of trustees, culminating sixteen years of service. Whereas Henson focused on the daily tasks of administration and the ever-present need for fundraising, his successor, William Tucker, took a more active role in the leadership of the seminary. Tucker served as a transitional figure in Brite's history and was Brite's first dean to hold a PhD. Though ordained, he did not arrive from a church setting, but rather possessed only academic credentials. Aware that some might be suspicious of his academic background, Tucker sought to assure skeptical pastors and other potential supporters that Brite remained focused on its primary mission of educating men and women for pastoral ministry.[117]

Within six months of becoming dean, Tucker submitted a proposal to change the composition of the board of trustees in Brite's Articles of Incorporation. Where the 1963 articles only required a majority of board members to be residents in Texas, Tucker proposed that all board members (from nine to seventeen in number) "had to be active church members, four-fifths of whom had to be members of the Christian Church (Disciples of Christ)." Further, Tucker solidified the board's connection to TCU by proposing that at least "one fourth of the members of the Board of Trustees must be members of the Board of Trustees of Texas Christian University."[118] Though not a new practice, from this point on, the revised articles mandated an interlocking relationship between the two boards.[119] Additionally, Dean Tucker created a student relations committee, which included representation from Brite's trustees.[120]

Under Tucker's leadership, Brite also began an aggressive new development plan, largely dependent on the efforts of Ed Kallenberg, Director of Planned Giving, and Gilbert Davis, Director of Church Relations, both located in the development offices within Texas Christian University. The two developed a "program for Brite to increase giving" and gain greater financial security.[121] In the first three years of the program, the two raised $840,120, doubling Brite's endowment. Their work ultimately provided long-term security for Brite. Not all Disciples schools were as fortunate. Drake Divinity School, for example, closed its doors in 1968 due to financial problems. When Gilbert Davis assumed his position in 1971, Brite's endowment was $1.25 million; when he retired in 1992, the endowment had grown to $70 million.[122] The vast majority of that financial growth rested in both the early work done by Kallenberg and Davis together, and the later work continued by Davis once Kallenberg retired.

Chancellor Moudy used the occasion of the approaching university centennial celebration to create a fund-raising campaign calling for a forward-looking vision. The New Century Program brought $35 million in new resources to fund operations, endowments, and capital for the university (though this fell somewhat short of its $43 million goal).[128] This campaign provided the means for Texas Christian University to modernize itself, not only in terms of equipment and facilities, but also in terms of its identity as an institution; the funds enabled TCU to become a bit further removed from Sadler's Christian vision for the school in order to move toward Moudy's professional and academic understanding of the university. In 1964, Texas Christian University required all of its students to have nine semester hours of religion; by 1977, that requirement had dropped to three hours.[129]

By 1977, the culture of Brite Divinity School had shifted rather dramatically from that of 1964. In fact, the culture of the seminary changed more completely in those brief thirteen years than in the previous five decades combined. In 1964, the Brite catalog had portrayed women primarily as saintly mothers to their obedient children or dutiful wives to their scholarly husbands. The catalog defined women by their relationships and roles in the family. By 1977, women had assumed their place in the classroom, graduating alongside men and receiving both MDiv and DMin degrees. No longer did white male students, wearing pressed white shirts, sporting crew cuts, and sitting in straight rows, dominate the face of the school. By the 1970s, women, African Americans, Hispanics, hippies, and other faces regularly appeared. The number of women in Brite's classrooms grew from 2 percent to 10 percent, reaching 18 percent of the Brite student body by 1977. These percentages followed similar trends found in other university-related theological schools.[125] One unintended consequence of more women seeking MDiv degrees was a decline of those who enrolled in the master of religious education program. For more than six decades, Brite had directed women interested in theological education primarily toward the religious education program, as it was the most likely avenue for future employment.[126] By the 1970s, women had discovered that the MDiv degree provided a broader base for ministry. As a result, in both 1973 and 1976, Brite did not award any degrees in religious education.[127]

Contributing to the tension between church and academy, well-qualified women graduating with MDiv degrees found employment in churches difficult to come by. Although several mainline denominations had officially recognized the ordination of women for decades, it would be another twenty years before women grew in significant numbers behind the pulpit.[128] A December 1973 issue of the *Fort Worth Star-Telegram* starkly illustrated the paradox between the emerging service of women in the church and the prevalent view of women in society. In the paper, a half-page article entitled "Women Ministers Work to Beat Stereotypes" featured women who had graduated from Brite and who went on to serve in church leadership roles. However, an article on the opposite side of the page was titled "Several Techniques Can Help Fill Out Bustline."[129]

Disciples of Christ had actually ordained their first women in the late 1880s, but their church culture remained about as unsupportive to women in ministry as most of the other mainline denominations. Walter Naff recalled his experience of placing women in the pulpit through the field education program. He described the gap between the "influx of good competent women" in the seminary and the "church that was not about to accept them into ministry" as "the greatest heartbreak I felt in the twenty-two years I was here." Naff also recalled, "Trying to find placements for black students was just as heartbreaking."[130] Of course, black congregations also had cause to be suspicious of ministers educated primarily in white theological educational settings.

In 1975, Dean Tucker wrote a letter to the congregations participating in Brite's Field Education programs challenging them to reconsider their hiring practices. In the letter, Tucker noted that, while Brite had in recent years primarily educated white, male "preacher boys," the seminary had grown to include women, blacks, and Hispanics. Tucker called on these congregations to provide all students, "regardless of race or sex," a place to serve, arguing that all students "must have meaningful field experience if they are to receive adequate preparation for ministry." If Brite is "to move forward with our policy of non-discrimination," Tucker wrote, "we are in need of your cooperation and support."[131]

The Brite faculty always lived in the tension between the type of student body it wanted to teach and the reality of the churches in the American Southwest. Although Brite offered full scholarships to minority students and recruited regularly from Jarvis Christian College, minority diversity made up only about 5 percent of the Brite student body. These percentages were similar to those found in other majority-white theological schools across the country. Though Brite did not have much success in these years in recruiting minority students to its academic programs, faculty sought to address the needs of the ethnic communities in Fort Worth in other ways. In 1971, for example, Charles Kemp taught a noncredit pastoral care class to sixteen black pastors in Fort Worth.[132] Although Brite sought greater racial diversity for both its faculty and its student body, the school experienced little success during these two decades. A 1969 survey reported that no white seminary had more than twenty or twenty-five black students, and only a dozen seminaries had black faculty.[133] By 1972, Perkins School of Theology had hired its first African

American, Mexican American, and female professors.[134] Yet, at the same time, the Brite faculty remained 100 percent white and male.

In 1974, Brite hosted its first class, The Black Religious Experience in America, taught by a black professor, Mr. Reby Cary, an associate dean of the University of Texas at Arlington. Several students noted this was the first opportunity in their academic careers to take a class from a black professor. Sir Walter Scott Jr., a black Brite student, commented, "The course had helped piece together enlightening truths concerning historical facts that have been distorted in the past. Hopefully, the course has done even more for my Anglo-Saxon brothers and sisters!"[135]

By the middle 1970s, diversity began to show up on the program for Ministers Week. In February 1975, Brite invited its first woman, Dr. Muriel James, to deliver the McFadin lectures. Dr. James served as an ordained minister in the United Church of Christ and worked as a licensed marriage and family psychotherapist.[136] These lectures were founded in 1943 by an annual gift from the McFadin ministerial loan fund set up by D.G. McFadin of Dallas, Texas, and they cover a broad range of theological and pastoral concerns. In the year following Dr. James's lecture, Bishop Joseph A. Johnson, the first African American to attend Vanderbilt University, gave the Wells Sermon Series.[137] The Wells series, also founded in 1943, was made possible by an annual gift from the East Dallas Christian Church in honor of its former minister, L.N.D. Wells. Also reflective of the changing times, in 1975 Brite mandated that all master of divinity students must have at least one class in minority studies as a graduation requirement. Students met this requirement by taking a course in black, Hispanic, or women's studies.[138]

Even in the midst of transition, Brite realized the difference between the work it hoped to do and its own complicity in continuing racial advantage. In a 1970 faculty meeting, professors Richard Hoehn and George Smith, the first non-Disciples teaching faculty members at Brite, gave a report in which they traced the history of Brite seeking to educate minority students (principally African American) but noted that "the principle has been difficult to implement in practice." The faculty minutes state:

> We recognize that all of the faculty of Brite are white anglos; that the best paying and prestigious administrative positions are filled with white anglos; that minority groups are woefully under-represented in the student body in proportion to their members in the general population. This results in a number of detrimental

> effects to our school. A disproportionate amount of the funds we spend go into white anglo pocket books, thus perpetuating and continuing to accentuate economic disparities between whites and minorities. The ways in which our current recruitment practices are structured accidentally tend to minimize minority participation. . . . We therefore recognize that without intending to discriminate our school nonetheless continues to work to the advantage of white anglos and the disadvantage of minority persons. . . .[139]

Not only did the Brite faculty acknowledge its complicity in systematic racism, but also, in the same meeting, the faculty voted to support a number of initiatives to address the issue. These actions included beginning a more intentional effort to recruit minority students, asking ATS to grant academic exemptions for these students, and providing special consideration for minority candidates in hiring practices.[140]

The dominance of white male faculty continued throughout the decade of the 1970s. However, as Dr. Suggs noted in a 1976 report, this was not a systematic choice. Suggs reported that Brite offered a position to a Hispanic professor who chose to teach at an eastern seminary and to a woman who took a position at a secular university. Although Suggs expressed the hope that future faculty hiring would include women and those representing traditionally underrepresented ethnic groups, his report did not explore what issues may have caused those who were offered jobs to accept other employment.[141]

Through the middle 1970s, Brite struggled mightily with limited finances, but somehow managed to grow nonetheless. From the middle 1960s to the early 1970s, the average size of the student body increased from 150 to 200 students. This growth contrasted with national trends that saw a dramatic decline in enrollments in theological education beginning in 1969.[142] Part of Brite's growth likely resulted from students seeking to avoid the Vietnam draft.[143] At the same time that the student body increased, and Brite took on the Doctor of Ministry Program, inflation affected all areas of the economy in the United States. By the middle 1970s, Dean Tucker viewed limited funding as the greatest challenge Brite faced. Although Brite's annual shortfall was reduced from over $100,000 to $25,000 per year, through the work of Ed Kallenberg and Gilbert Davis, annual deficits continued to prohibit further growth in either program or faculty.[144] Although TCU consistently underwrote Brite's losses, the university also raised money in the name of providing ministerial education that went directly into TCU's own coffers. From 1964 to 1971, Disciples of Christ congregations in Texas donated over $890,000 to the University.[145]

Conclusion

Undoubtedly, the campus of Texas Christian University and the halls of Brite Divinity School were very different places in 1977 than they were in 1964. In a 1975 address to the trustees, Chancellor Moudy noted the problems that came with "the acceleration and complication of cultural changes with which we have been faced, particularly in the recent decades of the twentieth century. A campus is no longer the sheltered asylum it once was."[146] While Moudy understood the cultural changes of the day as an impediment to the purposes of the curriculum, in a 1976 dean's report to the Brite trustees, Dean Tucker offered a much more optimistic vision of the new culture:

> Today the seminary faculty, while not as large as projected in a flush of optimism several years ago, is strong and productive; scholars and ministers, our professors figure prominently in the activities of both church and academy in North America. The current student body – black, brown, and white – has been attracted to the seminary from homes across the nation, not to mention India, Taiwan, Ethiopia, and Kenya.[147]

While Tucker's words may overstate the diversity found at Brite, the words and actions of Brite during the 1970s reveal a different institution from the one that Sadler had tightly controlled. By the mid-1970s, the proportion of women in the study body passed 20 percent (double that of Perkins Theological Seminary), international students made up approximately 10 percent, African American students composed over 5 percent, and Hispanic students averaged 1 percent. While these percentages did not compare well with those found in the US population, they represented a marked contrast to the nearly 100 percent white male student population of the middle 1960s. Additionally, diversity expanded in terms of denominational affiliation. By 1975, 55 percent of students came from a Disciples background, while 23 percent were Methodists, and 22 percent hailed from a mixture of fifteen other denominations.[148]

The growth of Brite over these years could be more directly attributed to the strength of personalities than intentional systematic development. By the mid-1970s, Brite remained financially dependent on the university. Throughout the first six decades of Brite's history, the university simply underwrote any losses, while it took a considerable share of the fundraising proceeds in Disciples circles that focused primarily on supporting the education of ministers. While the immediate concern of this era focused on adapting to cultural upheavals, Glenn Miller notes that the long-term financial strain on seminaries presented an equally important, if not yet fully realized, challenge.[149]

Despite TCU's continued support of the divinity school, in the 1970s, Texas Christian University began to define Brite differently than its other schools. After a major university restructure in 1972, an organizational chart no longer listed Brite among the Colleges of Arts and Sciences or Business, or even the Harris School of Nursing. Rather, the chart listed Brite as a separate entity, yet one that reported to the newly created office of vice chancellor and dean of the university. Additionally, in a 1976 report to the Brite board of trustees, Chancellor Moudy characterized Brite as "self-standing, having strength, and moving forward."[150] While this reorganization of the university began to recognize the "self-standing" nature of Brite, at this time the seminary did not possess the financial viability to live fully into the independent organization its charter had created for it in 1914.[151]

Many of the cultural changes experienced at Brite from 1964 to 1977 resulted from external forces as the American culture surrounding the school had changed. However, to attribute all of these changes to exterior forces would fail to recognize the leadership of Brite faculty and students. On June 30, 1977, right at the end of this period, one of the most significant leaders on Brite's faculty retired. Responsible for bringing social awareness to Brite over a twenty-one year career of teaching, Dr. Harold L. Lunger, Professor of Christian Ethics, provided a consistent and challenging voice for greater awareness of social issues, well before those issues became popular cultural themes for social protest groups. Lunger's leadership provided just the right mix of social awareness and academic concern as he raised student awareness about issues ranging from race to labor movements. Lunger led efforts at Brite to increase requirements for the Doctor of Ministry Program and, after his retirement, provided, along with his wife Alberta, the funds to establish the Harold and Alberta Lunger Professorship of Spiritual Resources and Disciplines.[152] The leadership of people like Lunger enabled Brite to begin a significant cultural transformation between 1964 and 1977, one that would change the face, ethos, content, and curriculum of Brite Divinity School for years to come.

5

The Suggs Era: Church and Academy, 1977–1989

LISA BARNETT

In February 1977, Dr. M. Jack Suggs officially became the sixth dean of the Brite Divinity School.[1] Suggs, a New Testament scholar well-known in the academy, received his PhD from Duke University and was also an ordained Disciples of Christ minister who had previously served as a pastor.[2] As a longtime faculty member at Brite, Suggs had been a leading voice on the faculty. This combination of roles guided him during his time as dean to transform the climate and ethos of Brite to reflect a commitment to professional theological education at the graduate level.[3] This paradigm shift is most evident in a comparison of the purpose statements printed in two different Brite catalogs. Prior to Suggs's assumption of the office, the purpose statement emphasized "preparing men and women for the varied ministries of the Church of Jesus Christ" and "leading students into a deepening and maturing Christian experience."[4] This statement is in stark contrast to the goals outlined in the next edition of the catalog, printed during Suggs's deanship, where emphasis was placed on the "seminary's special vocation . . . as a center in which the church's faith and mission are examined, clarified, and articulated." The new statement also stressed that the "intellectual discipline, which Brite accepts as a community of learning, is that appropriate to graduate, theological education in the context of Texas Christian University, a PhD-granting institution."[5] The Brite report given at the TCU trustee meeting in March 1981 noted this change of vision: "The Seminary was progressing on its goal of becoming a great theological educator."[6]

This commitment to professional graduate education in the divinity school became the theme not only for the programs Brite offered its students, but also for the enhancement of faculty selection and retention. In a report to the Brite board of trustees in 1984, Suggs highlighted the accomplishments of two specific faculty members and expressed his understanding of academy and church as integrated rather than disconnected locations:

> They epitomize what we want faculty to be: master teachers; significant scholars of national reputation; in their distinctive ways, important contributors to the life of the church; and cooperative, hard-working servants of the seminary and the university. By them, we are reminded that none of the stereotypical either-ors holds: it is not either professors or church leaders; it is not either scholars or solid committee workers. . . . You have people who incorporate those roles in a balanced and effective manner.[7]

As dean, Suggs also reduced faculty workload to make room for scholarly research and participation in professional organizations. Repeatedly, Suggs reported to the board on faculty searches and the need to diversify with regard to gender and ethnicity. While these were pressing concerns, Suggs refused to sacrifice the quality of the faculty for the sake of filling positions. Many faculty searches continued longer than expected so that highly qualified candidates could emerge. Commitment to the church remained a priority for Brite, as Suggs often noted ways Brite's faculty served church constituencies:

> Given the changed character of graduate education since 1960, it is not easy to put together a faculty with the commitment to the church this faculty shows—but it can be done, if you work at it. I'll say only one more word about these appointments: in 1976, the faculty was all-White, all-male. We now have three women and one black—which is important to the changing shape of the world in which ministry takes place.[8]

Suggs also worked on developing better ecumenical diversity within the faculty through the appointments made during these years. His efforts proved successful enough to provide some concerns among trustees and other supporters of the institution.

As indicated in the previous chapter, throughout the 1960s, Brite's faculty had become more aware of diversity and its importance for ministry. According to Conrad Cherry, "The emphasis on globalization in the 1980s exemplified the growing importance of religious, cultural, ethnic, racial, and class *difference* in theological education."[9] "Multiculturalism and multiracialism," he writes, "would characterize the emphasis on 'globalization' in the divinity schools in the 1980s."[10] The diversity of Brite's student population increased considerably during these years. A greater representation of ethnic and racial groups appeared at Brite. Women formed a greater percentage of the student population as well. Second-career students also enrolled in strong numbers by the mid-1980s. While these increases signaled a positive change for admissions at Brite, the practical realities occasioned by them offered challenges of their own. Brite struggled to balance concerns for academic excellence while providing proper attention for deficiencies. Finding places for all students to serve in field education settings remained difficult. By the end of the period, faculty members urged the dean and one another to become more hospitable to the roles homosexuals could play, both in the school and in the church. Ultimately, increasing diversity found within the student body at Brite required changes in curriculum, programs, and policies that affected the entire academic climate of the school.

Cultural pluralism, emerging ever more starkly during these years, presented faculty members with yet one more factor they knew theological education must address. Conrad Cherry notes the effect that pluralism had on university-related divinity schools:

> The preponderant cultural and social reality with which university divinity schools have had to contend in the late twentieth century is American pluralism, not American secularism. The assertive diversity of religious and cultural worldviews, not the marginalization or elimination of sacred worldviews, constitutes the heart of the challenge. . . . The reality of pluralism thus has presented an intellectual as well as a social summons. In responding, divinity school intellectuals have faced the difficult task of honoring the integrity of diverse worldviews and their contents while probing their own religious traditions and the democratic culture for values, views, and social goals constitutive of the common good.[11]

Suggs noted this concern directly in his dean's report of 1979 when he mentioned William Hall's retirement from teaching mission and world religions. This position, Suggs argued, is the "place where the church has to deal with frontiers—the frontier of the larger world beyond our national borders

Jack Suggs, top center, hosting a seminar in his home.

which is predominantly non-Christian and the frontier of a future of uncertain shape." Suggs mentioned "Iran, Mexico, Zaire, and Thailand" and concluded "it is just not the same world." Because of the "careful deliberation" required by faculty to fill this position appropriately, Suggs informed the board of his intention to postpone the search "for a year."[12] As it turned out, it took six years for Brite to hire someone for this position, when the school finally hired Don Pittman (PhD, University of Chicago) to teach the history of religion, including world religions. During the interim, Brite used several visiting professors to teach courses in global Christianity and world religions.

During the Suggs years, Brite continued to struggle with its own location as a university-related divinity school. Though the Brite board of trustees continued to function for the divinity school, it operated fully within the confines of the university. The board always chose the university's executive leadership as its own. Because of scarce financial resources, Brite had developed a relationship of dependency on Texas Christian University. With interlocking board members between Brite and TCU, and with its chief officers also located in the university, Brite remained in an ambiguous position with regard to its ability to make its own decisions. The 1989 ATS self-study highlights this equivocal relationship between the two institutions:

> There are unquestionably ambiguities suggested by Brite's position as a corporation within the administrative structure of Texas Christian University. Some types of decisions that ordinarily belong to a governing board are ceded in practice to the TCU board: from key personnel decisions in upper administration to the basic shape

> of benefit packages. Financial strategies of the "parent" corporation tend to establish boundaries for seminary planning.[13]

Some key events during these years would test the nature of this paternalistic relationship with Texas Christian University.

In a changing world, the vision and purpose of Brite Divinity School also changed to reflect a greater commitment to professional theological education at the graduate level. Successful efforts to increase sources of funding for Brite equipped both programs and faculty to undertake the responsibility of educating theological students in a multicultural and pluralistic world. This chapter traces the developments during the Suggs deanship that demonstrate a paradigmatic shift at Brite toward taking academic quality more seriously.

Church and Academy

Jack Suggs placed new emphasis on the scholarly performance of the faculty at Brite. This focus motivated many of the decisions and policies during the last dozen years of his career. Although a new focus on scholarly work emerged, the underlying commitment to the church, consistently a part of the mission and vision of Brite, remained a strong factor in faculty appointments. Suggs commented in 1979, "We promised that we would bring in only fully committed church theologians with high scholarly and professional competence. And, we have been fortunate, indeed, in our appointments. . . . We have been able to maintain a faculty which shares the fundamental goals to which the school is committed."[14] He elaborated more on this position in a 1981 report to the Brite trustees:

> I think that the first word you need to hear [about this faculty] is about their commitment to the Church. Brite's very clear sense of purpose and vocation has been a major factor in our ability to attract a group of very capable scholars under forty who want a teaching position in which they can do <u>church</u> theology. . . . I want you to have the sense that we are appointing people who have real ability. But I also want you to understand that they are people whose choices have been determined in large measure by their sense that we are serious about the church and represent a climate in which their serious scholarship can serve the church. . . . One of our important concerns will be retention—which means adequate rewards and a working environment, which becomes increasingly supportive of their efforts.[15]

In a 1979 report to the Brite board of trustees, Suggs highlighted one significant concern raised during the 1978 Association of Theological Schools ten-year review. The commission "requested a report in December on policies with respect to sabbatical leaves, tenure, and promotion." The visiting team had noted that Brite had not "advanced anyone from associate professor to full since Bill Tucker was promoted in 1968." Brite's self-study had likewise indicated concern on this point. Suggs instructed the board of faculty to "resolve to develop an interpretation of criteria for promotion appropriate to graduate professional education which will insure that all faculty are treated equitably."[16]

The 1978 self-study report also described the struggle to find a balance between Brite's responsibility to the church and to the academy within the context of operating as a part of TCU. Faculty members stated their concern about a workload that "simply crowded out" much ability to produce "scholarly research and publication." One faculty member "suggested that if we emphasize graduate education, class loads should be cut and research and publication demanded." But, if the emphasis is to be placed on "professional education, due recognition and credit should be given for professional activities, services to churches and community, and other relevant work."[17] Some faculty hoped that Brite would find ways to recognize, through promotion, their involvement in church-related activities. Others emphasized publication, stating that genuine graduate education depended on a faculty regularly making a scholarly contribution to the literature of the field. The faculty and the dean's office would struggle with this tension for years to come.

Improvement, however, did occur, and the next professor to advance from associate to full professor in 1980 was Dr. Marcus Bryant.[18] Bryant had been Associate Professor of Pastoral Care and Pastoral Psychology at Brite since 1967.[19] Although six other faculty members had been at Brite as long, or longer, than Bryant had, he was the only one of them to have a PhD and who was not planning to retire soon.[20] An ordained Disciples minister, one who maintained strong connections to work in the church throughout his career, Bryant had published one book.[21] Dr. James Duke, also ordained, but oriented more toward scholarly work than ministry, received tenure in March 1981, having served as Assistant and Associate Professor of Church History at Brite since 1976.[22]

The 1978 ATS self-study report also made several recommendations dealing with research, professional involvement, and workload. The self-study encouraged Brite to find ways to reduce the faculty teaching load, support faculty leaves, and reduce faculty participation on committees. The report also encouraged administration to find ways to support faculty attendance at professional scholarly meetings.[23] By 1989, a decade later, faculty reported several improvements when the self-study rolled around again:

> Junior faculty are funded for one meeting of their primary national society during each of their first two years at Brite. After two years of service, all Brite faculty receive seminary support based on a three-year cycle. Without program participation, full support is available for one meeting in a three-year cycle; fifty percent support is provided for any other two years. With program participation, full support is available each year of the three-year cycle. . . . In the fall of 1982, the importance of preparation for teaching was enhanced by the reduction of the course load for faculty from five courses, plus participation in the D.Min. program, to four courses and D.Min. participation. Each professor may now request a student assistant who receives a $500 stipend per semester for which five hours of research assistance per week can be expected.[24]

However, "the single strongest complaint of the full-time teaching faculty about their workloads is the time spent in meetings."[25] Yet, faculty found in Brite a working environment that generally supported their scholarly work. Suggs continuously updated the Brite trustees with their publishing accomplishments and, on one occasion, took special pride in their mention: "I found a table in Vice Chancellor Koehler's annual report for 1983–84 too interesting not to share with you. According to that table, with only twelve full-time continuing faculty last year, Brite faculty produced twenty-five percent of the books authored by university faculty and eighty percent of the books edited on campus."[26] Suggs said, "We are serious about the church and represent a climate in which their [Brite faculty's] serious scholarship can serve the church."[27]

Brite's commitment to improving academic excellence extended as well to policies affecting the composition of the student body at Brite Divinity School. E. Brooks Holifield commented on a major criticism of the education for professional ministry:

> Seminaries suffered from many of the same problems that had beset them in the 1930s. They accepted 87 percent of their applicants, and the range of academic abilities was therefore wider among their students than in more selective professional schools. . . . Too many schools still had less than demanding academic standards and little willingness to dismiss underperforming students.[28]

Brite began to take steps to address this critique of theological education. Because of the high enrollment at Brite in the early 1980s, the "non-probationary admission level has moved from [a grade point average of] 2.25 to 2.5, a level matched by only one seminary in the Southwest."[29] Suggs also added, "Just a few years ago, merit scholarships were awarded with fair frequency to students with an undergraduate GPA of 3.3. Now, though we award above a dozen merit scholarships, the recipients' GPAs are typically 3.6 or above."[30] Suggs commented on the results of this increased level of academic expectation in a 1985 report to the board: "The church deserves better minds than we once admitted."[31] Along with these measures, the faculty recommended raising the GPA for graduation to 2.30 in 1987, as well as a new plus-and-minus system grading scale.[32] The concern about grade inflation resulted in a 1988 change to a pass/fail grading system for choir, and a recommendation in the 1989 ATS self-study report that consideration be given to a pass/fail grading system in supervised ministry.[33]

In March 1987, the Brite faculty also recommended appointing a committee "to study of the need and possibilities for a formal program to improve the writing skills of Brite students."[34] At the August 1987 faculty meeting, Assistant Dean Don Pittman reported for this committee, named the Task Force on Fundamental Academic Skills, that "Ms. Wanda Russell has accepted an appointment as Consultant for professional Writing for the 1987–88 academic year. A diagnostic writing test will be given to entering students to ascertain the need for help in improving their writing skills."[35] In an effort to raise academic expectations associated with writing papers, the Brite faculty approved a recommendation from the Brite Academic Procedures Committee. Faculty now required all students to observe the guidelines found in Kate Turabian's book, *A Manual for Writers of Term Papers, Theses, and Dissertations*.[36]

Naturally, these academic expectations in the preparation for professional ministry caused some concern among the students. One student sent a letter to the Academic Procedures Committee in 1989 expressing consternation over increasing academic expectations. Suggs responded to the letter by stressing the importance of graduate professional study:

> What I am convinced of is this. (1) Education must begin with students where they are. Many of them do not have religion majors in their background. A good many of them come to seminary because they are religious and believe religious institutions to be important in meeting human need—doubtless, because they have experienced

> the church in that way. They have to learn, not only to be theological, but why it is important to be theological. (2) Beginning with students where they are does not mean surrendering of graduate professional study. It does mean making graduate professional study possible by accepting the level of interpretation students need in order to engage the theological enterprise. And that is a pedagogical issue which might be important to consider among all faculty.[37]

Dealing with Diversity

The 1978 ATS self-study report had recommended "that deliberate attempts continue to be made to include women, blacks, and Mexican Americans among future faculty appointments."[38] The issue of diversity would take on more significance during Suggs's deanship. Holifield writes, "Women flowed into the seminaries, increasing their enrollment from 5 percent in 1972 to 22 percent in 1988."[39] However, as Cherry points out, "Women faculty had not attained the same representation in theological education."[40] Brite called upon Dr. Kathryn Williams, the associate minister of the Christian Church (Disciples of Christ) in the Southwest, as an adjunct faculty member in 1978 to coteach, with Dr. Richard Hoehn, the course Studies in American Culture: Women.[41] In 1980, Brite appointed Toni Craven as Assistant Professor of Old Testament.[42] Craven, a Roman Catholic, received her PhD from Vanderbilt in May 1980.[43] She became an associate professor in 1985 and received tenure in 1986.[44] In 1984, Suggs announced that Nancy Duff, a Presbyterian, would assume duties as Assistant Professor of Christian Ethics in the fall of 1985,[45] following the completion of her dissertation at Union Theological Seminary in New York.[46] Suggs told Brite trustees that "at Union, she was a teaching assistant to noted scholars Christopher Morse, James Cone, Geoffrey Wainwright, and Dorothee Solle. . . . She has also been a teaching assistant to James Forbes in homiletics in New York."[47] The Reverend Sharon Iverson also joined the staff as an assistant director of admissions and instructor in religious education in a non-tenure track appointment in June 1985.[48] With these appointments, Brite took a few steps toward creating a more diverse faculty presence.

The process of appointing racially and ethnically diverse persons to the faculty at Brite proved a more difficult endeavor. As with the hiring of women, the hiring of an African American professor began at the adjunct level. Brite named the Reverend Dr. Jesse Truvillion of Fort Worth's St. Peter Presbyterian Church as an adjunct professor of black studies for the spring term of 1980.[49] He continued in that role through most of the 1980s. In addition, Dr. James

Cone returned to Brite (Cone had visited Brite in 1972) as a speaker for the Brite Series, a lecture series sponsored by the student body.[50] Finally, in the fall of 1988, Darryl Trimiew, Brite's first full-time African American professor, joined the faculty.[51] Trimiew, an ordained Presbyterian who later joined the Disciples, held a JD degree from Rutgers School of Law, an MA from Northern Baptist Theological Seminary, and in 1988 was a PhD candidate at Emory University.[52] Despite this progress, the Brite faculty knew much work remained to diversify its makeup. The 1989 ATS report recommended faculty give deliberate attention to "developing a program addressing the needs of the Spanish-speaking community and the corollary need for Spanish-speaking faculty."[53]

As Suggs sought to increase the academic qualifications of the faculty at Brite, ecumenical diversity naturally followed. Interestingly, this would raise some concerns among the Brite trustees. Shortly after Suggs became dean, William Longsworth, an ordained United Methodist Church minister, became Assistant Professor of Christian Ethics.[54] In 1979, Dr. L. William Countryman became Assistant Professor of New Testament at Brite. Besides having a PhD from the University of Chicago, Countryman was also an ordained Episcopalian.[55] In 1979, faculty hired Dr. Howard Stone as Assistant Professor of Pastoral Care and Counseling. Ordained in the Lutheran Church in America, Stone earned a PhD at Claremont School of Theology.[56] Following these announcements by Suggs to the Brite board, a Brite trustee sent a letter containing remarks made at the board meeting as an attachment to the minutes:

> As Dean Suggs announced the new faculty appointments, giving impressive academic qualifications and achievements of each, I, as well as other members of the board, voiced concern as to whether or not the other qualifications of character of these men meet the standards we, as Christians, must set for our lives. This is a prime concern to those of us who may be low on the "academic totem pole," but who sit in the pews of our churches, each and every Sunday. We want to know of these qualifications, and they should be included. What kind of men are they? In seeking God's goal for Brite Divinity School, not our own, do these men have a vision of a totally Christian world? Are they men who have surrendered to the Lordship of Christ, and who will participate in bringing the kingdom of God "here on earth as it is in heaven?" The Apostle Paul's message

> in I Cor. 13, ". . . and if you have all knowledge, and have not love, you are as nothing," speaks to those who teach as well as those who hear—and speaks especially to those who teach in a seminary. Brite Divinity School must never exist to serve one particular group or one denomination, but since most of their support comes from the Christian Churches and members of the Christian Church, do these men share in a devotion to our common cause?[57]

Although not prominently publicized at the time of her appointment, Professor Craven's church affiliation created a considerable stir as well. Suggs told the board in 1982, "I still find a bit of perplexity among some people about our appointment of a Catholic in Old Testament—but never where Toni Craven's personal impact has been felt."[58] The year following Craven's appointment, Brite hired "three Davids to challenge Secular Goliath," at least according to the sensational headline found in the *Brite Newsletter*. First, Dr. David Gouwens assumed his position as Assistant Professor of Systematic Theology. Gouwens had received his PhD from Yale University and possessed a denominational connection with the Reform Church in America (though he was later ordained in the Presbyterian Church, USA).[59] Dr. David Balch became Brite's Associate Professor of New Testament. He also received a PhD from Yale University and maintained membership, at that time, in the Presbyterian Church (though his ordination soon resided in the Lutheran Church in America).[60] Dr. David Polk, an ordained Disciples minister, rounded out the trio of "Davids." He held his PhD from Claremont and began his work in 1983 as the Harold Glen Brown Associate Professor of Pastoral Ministry.

At the November meeting of the Brite board, a few trustees expressed concern about the ratio between Disciples and non-Disciples on the faculty. The next year, two more Disciples arrived: Don Pittman, from the University of Chicago, to teach as Assistant Professor in the History of Religions and serve as an assistant dean, and Joey Jeter, who held a PhD in history from Claremont, though he was hired as Assistant Professor of Homiletics.[61] Around this time, the board appointed a committee to study the desired Disciples ratio on the faculty of Brite Divinity School.[62] A year later, a statement emerged from the Faculty Committee of the Brite Trustees addressing the issue of ecumenical diversity among the faculty at Brite:

> We move that the Brite Divinity School Board affirm that Brite Divinity School is primarily a seminary of the Christian Church

> (Disciples of Christ). Therefore, it is our considered judgment that a majority of the faculty should be from the Disciples tradition, while not compromising the quality of any faculty appointments. However, we believe that it is of particular importance that the person to be selected for the position in Church History be a Disciple.

Discussion on the motion ensued with Chancellor William Tucker raising a question about the trustees becoming involved in hiring faculty, though affirming the position of keeping Brite as a Disciples seminary. On vote, the motion carried. However, Dean Suggs offered an administrative interpretation of the action and the discussion:

> I understand the motion to be supportive of already existing concerns of the administration and faculty of Brite and that it is intended to express a guideline rather than a mandate. I also understand that the guideline's goal is controlled by the aim of not compromising the quality of faculty appointments.[63]

The next-to-last faculty hire made during Suggs's deanship (the last being the hiring of Darryl Trimiew in 1988) was Dr. Mark G. Toulouse. Toulouse, an ordained Disciples minister holding a PhD from the University of Chicago in the History of Christianity, came to Brite in 1986 after teaching at Phillips Theological Seminary for two years.[64] Appointments of three Disciples in two years helped to alleviate trustee concern, but the issue would arise again in the next decade, when the majority of faculty hires, during the years of Deans Perdue and Toulouse, moved well beyond Disciples identification.

New diversity also appeared within the student body at Brite during these years. The 1978 ATS self-study report noted, "Within a generation, the typical Protestant seminary student body has changed from largely single, white males, to today's predominately married student body, a considerable number of women, some racial-ethnic minority students, and the newest phenomenon—an increase in older and/or 'second career' students."[65] Suggs placed increased emphasis on recruitment in 1978 when he hired D. Newell Williams, a newly-minted PhD in American Religious History from Vanderbilt, to serve as an assistant dean primarily charged with improving Brite's recruitment efforts. Williams provided an early report for the *Brite Newsletter* that reflected the following diversity in Brite's student population at the time of his arrival:

> Fifty-five percent of this year's students are from the Christian Church (Disciples of Christ). Almost twenty-two percent are United Methodists, seven percent from the Assemblies of God, and five percent Baptist. Five [students] are Episcopal and five, Presbyterian. A total of seventeen denominations are represented in the student body. . . . Among the students enrolled [228 at this time], there are forty women. Eighteen blacks are students in all degree programs. There are four Hispanic students.[66]

An analysis from the 1989 ATS self-study report reveals the extent of student diversity during the years Suggs served as dean. Though black and Hispanic numbers did not grow much over that twelve-year period, the number of women grew significantly, as did the number of second-career students. In 1988, black students represented about 10.8 percent of the student body; three Hispanics, one Asian American, and one American Indian were also enrolled. Women now made up about 30 percent of each entering class, and they came with better academic credentials than the average male student. The average age of Brite's entering students continued to rise, reaching 34.3 by 1988. Disciples constituted the majority of students entering either the MDiv or MRE programs (around 34.7 percent), while Methodists were catching up dramatically. More Methodists than Disciples entered all Brite's programs in 1988 (32.7 percent of all entering students).[67]

Issues related to gender and racial diversity at Brite continued to raise concerns about the role of theological education in relationship to minority groups. Cherry notes concerns regarding theological education and women:

> Women theological educators warned that these statistical gains should not be confused with significant structural and curricular change—in fact, the gains seemed to point to the compelling need for such change. . . . The marginality was apparent, for example, in the theological school curricula: "In introductory courses the works of feminist or liberation theologians still appear at the end of the syllabus as optional choices for papers."[68]. . . To the eyes of feminist theological educators, the shape of divinity school education at the end of the 1980s was characterized by statistical gains in social diversity that had not yet significantly transformed the structures and processes of learning.[69]

A student at Brite noticed the faculty's lack of attention to feminist and liberation theologies and sent a letter to Dean Suggs making a recommendation:

> Having just read *God's Fierce Whimsy*, ed. By Carter Heyward, Katie Cannon, et. al., I would like to recommend this book to you and the Curriculum Committee since it addresses in a fundamental way seminary education in light of feminist studies. I would like to propose that our seminary look at its curriculum in light of the insights of *God's Fierce Whimsy*. At the very least, it challenges us to integrate feminist scholarship into our existing curriculum, and at the most, it challenges us to rethink what we count as theological education.[70]

In 1986, Brite professor Nancy Duff presented a recommendation from the Human Relations Committee for "Revised Guidelines for Inclusive Language" that the faculty approved.[71] In spite of the addition of women faculty members and the increasing number of women enrolled at Brite, there were still practical issues within the life of the church. One faculty member expressed concern at a faculty meeting about the difficulty of placing women ministers in the churches and urged the seminary to initiate some effective form of action.[72] The 1989 ATS self-study report also acknowledged some resistance to the inclusive language policy at Brite as it noted, "Twenty-four percent [of students] do not support the 'continual emphasis upon inclusive language at Brite.' Some students perceive their theology is discounted when they employ God-language consistent with their beliefs."[73]

Cultural attention to racial diversity raised serious questions about Brite's curriculum and policies throughout the period. The 1978 ATS self-study report pointed to deficiencies in this area:

> As regards Mexican-American and/or Spanish-speaking recruitment, Brite has probably not done as much as it could. . . . (Most Mexican-American Disciples of Christ congregations in this region are served by lay ministers.) We have made regular annual visits to Jarvis Christian College, Hawkins, Texas, and have participated on an invitation basis in the career day program of Bishop College, Dallas. . . . At least three factors . . . have a bearing on our ability to launch a more aggressive program of racial-ethnic minority recruitment. One factor is the need of many of these students for financial

> assistance beyond the full-tuition grant. Another factor is the difficulty black students have in securing a part-time ministry position. A third factor is the absence of a minority staff person who can teach, or assist with recruitment, or who can serve as an "advocate" for minority students.[74]

In 1979, Brite received a challenge grant from the Division of Homeland Ministries of the Christian Church (Disciples of Christ) to "make possible an enriched program of field education for black Disciples students."[75] In 1980, the Human Relations Committee at Brite discussed ongoing issues demanding more attention in the future. These included, "The possibility of a more permanent black presence on the faculty, the possible assignment of blacks in white field education settings, and some sort of open forum on minority (especially black) concerns."[76] A report from the Human Relations Committee to the faculty in 1986 suggested "studying the need and opportunities to improve the writing skills of ethnic minority students."[77] A 1987 report from the Human Relations Committee addressed perceptions surrounding the racial diversity at Brite:

> The Committee has given attention to a communication from the Academic Procedures Committee, which reported that some minority students have the perception that they are being more strictly graded than other students.... The Human Relations Committee thinks that this issue needs further investigation. The Committee urges faculty members to give attention to minority concerns and feelings, and make efforts to build relationships with minority students, which can allay these fears. The Committee has given attention to expressions by minority students in regard to their sense of not being fully participant in the Brite community. Faculty discussion of this matter emphasized the need to develop rapport among the various constituents of the Brite community.[78]

Soon, the matter of diversity expanded to include sexual orientation. As homosexual orientation and the clamor for civil rights became more culturally prominent, theological seminaries found themselves dealing with the issue of sexuality as well. The 1978 ATS self-study report provided the following report:

> Brite Divinity School has no stated policy on the admission of ho-

> mosexuals. Applicants are not asked to state their sexual preference. Homosexuals have been admitted to the seminary, but it was not known that they were homosexuals at the time of their admission. Some faculty and students have discussed this matter informally with the present dean, but it has not been raised for policy formulation. There is some feeling that in light of current church discussions of the ethical attitudes and actions toward homosexuality and the ordination of homosexuals to ministry, it is appropriate that the seminary give formal consideration to the issue.[79]

A discussion of the issue occurred at a meeting of the Human Relations Committee in 1980, and Dr. Richard Hoehn suggested consideration of a statement on admissions policy for the Brite catalog. He referenced the catalog of United Theological Seminary that included such a statement.[80] However, the Human Relations Committee and the Recruitment and Admissions Committee concluded, "Such a statement would not be appropriate in the Brite catalogue."[81] In 1987, a faculty conference on homosexuality and the ministry took place.[82] The 1989 ATS self-study report provided faculty comment on the continuing lack of attention given to this issue by Brite: "Only twenty percent [of faculty] perceive most students to be supportive of homosexual students. Central to the concerns as expressed by the students is the lack of clarity as to the seminary's policy and procedure in relation to admission of homosexual persons and to open discussion among faculty and students of the issues involved."[83] The issue remained unresolved during the Suggs years.

A new ecumenical awareness arose in the 1980s that challenged theological education to rethink its approach to teaching. Cherry writes:

> Visions of the social influence of Christianity springing from unity of religious purpose and strategy have been replaced by views of a global relatedness engendered by knowledge of cultural and religious difference. Throughout the 1980s, proponents of revision in theological education issued calls for the "globalization" of the educational task.[84]

Brite Divinity School took seriously the task of rethinking theological education in a pluralistic world. The retirement of Bill Hall from mission and world religions in 1979, and the decision to postpone the search for a year, gave Brite an opportunity to evaluate its task of theological education concerning the role of missions in a global context that would offer a new teaching role. Brite professor Richard Hoehn shared his observations on this new emphasis in a January 1980 memo:

> Missions refer to the sentness of the Christian calling. We are sent to witness the Gospel. We are called to missionize in all the human spaces of life—the continual reformation of our own hearts and lives, the witness to our neighbor, city, nation, and world. . . . The major challenges confronting mission are how to express the faith on the world order, and how to interface appropriately with other faiths. It seems to me that we need someone to fill a position in Christianity and World Culture. Primary competency should be on appropriate Christian responses at the international level. . . . What does our sentness today indicate that we ought to be doing at this level? Since a great deal of what can and may happen at this level will be dependent on our interface with other faiths, the person's other competence should be knowledge of other religions. The person would have to be fully aware of liberation theology as one important expression of the faith seen from the perspective of the Third World.[85]

James Duke also offered his views on the teaching position in a letter to the faculty committee later that year:

> In my judgment, we need to identify with precision the curricular needs before we can even begin to debate the various options for meeting it. I can identify several alleged concerns that are quite distinct. Every ministerial student needs to understand: (1) the nature of religion as such and the forms of religiosity within the human community, (2) at least one non-Christian religion, (3) Christianity in a non-European and non-North American context, (4) the history of the expansion of Christianity, (5) the theology and practice of mission(s), (6) how Christianity interacts, positively and negatively, with other religions and/or non-Western cultures, (7) the situation of third world persons, preferably from the point of view of those persons, (8) the relations of "church and society" in a global context. . . . I am leery of the prospects for combining several items on my list into one job for one person. . . . Our confusion about this

> post is neither accidental nor unique. My survey of seminary curricula convinced me that confusion is widespread and that "solutions" are, with precious few exceptions, unstable arrangements. The very notion of combining elements of mission(s), world Christianity, non-Christian religions, global social concerns, and cross-cultural sensitization under some "umbrella" within the seminary is shaped more by historical forces than by budgetary constraints.[86]

While the faculty search and the redefinition of this position continued, Brite called upon several visiting professors to teach courses in global Christianity, including Dr. Orlando Costas,[87] Dr. Tokiyuki Nobuhara,[88] and Dr. Jorge Pantelis.[89] Finally, in 1984, Suggs announced that faculty had called Don Pittman to Brite to serve as Assistant Dean and as Assistant Professor of History of Religions. Suggs added to this announcement, "His teaching field . . . adds an important dimension to curriculum in an age where it is important to know what a Shiite Muslim or a Mahayana Buddhist is."[90] Suggs announced the following year the addition of Dr. Kenneth Teegarden, retiring general minister and president of the Christian Church (Disciples of Christ), as the distinguished minister in residence at Brite for a three-year period. His teaching assignment covered both ecumenical and global Christianity.[91]

In spite of Brite's recognition of the need to study non-Christian religions and converse in an interfaith environment, in practice Brite had paid precious little attention to Christian dialogue with other religions. In 1987, Nancy Duff proposed a course in Jewish-Christian relations:

> In response to the [Curriculum] Committee's request for a rationale for offering a course in Jewish-Christian relations . . . I would submit the following considerations. The Ethical Guidelines for Seminaries and Seminary Clusters adopted by the Association of Theological Schools states the following: An Institutional commitment should be made by the Christian seminary to overcome anti-Semitic tendencies and expressions in the Church and theological education by (a) analysis of sources of anti-Semitism in the Christian tradition and (b) by increased knowledge of the Jewish interpretation of the Bible, Jewish traditions, and the history of Judaism. I believe that this guideline from the ATS justifies a course in Jewish-Christian relations at a theological seminary.[92]

Shortly thereafter, Brite began a relationship with Rabbi Ralph Mecklenburger, of Beth-El Congregation in Fort Worth, who regularly cotaught a course with Don Pittman and, in later years, with Kenneth Cracknell.

During the Suggs era, Brite's experience of dealing with the issue of pluralism tracked with the approach of Protestant theological education in general. According to Conrad Cherry, "With the growing awareness of the radical diversity of peoples occupying the 'global village,' . . . the final purpose of understanding other religions inclined toward the appreciation of their distinctive otherness. . . . One of the chief goals of understanding would prove to be understanding itself."[93]

Diversification of Programs

Diversification of programs would be a resounding theme during the years of Suggs's deanship. Graduate theological education provided increased attention to the relationship between theory and practice. In their 1978 ATS self-study report, faculty concluded, "The single most demanding need, identified by our self-study and the consensus of all of our constituencies in numerous consultations, is for the addition of a mature and experienced professor in the general area of church practice."[94] The trustees addressed this concern quickly by "voting to establish a new position in pastoral theology."[95] Brite chose Dr. Harold Glen Brown to fill this position the next year.[96] When he retired in 1983, Brite named the position to honor him, and Dr. David Polk was hired.[97]Mr. and Mrs. Robert Leibrock, of Midland, Texas, provided funds to endow the Brown professorship.[98]

The addition of this faculty position allowed Walter Naff to devote his full-time attention to field education. Brite's focus on developing new forms of contextual education mirrored developments in other university-related divinity schools, as described by Cherry:

> During the 1970s and 1980s, divinity school educators differed in their ways of treating training for the ministry as a process of contextual education, but they shared the supposition that practical education in the ministry should amount to something quite different from training in the use of fixed professional skills. . . . At the university divinity schools, contextual education entailed replacing "fieldwork" with programs in "supervised ministry" or "field education" that required regular supervision and evaluation by faculty and academic analysis by students.[99]

The 1989 ATS self-study report reviewed the weaknesses found in Brite's field education program that faculty had identified in 1978, including a "perceived failure of the program to focus on educational objectives and [its tendency] primarily to function as an opportunity for field education with financial remuneration."[100] Brite's "overhaul," with its emphasis on "educational integrity," included many changes. The underlying context for rethinking the program included attention to the nature of professional theological education at the graduate level:

> The primary objectives of field education are to provide the student with an opportunity (a) to gain competence in correlating Christian theology and practice of ministry, and (b) to gain a sense of personal and professional identity in the context of a supervised and evaluated experience in, and exposure to, the full range of ministerial tasks in a setting related to the student's vocational goal.[101]

A new field education program at Brite began in 1979 as a pilot project with full implementation by 1980. Changes to Brite's program fell in line with those at other divinity schools. The program included recruiting congregations and educating their leadership to create teaching parishes. Resident pastors became supervisors; a contract between student and supervisor set out "personal and professional goals to be pursued during a given semester." With Brite's help, congregations formed lay committees to help supervise and evaluate student work. The program encouraged faculty members to "become involved in weekly field education conferences" where students would share their field experiences and learn how to think theologically about them.[102] This direction in field education provided new opportunities to connect church and academy.

The DMin program at Brite constituted the other area where church and academy most naturally connected. Faculty remained concerned about both the quality of students in the program and the fact students could graduate from the program without demonstrating a clear ability to think theologically. Dean Suggs noted in 1981 that the instructional staff was too small for the tasks of the program.[103] In 1984, faculty recommended revisions to the program by creating a pastoral care and counseling track "suited for students who wish to pursue specialized professional study in pastoral care."[104] The Curriculum Committee proposed to the faculty in 1986 a recommendation that a "D.

Min. in Parish and Institutional Ministries be designated for students working in general ministry as distinguished from a concentration in Pastoral Care and Counseling."[105]

The master of religious education degree offered at Brite suffered from attrition. The 1978 report noticed the reduction in the number of students entering the program and delineated the factors contributing to that decrease. Women turned from an emphasis in education toward "full parish ministry and from the MRE to the MDiv as preparation toward that goal." Faculty noted that the "Methodists are finding little demand for the MRE degree, as indicated by the Perkins decision to drop their degree program in Religious Education." Faculty believed the degree could be saved "by raising the level of preparation of those who seek this ministry."[106] Despite efforts to tend to the program in various ways, the number of students enrolling in the program remained small. The 1989 report concluded that the MRE program posed some difficult questions. While faculty recognized that congregations wanted to take Christian education more seriously, few were able to hire more staff dedicated to that purpose. Students attending seminary preferred "to prepare for a broad-based ministry rather than specialized ministry." Faculty concluded that the MDiv degree, perhaps with a concentration in religious education, should be "the preferred degree for a career in religious education."[107] The MRE at Brite neared its end.

These concerns about ministerial practice, evidenced in discussions about field education, the DMin, and the MRE, reflected a larger issue facing theological education during these years. Cherry observes, "In the 1970s and 1980s, faculty committees were still fretting about how to link the community of the church with a divinity school community shaped by the university ethos of specialization and academic professionalization. The establishment of that linkage was rendered difficult by the churches' developing expectations of their ministers."[108] Increasingly, faculty emphasized the role ministers must play in empowering laity for the ministry of the church. Brooks Holifield makes the following observation on this matter:

> Mainline Protestants embraced the ministry of the laity with enthusiasm. For some of them, the most important statement on the nature of the pastorate was the 1982 ecumenical document "Baptism, Eucharist, and Ministry," produced by the Commission on Faith and Order of the World Council of Churches. It identified widespread agreement that Christian ministry was the work of

> "the whole people of God." The document acknowledged that the churches needed persons who were "publicly and continually" responsible for reminding it of its witness, and it defined the ordained minister's chief duty as the building of the body of Christ by preaching, teaching, and celebrating the sacraments, but it insisted that these tasks had as their goal the "mission" and "caring ministry" of the whole church.[109]

In response to the publication of *Baptism, Eucharist, and Ministry* (World Council of Churches, 1982), the board added a paragraph to Brite's "Purpose and objectives" statement. The additional wording read, "While a seminary's special mission is education for professional ministry, Brite also attempts in various ways to enhance the ministry of the whole church through programs and services which strengthen the basis of Christian lay vocations."[110]

Brite's emphasis on the diversification of its programs refined its focus to attract persons interested in the lay ministry and/or nonordained ministry in the church. In 1986, Suggs charged the Curriculum Committee with exploring the issue of diversification and "finding new ways to use our resources for the edification of the church."[111] After a year of studying the issue, the committee offered a proposal to develop a new program, the master of theological studies (MTS) degree, along with an accompanying nondegree certificate of theological studies (CTS).[112] The MTS filled a need particularly found among Methodists. It met the denomination's concerns to provide theological education for diaconal ministry and, thereby, provided a new stream of students for Brite. The program also sought to attract "persons who wish to examine and develop religious and theological perspectives on their life situations." The certificate, on the other hand, offered the opportunity for college graduates to enter the seminary classroom "in order to enhance the quality of their lay leadership within the church and broaden their perspectives on contemporary faith and life."[113]

These new programs began in January 1988.[114] The United Methodist Church formally approved the new program for its diaconal ministers.[115] Endorsement for the programs also came from the Catholic Church, as noted in correspondence early in the planning stages. Daniel Luby wrote on behalf of the diocese of Fort Worth, "I do believe there is a market among Fort Worth area Catholics for the kind of program you are considering at Brite. . . . I am excited about the possibilities it offers Catholics, especially for those Catholics in our diocese who are interested in pursuing full-time work in the church."[116] With these two new programs, Brite gave formal attention to the education of laypersons, an agenda that remained central to Brite's work in the decades ahead.

Finances and an Ambiguous Relationship with Texas Christian University

Shortly after Suggs assumed the dean's office, he inherited the Investment in Ministry Campaign, a financial campaign that began in 1977 with the stated goal of raising $7.5 million dollars for Brite. Gilbert Davis and Ed Kallenberg provided leadership for the campaign.[117] In the three-year effort, the campaign raised over $8.1 million, some of this amount dedicated to operating expenses.[118] Through a grant from the Lilly Endowment, Ron Moss became assistant director of church relations, the first development officer to serve Brite exclusively.[119] The influx of money provided for Brite's budgetary support by investment income, something that was not characteristic of most seminaries.[120] However, Cherry observes that most university administrations were asking divinity schools to take more responsibility for funding their own work.[121] Brite's successful fund-raising also raised expectations within the university that Brite could now move toward fully paying its own way.

In 1978, the Brite board of trustees and the TCU board of trustees considered a joint resolution to revise the financial obligations between the schools and to clear up some of the ambiguity over finances. The agreement provided that Brite must pay a pro rata charge for operations and for maintenance of the physical plant based on the amount of space occupied by Brite. The plan called for a phased-in cost, with the charge increasing each year until it reached a level of 100 percent of costs in 1983–1984 and subsequent years.[122] The ambiguous relationship between Brite and TCU was also evident in discussions related to student housing for Brite students (paving the way for Brite to give sustained attention to the sad state of Brite housing during the 1990s). The 1989 report reflected on this matter:

> From 1966–1988, an "unincorporated entity" known as the "Texas Christian University Apartment Fund" was created to manage apartments, some of which were occupied by TCU students and others by Brite students. An agreement between the two corporations recognized the Chief Executive Officer of the two corporations (the Chancellor) as the primary authority in the Fund and provided that the Fund "shall employ a manager." The manager so employed was the TCU Housing Office. Subsequently, the University disposed

> of the apartments used by TCU students. The remaining facilities have been continuously occupied by Brite students. The agreement requires the active participation of the dean of Brite Divinity School in management decisions. In 1988, the Texas Christian University Apartment Fund was dissolved and ownership of the apartments was transferred to Brite. Under this new arrangement, the apartments became an auxiliary enterprise with management and budget within Brite and under the dean's supervision. The TCU Housing Office continues as manager for the apartments.[123]

Relations between the two schools remained harmonious until the closing years of the 1980s, when heightened tensions between Brite and TCU appeared primarily over the issue of apartheid in South Africa.[124] Although the Christian Church (Disciples of Christ) passed a resolution at the 1983 General Assembly that all affiliated institutions should create a plan for divestment by 1985, the TCU and Brite trustees took no action on the issue. The faculty of Brite adopted a resolution in 1987 requesting the Brite board of trustees to divest funds from companies that support apartheid and to encourage the TCU board to do likewise.[125] In a meeting of the Executive Committee of the Brite Trustees, Chancellor William Tucker told the trustees that the TCU board of trustees had already considered this issue and "their decision had been to 'take no action' since they considered their primary responsibility to be related to protecting the income from endowments. They felt that the donors of such funds expected them to manage the funds so as to produce the highest yield."[126]

Discussion among the executive committee led to its recommendation that Brite trustees reject the resolution presented by the Brite faculty and, instead, "wholeheartedly endorse the action of the TCU Board at its fall 1986 meeting."[127] However, when the issue came before the entire Brite board of trustees in Spring 1987, one member made a motion that the Brite board of trustees have the portfolio of investments reviewed, as "the issue is not fiduciary or political, but moral." The Brite board voted to review Brite's current investments linked to targeted companies after a discussion of the moral issues involved in the matter of apartheid.[128] At the fall 1988 meeting, the Brite board asserted its role as a separate body and voted to affirm the following policy statement:

> Board members are in general agreement on the following items: a common abhorrence of apartheid or oppression of people anywhere

> in the world . . . [and] acceptance of fiduciary responsibility, which carries an added dimension because of our sense of Christian stewardship. . . . In light of the foregoing, when a company in which the School is a shareholder operates under policy or engages in conduct that seems in need of modification or reform, the Board should seek appropriate means to influence the company's performance. . . . If determined, constant efforts to affect the desired reform fail, the Board regards divestment as a strategy to advance a Christian witness, which under certain circumstances may be pursued in a manner consistent with their duties as Trustees.[129]

Chancellor William Tucker reported at that meeting, "The Administrative Committee of the Church in [its] June, 1988, meeting heard a report which indicated that ten or more of the Higher Education institutions have not yet divested from companies doing business in South Africa." The minutes also indicated that "Dr. Tucker feels that TCU is unjustly criticized, and that TCU is being discriminated against by the Church."[130] The arguments surrounding apartheid highlighted the fact that the autonomy of the Brite board could be asserted whenever the board decided to assert it. The board simply rarely chose to do so.

During Suggs's time as dean, the vision and purpose of Brite changed to reflect a greater commitment to professional theological education at the graduate level. Furthermore, successful efforts to increase the endowments and funding for Brite allowed for many changes to curriculum, programs, and faculty. Each of the changes made during these years reflected a commitment to educate theological students in a world that was becoming increasingly diverse and pluralistic. Each change also manifested a clear commitment from the church world to take the academy seriously in order to provide a credible ministry within this changing environment.

6

Living into Brite's Incorporation, 1989–2009

JEFFREY WILLIAMS AND DYAN M. DIETZ

In 1989, Brite submitted its self-study for reaccreditation to the Association of Theological Schools. The document defined the historic and ongoing relationship between the divinity school and TCU as "like [the] other colleges in the University." The authors of the self-study made clear that the vice chancellor for academic affairs exercised general oversight of the seminary and the graduate council in the university oversaw Brite's academic programs. Clearly, some in the divinity school saw the significance of this arrangement as more than mere historic practice and extremely beneficial to Brite. The self-study declared, "The seminary finds the accountability structure with respect to curriculum, promotion and tenure, appointment policy and procedures . . . and calendar strong and advantageous."[1] Outgoing dean Jack Suggs reinforced the nature of the relationship by emphasizing that Brite was and needed to remain a "constituent" school of TCU.[2]

Despite the strength of these sentiments in 1989, ten years later Brite and TCU officially clarified that the two schools were distinct corporations with autonomous governance structures. No officer or other body within TCU exerted direct authority over the affairs of Brite. While both schools underscored the fact that Brite had, since 1914, been separately incorporated, and both pointed to the improved relations that resulted from a more distinct governance structure, many within Brite also quietly celebrated the new-found freedom and opportunities they believed full recognition of their governing autonomy created.

The story of Brite's changing relationship with TCU has helped to define Brite's history since 1989. The clarification reflected profound concerns on the part of Brite's faculty, administration, and trustees about the enduring benefits of the constituent arrangement. However, more than a distinct event in the midst of other significant matters, the clarification reflected, and in most cases depended upon, Brite's identity, financial security, and mission. Ultimately, the clarification in the relationship between Brite and TCU would not have taken place had Brite's board, administration, and faculty not defined an aggressive vision for the school and possessed the human and financial resources to pursue that vision. The new arrangement allowed Brite to undertake the challenge of pursuing the educational quality, breadth of programming, and academic rigor historically associated with the major university-related divinity schools while achieving the financial and administrative independence of a stand-alone seminary. This vision for Brite and its implications for the school's relationship to TCU is the focus of this chapter.

Brite at the Close of the 1980s

As the 1980s came to a close, Jack Suggs announced his retirement, leading Brite to open a search for a new dean, who would enter a school that had experienced important changes over the course of the previous decade. The percentage of women enrolled in Brite's degree programs steadily increased between 1980 and 1990, as did the percentage of United Methodist students in relation to Disciples students, finally surpassing the latter within the MDiv program in the 1990s. The number of African American students doubled over the course of the decade. In the 1980s, Brite's full-time faculty finally included both a woman and a person from a traditionally underrepresented ethnic group. Through its faculty hires, recruitment efforts, and stated goals, Brite sought to improve the quality of the institution by providing educational resources in the form of teaching and research that took seriously the role of the seminary as the intellectual center of the church. In this sense, Brite did not accept the common opposition between academy and church. Rather, the school's faculty and leadership sought to bring the two closer together by granting the academy a pivotal role in the life of the church.

In the midst of these changes, Brite's board of trustees authorized the drafting of new bylaws for the school that ultimately brought Brite's governance into closer congruence with that of other university-related divinity schools. Dean Suggs indicated that pragmatic matters, rather than any significant concern about the nature of Brite's incorporation or its relation to TCU, drove the revision. The month before his retirement, Suggs explained in a letter dated May 1, 1989, "The need of the Board of Trustees for contemporary revision of by-laws has probably been clear for a good long while, but became especially clear two years ago in the midst of the confusion about the appropriateness of proxy votes." Suggs went on to explain that the Brite trustees had, for some time, utilized proxy voters despite state laws forbidding the practice.[3]

Once the revision process began, Suggs took pains to control the process by editing bylaws drafted by Robert Ginsburg, the attorney for Brite and TCU, to ensure they reflected Suggs's vision of Brite as a constituent school of TCU. Suggs wrote:

> It is clear that Ginsburg is not at home with the ambiguities of our particular intercorporate relationship. We are incorporated as the graduate theological school of Texas Christian University—not as a completely free and autonomous body. I suppose that it will be advisable to try to proceed somewhat further on the by-laws without involving Tucker, who does have some other things to do. But it is just [as] clear that he has to be brought in at a stage that will prevent some accident occurring at the final stage which effectively redefines the relationship between the two corporations.[4]

Suggs, like so many divinity school leaders over the course of the twentieth century, associated the highest quality theological education with a school's integration into the life, values, and culture of a university. In contrast, Brite incorporated in 1914 as a separate corporation, independent of the university. In fact, the original charter (Articles of Incorporation) did not even mention TCU. The revisions made in 1963 to the Articles of Incorporation, however, changed the language to include Brite as one of the constituent schools of TCU. Suggs drew his image of Brite's relationship to TCU from the 1963 restated articles rather than the 1914 Articles of Incorporation. His revisions to Ginsburg's draft of new bylaws formalized Brite's integration into the administrative governance of TCU. Although for years Brite operated under the direct administrative oversight of the TCU chancellor, vice chancellor for academic affairs, and vice chancellor for finance, the 1963 version of the articles actually had instituted a more complex relationship in which these officers "together with the Dean of Brite Divinity School, shall be the chief executive officers of the corporation."[5] In other words, the 1963 articles identified Brite's dean as one of the chief executive officers, coequal with the TCU officers, though actual practice shortly after 1963 departed from these articles by subsuming the dean's authority under the university's officers.

The original 1914 bylaws mentioned nothing specific by way of governance other than that the board of trustees had full authority. An early draft of the 1989 bylaws proposed that TCU's chancellor serve as Brite's chief executive officer and the dean as "the second ranking officer of this corporation." Suggs, however, questioned whether TCU's vice chancellor for academic affairs should serve as the second ranking officer rather than the dean. The final version of the bylaws resorted to the de jure practice recommended by Suggs in which the "Chancellor, the Vice Chancellor for Finance and Planning, and the Vice Chancellor for Academic Affairs of Texas Christian University are, respectively, the Chief Executive Officer, the Chief Fiscal Officer, and the Chief Academic Officer of Brite Divinity School." The bylaws defined Brite's dean as the "Academic Dean and the Chief Operating Officer of the School," a position equivalent to the deans of the other colleges within the university who all reported to the vice chancellor for academic affairs.

Suggs also played a key role in revising another article in the proposed bylaws; this one related to the power of the TCU chancellor. Ginsburg's draft excluded Brite's dean from those the chief executive officer (the TCU chancellor) could dismiss "when, in his judgment, the interest of the School shall require it. . . ." Suggs countered that the chancellor should have the power to dismiss the dean.[6] The final version of the bylaws incorporated Suggs's suggestion, thereby ensuring the clear authority of the chancellor, rather than Brite's board, over the dean.[7]

Suggs's concern that Ginsburg might redefine the relationship between Brite and TCU also likely touched upon the bylaws' formulation of the nature of the relationship between Brite's dean and its trustees. Ginsburg's draft suggested that the dean "will work with the Board of Trustees in determining general plans and policies of the School, [and] in selection and appointment of key personnel." The draft went on to stipulate that the dean would "represent the School [and] in major educational organizations and have such other responsibilities as the Board of Trustees may from time to time indicate." The approved bylaws altered the arrangement by specifying that the dean would not only carry out these functions through work with the board, but also with "the Chief Officers" of the corporation, namely the TCU officers. In other words, the bylaws ensured that the dean would not act independently of the TCU officers when it came to the major issues in the life of the school.

Through these various changes to the 1963 bylaws, Brite legally ceded several of the most significant characteristics of an independent academic institution to TCU. The bylaws subsumed the authority of the dean beneath the university officers and granted the chancellor the exclusive power to appoint faculty and administration and to dismiss any of the employees of the Divinity School, including the dean. In exchange, Brite became more formally integrated into the life and structure of the university. Brite's board approved the bylaws in November of 1989, at the first official board meeting attended by the new dean, Leo G. Perdue. Dean Perdue encountered these changes only upon his arrival to campus—before accepting the position, he had become familiar with the 1963 bylaws. Thus, the structural changes recommended to the board surprised him, though all parties at TCU and Brite had agreed to them in the months immediately preceding Perdue's arrival to campus.

At the same time that the Brite trustees took formal action to solidify TCU's administrative control over the institution, the trustees attempted to continue to wield a degree of independence from TCU through Brite's stand on the issue of divestment in South Africa. In 1988, Brite's board indicated that divestment was a last resort.[8] However, in 1989, the board instructed the school's endowment fund manager to refrain from purchasing any stock in companies that had business interests in South Africa.[9] While not a formal act of divesting from stock in corporations doing business in South Africa, the move guaranteed that Brite at least would not expand its holdings in companies working in South Africa. The policy also continued a pattern of Brite's board exercising independent judgment from TCU when it came to issues of racial justice.

The Brite board's decision to depart from the TCU position on divestment seems puzzling in the midst of its approval of revisions to its own bylaws that ensconced Brite within the governance structure of TCU. However, the divestment controversy suggested the Brite board could exercise some measure of independent action, even if the bylaws made clear that the school's dean and faculty could not. In the 1990s, this rather complex governance arrangement finally reached a crisis point. To understand what led to the crisis, we need to look to Brite's new leadership and the goals associated with that leadership.

The Perdue Era

The search for a successor to Jack Suggs led to the appointment of Leo Perdue as Brite's Dean in 1989. Perdue received his PhD from Vanderbilt University and taught at Phillips University in Oklahoma. Like Suggs, Perdue was both an ordained Disciple and an accomplished biblical scholar. Though not immediately obvious to the casual observer, Perdue had Native American ancestry and, therefore, became Brite's first dean representing an ethnicity other than Caucasian.

Perdue brought with him a vigorous commitment to excellence in theological education. The torrid pace with which he pursued changes brought many new opportunities to the school and tested the relationship between Brite and TCU in ways that ultimately contributed to new bylaws and a clarified relationship between the two institutions. Perdue routinely summed up his goals for Brite in the brief phrase "excellence in theological education."

A more developed vision of Perdue's version of excellence appeared two years after he arrived at Brite in the school's new statement of mission, philosophy, and objectives. The document drew upon the school's notion of itself as, in H. Richard Niebuhr's words, "the intellectual center of the church."[10]In particular, the document focused on the role of the seminary as a place "in which the church's faith and mission are examined, clarified and articulated and in which the professional ministry is equipped to lead the church toward the fulfillment of its mission." This twofold purpose of intellectual reflection and professional education for Christian ministry had long been part of the school's identity. The document built upon the school's identity by asserting the goal of shaping a specifically "Christian identity." This goal, the faculty asserted, grew out of God's redemptive action in world history, particularly the "exceptional" work God accomplishes through the church. Though one might read a certain triumphalism in this assertion, the faculty intentionally sought to challenge such an interpretation while still "tak[ing] seriously the mission God sets forth for the church." The document located the burden of the seminary's work in forming a Christian identity through its courses of study, which fostered "critical inquiry, reflective thinking, increased understanding of culture, and development of the arts of ministry."[11]

Moving from vision to action, Perdue focused significant energies on enrollment. Building on the trends of the 1980s, the composition of the student body shifted dramatically between 1990 and 2000. While enrollment at Brite grew during the 1980s, it began to dip toward the close of the decade. By fall 1989, enrollment had declined more than 10 percent from just four years earlier.[12] Perdue felt alarmed enough about the decline, particularly as it intersected with similar struggles at other ATS schools and reflected a decrease in membership within mainline Protestant churches, that he made student recruitment the centerpiece of his earliest goals for Brite.

Beyond merely adding quantity to the school's headcount, Perdue emphasized that recruitment needed to consider the quality of students as well. He addressed the latter point directly in his first report to the board of trustees, arguing that the struggles of mainline churches, including those within the Christian Church (Disciples of Christ), meant that the church "must have gifted leadership to help us move through the challenging period when most churches are not growing."[13] Perdue identified preferred qualities such as greater academic ability as measured through a higher undergraduate GPA, demonstrated leadership skills, and abilities to establish positive interpersonal relationships.[14] In response to the school's enrollment problems, Perdue appointed the school's first full-time director of admissions and also recalibrated the dean's responsibilities to include additional activities intended to garner a more public presence for the school.[15] In the fall of 1991, Mark Toulouse moved into the associate dean's position at Brite, which coincided with the office's shift into direct academic administration, making it possible for the dean to work on fundraising, public and church relations, and the development of a strong board of trustees.

Brite felt the effects of Perdue's emphasis on recruitment almost immediately. Only a year after hiring a director of admissions, Brite's enrollment increased 10 percent from where it stood in 1989. Two years after that, enrollment rose another 20 percent. In 1992, Brite boasted that enrollment in its master of divinity program ranked fifth highest among university-related divinity schools.[16]

This influx of new students included considerable numbers of United Methodists. By the end of the decade, the denomination was the single largest group at Brite. This growth in United Methodists reflected a general shift toward a highly ecumenical student body as the total number of denominations represented by Brite's students more than doubled over the course of the 1990s. Demographic shifts also extended to women, who represented 36 percent of the student body in 1989 but 50 percent in 1999, and to traditionally underrepresented racial and ethnic groups. The number of African American students doubled between 1989 and 1999, and Brite finally began to attract a small number of Latin American students in the same period. Overall, Brite's enrollment of students from traditionally underrepresented racial groups increased 87 percent over the decade, and in 1999 its numbers of international students were higher than they had ever been.

Similar to Conrad Cherry's observation of divinity schools in general, however, Brite's commitment to diversification did not necessarily reflect the ethnic and religious diversity of global Christianity, particularly in the school's relatively small numbers of Pentecostal students and Asian, Asian American, and Latin American students from across the theological spectrum.[17] Nevertheless, the school had made great strides in diversifying its student body. Brite also attempted to move beyond inclusion of students from nonwhite racial backgrounds to address more directly the particular needs of the religious communities from which those students came to Brite. It did so through the creation of a borderlands program (later a center), a Korean (later, Asian) church studies program, and more recent emphases on a new black church studies program. These programs offered a combination of coursework, student mentoring, and public events to equip students for service in their respective communities. The programs also simultaneously educated students from the dominant culture about ministry within their own increasingly diverse communities.

By 2002, when Perdue and Toulouse returned to the teaching faculty, the total enrollment at the school had reached 272 students, with exactly 50 percent men and 50 percent women (136 of each). Of these, 181 students were enrolled in the MDiv program. The other students were spread across five other degree programs (MTS, MACS, ThM, DMin, and PhD). More than 15 percent of the student body represented either ethnic minorities or international students. Students came from thirty different Christian denominations (including five different Baptist groups and three different Presbyterian groups), and two students were Jewish.[18]

Brite also made important strides in becoming an open and affirming seminary for lesbian, gay, bisexual, and transgender (LGBT) students, faculty, and staff. Though Brite has never officially tracked LGBT student enrollment numbers, the school enrolled LGBT students in the late 1980s and early 1990s who were "out" about their sexual orientation. A fundamental turning point in the school's communication of itself as an open and affirming institution came in 1994 when Dean Toulouse recommended opening Brite housing to couples in committed same-sex partnerships. Until this point, Brite's housing policy permitted only married students or single students of the same sex to share an apartment. Because Texas law forbid same-sex couples from marrying, Toulouse reasoned that a same-sex couple who affirmed they would marry if permitted by law conformed to the housing guidelines. The move to open housing indicated Brite's willingness to present itself publicly as welcoming to LGBT students. At the end of the decade, this effort received further support when, with TCU, Brite amended its nondiscrimination policy to include sexual orientation and, later, to extend insurance benefits to same-sex partners. In 2008, Brite went beyond TCU and most other universities and seminaries in further amending its nondiscrimination policy to include gender identity. These collective attitudes and efforts not only drew students, they also drew faculty. By 2007, Brite counted two LGBT persons among its faculty.

This commitment to the diversification of the student body also extended to the curriculum, which included course requirements for masters students in what Brite called "globalization." The focus on globalization reflected a changing consciousness within theological education as a whole that began in the 1980s. Don Browning notes four different approaches to globalization within ATS schools in the eighties: a commitment to global evangelism, the hope for "ecumenical cooperation among Christians throughout the world," dialogue between world religions, and Christian social action "to improve the lives of the poor and politically disadvantaged around the globe."[19] In the mid-1980s and 1990s, Brite's attention to global issues within the curriculum focused primarily on issues of social action, ecumenism between Christians, and Christian theology of religions. For instance, Brite's 1991 mission statement emphasized the importance of an education that acknowledged "a diverse world," not only in terms of the diversity of Christian tradition and experience, but racial, ethnic, and cultural diversity.[20]

Brite's first faculty member whose teaching focused on the issue of globalization was a University of Chicago graduate, Don Pittman. Educated within the history of religions approach at Chicago, Pittman began teaching courses in interreligious dialogue, Christian theology of religions, and the history of religions during the mid-1980s. Pittman left the school in 1993 to accept a position in Thailand. In the fall of 1994, when Susan White (PhD from the University of Notre Dame) joined the faculty to teach Spirituality and Worship, her spouse, Kenneth Cracknell, first as an adjunct professor and later as research professor, assumed primary responsibility for courses on interreligious dialogue and courses dealing with the Christian theology of religions.

In 2000, the faculty adopted a new mission and goals statement that emphasized the work of justice in relation to Brite's understanding of global issues. The goals statement noted the importance of seeking reflection on and engagement with "the meaning of Christian faith in dialogue with the concerns and goals of justice and reconciliation in today's world."[21] In 2006, Namsoon Kang assumed from Kenneth Cracknell the responsibility of teaching the majority of Brite's course offerings in globalization. A native of Korea, Kang's research and teaching focused on feminist and postcolonial approaches to the study of world Christianity and Christianity's encounter with other religions. Continuing to develop its engagement with global issues, Brite's faculty incorporated a specific course requirement in the study of world religions in 2009.

In addition to their work on the composition of Brite's student body and curriculum, Perdue and Toulouse shared an emphasis on enhancing the quality of students enrolling at Brite. In 1992, Brite increased its minimum undergraduate GPA requirement to 2.75 for entering masters students, a level Perdue argued was "the highest of any graduate seminary in the South and Southwest."[22] The school also implemented a minimum GPA for continued matriculation and graduation of 2.5.[31] Students failing to maintain this level of achievement were initially placed on probation and thereafter dismissed if they could not raise their GPA back to 2.5.[23] In these ways, Brite attempted to address the complaint reaching all the way back to the Brown-May study of the 1930s that raised serious concerns about admissions standards in theological education.[24]

Perdue, Toulouse, and their successors Newell Williams and Nancy Ramsay also led the school in continuing its commitment to diversify its faculty. By 2005, more than a third of Brite's faculty members were women. Brite added its first full-time Latina faculty member, Daisy Machado, in 1993. Machado left in 1996 to serve for three years as the first director of the Hispanic Theological Initiative in Atlanta and returned to Brite in 1999. In 2001, Brite hired its first full-time Jewish faculty member, David Nelson. Nelson's appointment followed several years of fundraising and community work at Brite to create the new Rosalyn and Manny Rosenthal Chair of Jewish Studies. In 2002 Stacey Floyd-Thomas became Brite's first female African American professor and the director of the newly created Black Church Studies Program. That same year, Brite hired its first Asian faculty member, Tim Lee, as part of a grant procured by Dean Toulouse seeking support for Korean studies at Brite. While the number of faculty from traditionally underrepresented racial and ethnic groups remained smaller than many hoped, by the year 2002, it was also larger than it had ever been. Increasing the faculty complement in these areas also helped increase student numbers from diverse racial and ethnic groups. By 2008, these students represented 26.4 percent of a student body in excess of 260, including 8.8 percent of students hailing from international locations.[25]

The academic credentials of each of these new scholars at Brite also helped solidify Brite's efforts at not simply diversifying the faculty but also improving the academic quality of the faculty. Each of the faculty members from a traditionally underrepresented racial or ethnic religious group who came up for tenure successfully met the school's expectations for tenure. In the early 1990s, Perdue and Toulouse reduced the faculty's teaching load by eliminating the requirement that every faculty member teach a doctor of ministry course each year. At the same time, they shifted the school's grading policy to a plus-and-minus system and adjusted the school's calendar to one more suitable for graduate work: twelve weeks of classes and two reading weeks (moving away from the traditional undergraduate calendar associated with the university). Thereafter, faculty load consisted of two courses each semester, with the expectation that faculty could transfer the time previously dedicated to the required DMin courses to refined teaching and additional research. In conjunction with their expectation for additional research, Perdue and Toulouse moved to strengthen faculty research support by implementing faculty summer research stipends, increasing travel funds, and adjusting the school's leave policy. The latter policy shifted from a one semester's leave at full pay or a full year's leave with half pay every six years to the option of a paid one semester's leave every three-and-a-half years or a full year's paid leave every seven years.

If many of the changes at Brite reflected commitments and trends reaching back at least a decade, other changes represented Brite's evolution into a more highly complex institution serving a broader constituency. The introduction of PhD and master of theology (ThM) programs to Brite's curricular offerings played a critical role in this transition. The ThM is a master's degree that requires a previous master's degree in a theological school as a prerequisite. In 1989, Brite's degrees almost exclusively prepared people for ministry in congregational settings. While the focus on congregational ministry did not necessarily change with the introduction of programs primarily intended for careers in teaching and research, these degrees diversified Brite's offerings and brought an influx of new students. In 2008, less than ten years after their initial launch, the ThM and PhD programs accounted for nearly 25 percent of Brite's total student body.

Discussions related to the introduction of a PhD degree predate 1992, when Brite received permission from TCU's provost to form a committee to explore a PhD program.[26] By 1996, Brite received the provost's and chancellor's approval, as well as the approval of Brite's board of trustees, for PhD programs in Biblical Interpretation and Pastoral Theology and Pastoral Counseling with an anticipated start date as early as 1998.[27] Some alumni and church leaders, however, imagined that the introduction of PhD programs signaled a waning of Brite's commitment to preparing women and men for vocations in churches. Like most divinity schools, Brite sought to challenge the perceived tensions between the church and academy that gave rise to these concerns. The school did this by questioning the validity of the duality itself. Brite argued that it served the church by maintaining high academic standards for those pursuing ministries in congregational settings just as Brite served the church by providing a theological education that prepared women and men for a variety of vocations that extended the church's work in the world. Of course, as Conrad Cherry observes, divinity schools often experience difficulties in maintaining equal commitments to academy and church: "Faculty had their classes to prepare, their books and articles to write, their presentations before professional societies to deliver in order to enhance and maintain their standing as university educators. Students had their research papers to compose, their readings to do, their seminar reports to frame in order to meet the requirements of a specialized education." Cherry also notes the lack of a clear relation between the content of much of divinity school coursework and the work of ministry as another hindrance to balancing commitments to church and academy.[28]

One of the ways Brite sought to address the challenges of nurturing a commitment to academy and church was to continue to hire faculty who clearly supported both arenas. In 1991 Brite brought Jim Duke back to the faculty from his position at Pacific School of Religion (he had left Brite in 1985). Two other hires in 1992, M. Eugene Boring in New Testament and Nancy Gorsuch in pastoral theology and pastoral counseling, also represented these qualities well. This task, always difficult in hiring, became all the more significant for positions such as field education and supervised ministry, critical to the life of a seminary but often filled in schools by people who did not have the credentials for tenure according to university standards. The inability to earn this traditional marker of academic distinction seemed to reinforce the idea that practical training lacked academic rigor. Nevertheless, the person's teaching requirements and oversight of students in fieldwork required someone who held both academic and ecclesial credentials. When Brite needed to fill this particular position in 1994, the school hired Stephen Sprinkle, someone who held a PhD in Systematic Theology from Duke University. Sprinkle could perform the teaching and research tasks of a faculty member and, as an ordained and experienced clergy, also held the appropriate ministerial experience to oversee students' fieldwork.

Brite also made several efforts to expand and strengthen its program connected to congregational ministries. The faculty approved programs in United Methodist and Baptist studies in the 1990s to create and support the growing denominational representation among Brite's students. The programs met ordination requirements by providing instruction in the history, doctrine, and polity of their respective traditions. They also provided students the opportunity to receive formation within a particular denominational tradition while being educated within an intentionally ecumenical context. The faculty approved similar programs in Presbyterian studies (2003) and Episcopal studies (2009) in later years.

A second initiative to strengthen Brite's program related to congregational ministries occurred in 1999 when Brite's faculty developed the master of arts in Christian service (MACS) degree program to address the changing nature of ministry within churches. The degree is designed for laypersons interested in serving the ministry of the church, often as volunteers. The first impetus for the program emerged out of revisions to the accreditation standards for the master of theological studies (MTS) degree programs. Previously, Brite's MTS program, established in 1988, included an emphasis on preparing people for careers in the church. According to the original description printed in the *Brite Bulletin,* the program had four audiences in mind: (1) those pursuing deacon's orders; (2) those serving as lay church staff; (3) those who sought "to enhance the quality of their church leadership;" and (4) those who desired personal enrichment.[29] The description made no mention of preparing people for doctoral work. Alterations to the ATS degree standards, however, shifted the expectation for this degree to a general theological degree that provided "a basic understanding of theological disciplines for further graduate study or for general educational purposes" rather than service within a church.[30]

Brite's efforts to respond to these changes to the MTS degree opened up a larger conversation that identified three needs that the school's masters curricula could not adequately address. First, many congregations' reliance upon lay and bivocational leaders for primary clerical functions necessitated a course of study for those leaders that would satisfy each denomination's educational requirements related to licensure. Second, students pursuing ordination as deacons in the United Methodist Church also needed a context to pursue their denomination's educational requirements. Finally, the diversification and professionalization of staff in many congregations created a market for laypeople with specializations in a select area of ministry.

Brite attempted to address these needs through the formation of the MACS degree program. The program combined coursework in the tradi-

Leibrock Village (southwest corner) housing for students and families (2010).

tional theological disciplines with practical experience, particularly through a year-long field-based supervised educational experience. In addition, students selected a specialization that required the completion of nine credit hours in Practical Theology, Religious Education, Pastoral Theology and Pastoral Counseling, or Worship and Spirituality. The focus of the MTS degree shifted to educating those who sought an introduction to the general theological disciplines or planned to pursue an advanced graduate degree such as the PhD.

Through the development and revision of new degree programs, Brite expanded the populations it served to include those preparing for different vocations within and outside of the church. An integral part of the motivation included the reality of a changing church, which increasingly professionalized lay activity within the church in vocations such as Christian education, worship, youth ministry, and pastoral care. Other programs, particularly the PhD programs, also brought Brite into a larger educational arena. Through the growing number and aims of Brite's degree programs, its research, and continuing education efforts, Brite provided a broad and highly complex form of theological education at the close of the 1990s.

In the midst of these changes to the academic life of the institution, Brite undertook the construction of a new housing complex. Brite's enrollment growth, desire for a larger residential community, and recognition of the aging condition of its current housing called for resolution. Brite's board approved a capital campaign in 1993 and, after at least one significant false start, the school broke ground in 1999 on a fifty-six-unit apartment complex, Leibrock Village, on the east side of TCU's campus. The final plans included codevelopment of the area on the part of TCU, which constructed graduate student housing along the periphery of Leibrock Village.

The ambitious agenda to expand or enhance Brite's facilities, faculty, ad-

Brite Students (c. 1990).

ministration, and student body in the 1990s added significantly to Brite's budget. Between 1989 and 1999, the school's budget increased 63 percent from $2.87 million to $4.67 million. Endowment growth helped offset the increase. In 1989, the endowment stood just below $20 million. By June 1999, the endowment had grown to $52 million, helping the school simultaneously to increase spending, budget for six-figure surpluses, and decrease the percentage drawn from the endowment. By 2002, when Perdue and Toulouse returned to teaching, Brite had successfully moved to a spending policy limiting endowment use to 5 percent based on a twenty-quarter (five-year) trailing average, a more fiscally responsible approach than the nearly 8 percent annually in use when Perdue arrived in 1989.[31] Among all accredited theological schools in the United States in the late 1990s, Brite's endowment ranked within the top 10 percent.[32]

As Brite approached the new millennium, the school appeared in tremendous health. Brite possessed an ambitious agenda for excellence in theological education along the lines of the major university-related divinity schools. It was financially secure, enjoyed record levels of enrollment, introduced new programs that expanded the constituents the school served, and increased the size and quality of its faculty. The school was also well underway with plans to build new housing to increase its residential population. On the horizon, plans emerged for a new academic building, a Houston campus, and global partnerships with other seminaries. Among ATS schools, Brite was rich and successful. Yet, its relation with TCU, for so long integral to the school's existence, was rapidly declining. To this deteriorating situation, we must now turn.

Affiliation with TCU

The breadth of Perdue's vision for excellence in theological education, and the pace at which he sought to implement that vision, strained relations between Brite and TCU to a breaking point. Perdue repeatedly complained that TCU's administration either ignored Brite's aims or simply did not understand theological education enough to provide the necessary administrative support. For its part, TCU often considered Brite's ambitions overly taxing to the university's administrative procedures, and perhaps even naïve. During a meeting regarding the construction of Leibrock Village, for instance, Chancellor Tucker explained that all construction plans would be reviewed and approved by TCU's board to ensure that "Brite does not build a hacienda down there."[33] Brite's frustrated hope to build a new housing facility proved critical to the mounting tensions. In 1993, Brite's board approved a major capital campaign to build a new housing complex. The plan depended upon TCU approval and assistance in securing a location for the housing complex. Earlier efforts identified a suitable location on a plot of land on Cantey Street, located on the northwest corner of campus, near the football stadium.[34] As work progressed on procuring permits, TCU's board surprisingly reversed course and withdrew its approval for the development of the Cantey site. The move exasperated Perdue, Toulouse, and several Brite board members who believed TCU reneged on its commitment to Brite in order to serve its own interests, including retaining the land to use as parking for football games. Questions about whether leaders of one educational institution could adequately support the aims of another, particularly when the aims of the two schools seemed to conflict, rose to the fore.

After TCU rescinded its offer to provide the Cantey site, Brite began preparing to confront the governance relationship with TCU head-on. As the process gained momentum, the Brite board removed TCU's Vice Chancellor for Academic Affairs, William Koehler, from his role as chief academic officer of Brite in 1998 and appointed Dean Leo Perdue to this role. Shortly thereafter Perdue had to interrupt his tenure with a medical leave (November 1998 to February 1999). However, over many months, Perdue, Toulouse, and others, including board members, had discussed thoroughly the difficulties posed by current governance relationships. Perdue, particularly, had struggled for years to overcome them.

Based on these ongoing conversations, in mid-November 1998, Mark Toulouse produced a confidential document for members of Brite's board that raised questions about the current governance structure.[35] Among those who received the document were the three trustees (Roy Snodgrass, Gene Brice, and Jim Oglesby) who Perdue appointed to represent Brite on a joint divinity school and university committee established to address governance questions. In addition, on December 8, Toulouse met with Brice and Oglesby to discuss the document. Toulouse relied heavily upon the recently revised standards of the Association of Theological Schools to underscore the tensions in Brite's governance structure. Toulouse observed that the standards divided graduate theological schools into three groups: (1) the independent, incorporated seminary with full authority vested in the seminary, and not located on a university or college campus; (2) unincorporated schools related to and typically financially dependent upon colleges, universities, or clusters of theological schools; and (3) schools related to ecclesiastical bodies in particular ways where authority is shared by the institution and the church.[36]

Toulouse emphasized that Brite's governance structure did not fit any of these categories. While the school was separately incorporated and had a governing board, qualities of the first type, it "has . . . limited its own authority to model other University Divinity Schools, a feature of the second type." Because Brite had its own board, a feature of type one, Toulouse suggested that Brite had an obligation to conform to the ATS requirement for boards to exercise "responsibilities for maintaining the purpose, vitality, and integrity of the institution; the achievement of institutional policies; the selection of chief administrative leadership; and the provision of physical, fiscal and human resources." Toulouse pointed out "this paragraph addressing Type one institutions describes Brite's governance situation more clearly than the paragraph describing Type 2 (the University-related seminary). But the paragraph intends to speak to fully independent seminaries (Type 1)." Although Brite had a governing board, Toulouse noted that the board chose "'chief administrative leadership' that is unrelated to theological education in any integral or genuine way." More specifically, Brite's "chief administrative leadership" had "no day to day relationship with theological education" and "had no relationship to theological education except through its relationship with the dean of Brite Divinity School."[37]

While Toulouse admitted that the standards allowed boards to articulate the nature of a school's governance authority and that the board could, therefore, continue its practice of limiting the authority of Brite's dean by delegating executive authority to the three university officers, Toulouse used the confusion in governance structures as the basis from which to move beyond a simple question of whether or not Brite complied with ATS standards, to a more fundamental point about the significant tensions that the school's governance structure created. Toulouse began with the ATS statement on the theological nature of governance as a "bond of trust" that is "theologically informed." Toulouse responded by again underscoring the ideological distance between the university's leadership and Brite: "[It is] hard for Brite to defend theologically a shared form of governance with the University, the administration of which (Chancellor, Provost, Financial Officer) have no direct ties to our 'faculty, students, and ecclesial bodies.'"[38]

Toulouse also drew heavily from the ATS standards' reference to the "exercise of faithful leadership on behalf of the purpose of the theological school." Toulouse countered that TCU's leadership was "defined more by legal relationships than by [the ATS expectation of] 'patterns of responsibility and accountability.'" He insisted:

> The Chancellor, Provost, and Financial Officer have not understood the purpose of the theological school. These three officers have a primary responsibility, defined by their job descriptions, to govern the Divinity School by being faithful (first and foremost) to the purpose of a large mostly undergraduate liberal arts university, not according to the purpose of the theological school (which, at best, can only be a secondary consideration in their thinking about any particular issue). This context, more often than not, has set up a conflict of interest that is not easily resolved (graduate student seminary housing over against the needs for football stadium parking, for example. How does this latter interest have anything to do with the purpose of the theological school? And, if the purpose of the theological school has to take second place to the purpose of the undergraduate university, how can this be considered "faithful leadership on behalf of the purpose of the theological school?")

While the question of whether a chancellor or provost can fully understand the mission and identity of a theological school could be posed by most faculty and administrators at the major university-related divinity schools, the dilemma became particularly acute because Brite was separately incorporated and yet chose to submit itself to the governance of TCU in ways that seemed to undermine its mission. Toulouse therefore suggested that the board shift to a different conception of its relation to TCU. Most importantly, Toulouse argued that the school's chief executive leadership should come from within Brite rather than from TCU. Second, borrowing language from the ATS standards, Toulouse argued that Brite "should consider the University as one of its 'constituencies and publics,'" recognizing Brite's accountability to the university just as it recognizes its accountability to the church. However, just as the seminary did not invest the day-to-day operation of the seminary in the church, it should not invest operations in the university. As one of its constituencies and publics, the divinity school would be accountable to the university through the establishment and maintenance of a "responsible" relationship with the chancellor and with the university as a whole. It would not, however, "necessarily include an investment of authority (accountability) for its day to day operations in the Finance Officer's office, the Provost's office, or the Chancellor's office."[39] The arrangement also implied that Brite assume full obligations for faculty and staff appointments, tenure, and conferring degrees. Other suggestions for ongoing connections were more practical, including proposing that the "Chancellor of the University should serve on the Brite Board of Trustees as an ex-officio member," that "the Dean of the Divinity School should maintain regular collaboration with the Chancellor of the University," and that the "Chief financial officer [for Brite] needs to reside at Brite Divinity School."[40]

After discussing this document with members of Brite's board, Toulouse arranged a meeting in December 1998 with TCU's new chancellor, Michael Ferrari, about the prospect of clarifying the relationship between the schools. Ferrari had assumed his duties only a few months earlier. As an outsider to the nature of the Brite/TCU relationship, a non-Disciple, and a longtime university president with an academic specialization in organizational theory, Ferrari brought openness to pursuing an alternative relationship between the schools. The conversation between Toulouse and Ferrari yielded several talking points that steered the course of the conversation going forward. First, Ferrari suggested rewriting the bylaws in order to revise the governance relationship in ways that still recognized the historic relationship between the two schools and the desire to continue that relationship in ways that would "nurture the growth and development of both schools." In particular, Toulouse and Ferrari discussed the possibility that the bylaws would stipulate Brite's dean as the chief executive officer of the corporation rather than TCU's chancellor and that the academic and financial operations of Brite would also be housed at Brite rather than TCU. At the same time, the two men expressed hope that Brite and TCU might continue to relate to one another in informal ways through regular meetings between the dean and chancellor and in formal ways through the chancellor being named an ex-officio member of Brite's board, and that other members of the two schools' boards might interlock.[41]

The talking points did much to set the groundwork for the next several months. When Perdue returned from medical leave in February, he dedicated his first few months to the process and worked closely with Ferrari and Brite trustees to move the process along at a steady pace. His return meant that Brite's leadership could be fully represented in all discussions, including the joint committee exploring governance. At heart, Perdue, Toulouse, and Ferrari hoped that a clarified relationship would ultimately strengthen the ties between the schools while allowing Brite to pursue its interests in the directions and pace it desired. The task at hand was to convince the more skeptical within TCU and Brite that this was both necessary and possible.

To this end, in the fall semester of 1998, Perdue and Ferrari had formed a committee made up of trustees from Brite and TCU. The committee assumed the task of identifying problems and making recommendations concerning issues of authority and governance for Brite. Perdue and Ferrari also drafted a resolution that, after some revision within the committee, was approved and forwarded to the TCU and Brite boards in November of 1999, just one year after serious discussion on revising the governance relationship began. As originally imagined during the conversation between Toulouse and Ferrari, the resolution emphasized the historic ties between the schools as well as the mutual benefits of continued collaboration. It also indicated the intention "to strengthen the existing affiliation and collaborative relationship" through the clarification of governance matters and a new financial relationship. The new terms of the Brite/TCU affiliation included TCU's continued provision of administrative support, maintenance, operational, and any "other services . . . comparable to services provided to other colleges and schools of the University." In exchange, Brite agreed to pay TCU 15 percent of its annual budget and not more than 3 percent of the cost of any additional services that TCU might add to the university for which Brite derived benefit. Brite also agreed to take on "full financial responsibility" for any facility construction or renovation it undertook.

Chancellor Ferrari had his work cut out for him to satisfy some members of the TCU board who expressed significant reservations about TCU relinquishing its control over the governance of Brite.[42] Ironically, the very intermingling of Brite's governance with that of TCU helped serve Brite when it came to the TCU board's vote on the joint resolution. Roy Snodgrass, chair of Brite's board, also served on the board of TCU. According to Ferrari, the respect and influence Snodgrass enjoyed with members of TCU's board ultimately helped persuade skeptics that a clarification of governance served both institutions.[43] TCU's and Brite's boards signed the resolution in November 1999. The agreement was implemented on June 1, 2000, and reaffirmed with slight changes in 2004.

Shortly after the implementation of the agreement, members of Brite's faculty reflected on the changed relationship in Brite's self-study for the Association of Theological Schools, explaining, "With the 1999 Resolutions, Brite and TCU have not set upon 'new,' separate paths, but rather have defined their legal relationship more clearly and fully, permitting a partnership which is more appropriate, flexible, and mutually beneficial than it has been in the recent past."[44] The positive assessment expressed by Brite's faculty intersected with Chancellor Ferrari's comments to Brite's board about the broader significance of the clarification of Brite's governance and the school's ambitions. Ferrari congratulated the board "on their desire to become one of the very best theological schools in the nation."[45]

The clarification of the relationship between Brite and TCU resolved the governance ambiguity that had clouded Brite for decades. Brite obtained the independence its original charter guaranteed and finally had the financial resources to carry out its mission. But just what the mission would be and how it might change as the school entered the twenty-first century remained to be seen.

Conclusion: Brite in the Twenty-first Century

Brite's attempt to establish a self-governing seminary with the academic and professional quality historically associated with university-related divinity schools continues. The effort institutionalizes William Rainey Harper's assumption that theological education as a whole and ministerial preparation in particular is best accomplished within the confines of the university. Brite preserves much of what Harper and others found valuable about the university: specialized learning that integrates academic knowledge and practical skills, connections to other academic departments, and the cultural prestige associated with university education. Yet, Brite's leaders hope that the school's independence might actually enhance rather than detract from the rigor and quality of the institution by allowing the school to pursue its ambitions on its own terms. In this sense, Brite's rationale turns Harper's vision on its head more than nuances it. William Rainey Harper could never have imagined that a university might hinder the progress of theological education.

But is Brite's effort sustainable? Can a school draw the best of both a university association and independent governance? The success of any school depends on many factors, but good governance is among the chief contributors to success. The Executive Director of the Association of Theological Schools, Daniel Aleshire, notes regarding governance, "Across the past twenty years, almost all of the serious accrediting sanctions issued by the ATS Commission on Accrediting have related to failures in governance, administration, or finances, and for many of the schools with sanctions related to finances, the underlying problem had as much to do with governance or administration as financial resources."[46] Brite's effort will, in important ways, depend upon its leaders successfully stewarding the governance responsibility the school fought so hard to obtain.

Observers witnessed some of the consequences of Brite's ability to govern itself in the spring of 2008 when the school's recipient of its Black Church Leader Award, Jeremiah Wright, hit the news for his comments about white Americans and American foreign policy. Wright, an African American, enjoyed a long and distinguished career as a community activist, educator, and pastor of Trinity United Church of Christ in Chicago. As then presidential candidate Barack Obama's pastor, Wright came into the spotlight after word broke that, in one of his sermons, Wright discouraged African Americans from singing "God Bless America." Wright proclaimed "God damn America" for its treatment of African Americans. In his sermon, Wright asserted, "The government gives them the drugs, builds bigger prisons, passes a three-strike law and then wants us to sing 'God Bless America.' No, no, no, God damn America, that's in the Bible for killing innocent people." Wright continued, "God damn America for treating our citizens as less than human. God damn America for as long as she acts like she is God and she is supreme." As conservative groups and the press mined Wright's other sermons for similar rhetoric, they discovered comments criticizing the United States after the September 11, 2001, attacks on the World Trade Center in New York. Wright argued that the United States had committed its own terrorist acts in its use of atomic weapons in World War II and had supported state terrorism in South Africa and Palestine.

Brite had selected Wright for the award nearly a year before the controversy emerged, and the school had planned to honor him at a banquet in late March 2008. When the controversy erupted earlier in the month, calls for Brite to rescind the award flooded the school. The TCU board and much of the university's administration joined the chorus of opposition. TCU Chancellor Victor J. Boschini issued a statement on March 17, 2008, that explained that while TCU valued the right of free speech, "giving an award is another matter, and in this specific case in light of Reverend Wright's recently discovered remarks, TCU [if it were up to TCU] would not give such an award."[47] Two days later, the executive committee of TCU's board, with the approval of Brite's administration, voted to move the event off campus "in light of security issues."[48]

In response to the public outcry against Wright, Brite issued its own statements, including an op-ed article written by Dean Nancy Ramsay and Brite Trustee Eugene Brice for the *Fort Worth Star-Telegram*. The article did not necessarily endorse Wright's language, but attempted to place it within the theological context of African American liberation theology and the biblical context of the prophetic tradition. Ramsay and Brice wrote: "The righteous anger of the prophet, as shown in Scripture, must not be confused with hate speech. In the tradition of the biblical prophets, Dr. Wright is challenging forms of oppression that demean any of God's children. He preaches regularly to persons who daily experience the stigma and oppression of racial and economic injustice that have plagued us since the earliest years of this country." The aims of Wright's actions, Ramsay and Brice concluded, "support the dignity and worth of all people while challenging actions and policies that threaten God's vision for peace and justice."[49]

TCU's explicit rejection of Brite's decision to recognize Jeremiah Wright suggests that had Brite operated under the older bylaws that ceded much of the school's governance to TCU, the outcome might have been much different. Despite the Brite board's ability in earlier years to exercise a measure of independence from TCU on issues it thought particularly important, namely racial integration and divestment, it never faced such public opposition from TCU. By clarifying the governance relation, Brite could act on its convictions while TCU could act likewise without either side compromising its position.

If the Jeremiah Wright event represented the benefits of a distinct governance structure, the tensions between Brite and TCU surrounding the event illustrate another challenge to Brite's ability to retain its vision for theological education: its relationship to the university. One event is not likely to scar the two schools' willingness to perpetuate their arrangement, but it does underscore the fact that while the joint resolution assures affiliation over a relatively short period of time, the required review of the arrangement routinely raises discussion about continued affiliation. If the two schools find a widening divergence in their interests, the affiliation could be jeopardized because it remains dependent on the perceptions and associations of each school's current leadership. Although financial issues help govern the agreement between Brite and TCU, and those financial arrangements have routinely been revisited in the past decade, the schools purposefully grounded their 1999 affiliation agreement in their shared history and interests rather than finances.[50]

The renegotiation of the affiliation agreement between 2009 and 2010 highlights several key issues in the Brite-TCU relationship. In October 2009, TCU submitted to Brite a draft affiliation agreement that varied in significant ways from previous agreements. In place of the relatively informal three-page agreements signed in 1999 and 2004, the proposed agreement stretched to thirteen pages and included new clauses allowing either party to terminate the agreement at any time during the period covered by the agreement, indemnification of TCU, and increased specification of the services and resources that would and would not be included in the agreement.

The agreement also employed a very different model for calculating Brite's payment to the university. The new agreement utilized an average cost basis to calculate Brite's payment rather than the marginal cost basis employed in earlier agreements between the two schools. The marginal cost basis proceeded from the fact that, given Brite's small size in relation to the overall university, TCU's expenses remained largely the same regardless of whether the university provided services to Brite. The university, for instance, would likely need to employ roughly the same number of staff and pay similar rates for insurance whether or not it had an agreement with Brite. Thus, Brite's "cost" to the university was relatively marginal.

An average cost basis approached the calculation of cost quite differently, in this case resulting in the appearance that a services agreement between the two schools cost TCU much more. Such a calculation considered Brite's use of services as a percentage of the rest of the university's use. For instance, if Brite students borrowed a certain percentage of the total number of books borrowed at the library, Brite should pay that percentage of the university's library circulation expenses. Where usage levels were more difficult to calculate, TCU based its cost calculation on Brite's student headcount in relation to the total student headcount and charged Brite the same percentage of TCU's costs for the service in question. Using such methods, TCU concluded that Brite annually "cost" the University over $2.1 million, or more than $1 million more than Brite paid under the existing agreement.[51] Although the two schools ultimately settled on a less substantial increase, the new agreement retained the use of an average cost calculation to determine Brite's payment to the university.

A shift in accounting standards might not necessarily reflect a difference in the nature of the relation between the two schools, though it is noteworthy that in 1999 Chancellor Michael Ferrari intentionally employed the marginal cost method for calculating Brite's payment to the university because he believed the method supported his larger goal of defining the relationship between the two schools in terms of shared values rather than finances. With the implementation of a new agreement in August 2010, Brite and TCU will now have the opportunity to discover if Ferrari was correct.

The schools will conduct their ongoing affiliation in the context of another significant feature of the new agreement, this one relating to Brite's property. A six-page "Memorandum" accompanying the final twenty-three-page agreement expanded upon clauses in the new affiliation agreement that provided TCU with a "preferential right" to acquire Brite's property should Brite receive a purchase offer from another entity. The agreement also placed limits upon Brite's ability to lease part or all of its property and granted TCU the ability to purchase Brite's indebtedness should Brite default on any Deed of Trust in to which the school entered.[52] The ability to gain control of Brite's property in the event Brite experienced significant financial difficulty or decided to relocate certainly represents a shrewd business decision for TCU, which would clearly be impacted by a decline in the facilities or relocation of a neighbor who occupies space within the larger TCU campus. For Brite, however, the agreement represents a new limitation on its ability to control its property. Brite's desire to maintain its affiliation with TCU now comes at the cost of ceding some of its control over its property back to TCU.

Another significant factor in considering whether Brite will be successful in its attempt to reap the benefits of university affiliation and autonomous governance is the school's ability to perpetuate the quality and diversity of programming typical of university-related divinity schools. In the 1990s and early years of the twenty-first century, Brite defined its goals for excellence largely in terms of heightening the academic qualifications and diversity of

Brite students (2009).

faculty who were also expected to take the church seriously; increasing the quality and diversity of the student body; expanding the types of degree programs in order to address a wider array of vocational paths; and revising the content of its existing degree programs to increasingly address the global scope of Christianity, its engagement with other world religions, and issues of justice and public theology in the modern world. How these goals evolve in the second decade of the twenty-first century and beyond is still unfolding.

In 2003, Newell Williams succeeded Leo Perdue as president of Brite. In 2005, Nancy Ramsay arrived as executive vice president and dean. Williams led the school in 2009 to adopt a new mission statement and set of institutional goals that shed some light on future directions. The new mission statement removed references to the school's affiliations with the Christian Church (Disciples of Christ) and Texas Christian University, though the placement of these affiliations within the school's institutional goals suggests that the two affiliations remain important to Brite's identity. Perhaps the most significant change in the mission statement was the removal of language specifying the kinds of educational endeavors the school pursues, specifically the phrase "programs of instruction, research and scholarship, and other forms of church and community service." Instead, the statement highlighted the vocations for which the school prepared people, namely "the ministry of Christ's church, the academy, and public life." Additionally, the mission statement shifted from a focus on producing people "for ministry, witness, and outreach of the church of Jesus Christ in the world" to the different task of producing people who will serve as "witnesses to God's reconciling and transforming love and justice." While the former statement seemed to limit the work of Brite's students to the church, the latter broadens the scope to include work that might be accomplished outside of the church. Taken as a whole, the new statement also more clearly embraces the broader constituents the school serves through its programs, though the removal of the reference to the school's research activity would seem to obscure a wider understanding of the ways that Brite can serve its constituents beyond its programming.

The new institutional goals lift up several commitments that have long marked Brite, such as recruiting and retaining a highly qualified student body and faculty, valuing faculty research, and promoting continuing education. The goals also highlight newer emphases such as greater attention to fostering student spiritual formation, something that the faculty integrated into its MDiv curriculum approved in 2009. Other goals, such as the focus on justice, might be taking new directions, as when the faculty agreed in 2009 to revise its scheduling practices in order to provide access to students whose financial constraints require them to maintain full-time employment. For the first time, Brite began offering all of the core courses required for the MDiv degree in a three-year evening rotation.

As Brite looks to achieve its goals toward excellence in theological education, it will need to consider the future of master of divinity education. The MDiv degree program is the largest program in the school, and it occupies a central place in Brite's identity. However, recent declines in enrollment in master of divinity programs at Brite and across graduate theological education, the shrinking numbers of mainline churches, and trends indicating fewer MDiv students are choosing to enter congregational settings suggest that the MDiv degree program may be heading toward a crisis. Between 2000 and 2008, the number of MDiv students at Brite dropped at a staggering rate of more than 25 percent. Beyond a decline in numbers, MDiv students also declined as a percentage of the total student body.[53] In 2008, MDiv students represented only 52 percent of the total student body, down from more than 70 percent just eight years earlier.

These declines come in the midst of serious questions about the identity and purpose of MDiv education. For many, graduate theological education, understood almost exclusively in terms of preparation for parish ministry,

Brite faculty (2010).

should focus on skills for ministry, particularly those that might counteract declines in church membership. As E. Brooks Holifield recently observed, "Some critics complained that the schools were *too* academic and gave insufficient attention to the practical work of ministry. Graduates sometimes grumbled that seminaries did not teach them how to deal with people, handle conflict, or perform the routine tasks of ministry." In addition, these critics argued that seminaries were "too attentive to the intricacies of theology and more interested in teaching students to read texts than to run churches."[54] They would substitute the older model of forming a learned clergy for theological reflection and articulation with the development of a particular skill set—ability to provide pastoral care, ability to increase church membership, ability to run a capital campaign, etc. Others resist the identification of theological schools as professional schools and push for an education that forms individuals in a pastoral identity emphasizing ministry as a form of art or an education that will develop particular emotional and spiritual qualities within students.[55] In still another attempt to characterize MDiv education, Holifield has suggested abandoning the notion of MDiv education as professional education in favor of the MDiv as vocational education that roots ministry in a divine call.[56] Brite will not be immune from the need to address these different conceptions of MDiv education in the years to come.

In addition to the challenges to MDiv programs from without, other challenges exist that are more particular to Brite. As the historic center of Brite's educational programming undergoes flux and its programming grows more complex, Brite faces obstacles naturally associated with the complex nature of its operations. Brite's degree programs now prepare people for a wide range of vocations from pastoral ministry to work in social service agencies to careers in the academy. But excellence in master of divinity education requires different structures and activities than excellence in PhD education. What is the optimal balance of faculty time, size, and institutional financial resources between programs preparing people for careers within the church and outside of it? This question becomes all the more critical given the fact that students in Brite's ThM and PhD programs now represent nearly 25 percent of the total student body whereas the number of students enrolled in Brite's MDiv program has declined by more than 25 percent and the number of students enrolled in the DMin program has declined by nearly 40 percent.[57]

At the same time, how can Brite recognize the challenges of different programs without defining those programs as in competition with one another for scarce resources or for the right principally to represent the identity of the institution? Rather, how can the school and its constituents imagine its programs as cooperative endeavors that enhance Brite's mission in ways that no single program could do on its own? Theological education serves a range of constituents from the students who enroll in its programs, to the church that depends on seminaries for trained leadership and critical reflection on the church's mission, to the public who benefits from its scholarly production and analysis of the role of religion in public life. In this sense, Brite's programs need to exist in symbiotic relationship with one another and in service to a larger mission rather than acting as warring factions.

Still another dimension to the sustainability of Brite's hopes to provide the highest quality theological education in the context of independent governance is the question of how Brite's programming will continue to evolve to reflect the reality of a changing church and social context. If graduate theological education provides a place "where people engage in the sustained, critical, and imaginative thought about human life before God," and we know that human life before God takes different forms in different times and places, then in what ways must Brite continue to evolve to meet these changes?[58]Brite's recent history offers evidence of its desire to continue to expand its programming through its introduction of an Episcopal Church Studies program to educate Episcopal students in North Texas. Other opportunities, including the growing importance of Christianity in Asia, Africa, and Latin America, the increasing numbers of adherents to the world's diverse religions in America, and the importance of making deeper inroads into the enormous Latin American population in the Southwest all loom large for Brite in the twenty-first century.

The decisions Brite will make about how it delivers theological education will also prove important to its understanding of excellence in theological education. Many schools have implemented distance and online programs as ways to enhance student access and strengthen enrollment.[59] Brite experimented with a distance program beginning in 2001 when it established a video-conferencing system in Houston that allowed the school to send a real-time sound and video feed of its courses to Houston. Students in Houston could interact with the faculty members and students in Fort Worth. However, Brite's faculty voted to discontinue the program in 2006, arguing that the program was too small, excessively expensive, and pedagogically less effective than they hoped.[60]

Interest in distance education within theological education as a whole, however, continues to increase.[61] The Association of Theological Schools currently prevents schools from offering degrees earned exclusively online. Instead, the ATS requires at least one year of residency at a school's main campus.[62] But many schools raise significant challenges to this standard with the hope that they might offer complete online programs. In the meantime, several schools offer substantial numbers of online courses.[63] In what ways will Brite engage this trend? If it chooses to resist online courses, will schools that offer such programs gain an advantage in recruiting students? Alternatively, if Brite chooses to offer online courses, how will it ensure formational learning that often takes place in direct contact with faculty and other students?

The financial cost of theological education represents still another challenge for Brite, particularly in light of the crash of the world's financial markets in 2008 and early 2009, which resulted in the loss of nearly 30 percent of Brite's endowment. This devaluation of the endowment within the context of declining support from the church and other revenue sources has required Brite to rely more heavily upon tuition revenue to sustain its operating budget. Between fiscal years 2000 and 2009, Brite's operating budget increased 63 percent. During these same years, tuition charges increased 90 percent. In the 1999–2000 academic year, net tuition and fee revenue was just under $148,000 in a budget of $4.825 million. The approved budget for the 2008–2009 academic year included net tuition revenue of over $815,600 in a budget of over $7.8 million. While Brite's tuition charges remain far lower than other professional schools at TCU, the relatively low salaries of those entering ministerial careers makes even divinity school tuition rates significant.[64]

Like students at many ATS schools, Brite students have turned to increasing levels of borrowing to finance the rising costs of education. A 2002 study found that just over 25 percent of Brite's students took out a student loan at some point during their studies at Brite. In 2005, nearly 50 percent of students took out a loan. Furthermore, in 2005, students borrowed 40 percent more in a single year than the students in the 2002 study that included cumulative statistics (approximately $2.1 million in 2005–2006 as opposed to approximately $1.5 million cumulative in 2002). The average student in 2005–2006 borrowed in excess of $14,000. A third of all borrowers (16 percent of the student body as a whole) borrowed $18,500 in 2005–2006—the maximum amount one could borrow in Stafford Loans that year. When placed in the context of a recent national study on seminary borrowing, Brite students are about average for borrowing.[65] Like other theological schools, Brite will need to confront how students will be able to afford theological education and whether a viable student body is possible if costs continue to increase at their current rate.

No doubt the known challenges to Brite's future will be compounded by those that cannot now be identified. In many ways, Brite's future is tied to that of mainline theological education as a whole. But the future of the school will also be determined by its own decisions about the way it will provide graduate theological education within a changing world. As Daniel Aleshire notes, "The future of theological education will, in many ways, be defined by the ways in which schools are shaped by and respond to changes in the church, higher education, and the Christian movement as it advances in the twenty-first century."[66] One thing is certain, the ability to address a changing environment while remaining true to its mission will be crucial for Brite as it is for all educational institutions.

Notes

Introduction

1. Randolph Clark, *Reminiscences: Biographical and Historical* (Wichita Falls, TX: Lee Clark, Publisher, 1919), 9.
2. Glenn T. Miller, *A Community of Conversation: A Retrospective of the Association of Theological Schools and Ninety Years of North American Theological Education* (Pittsburgh: Association of Theological Schools, 2008), 4.

Chapter One
Before Brite: Ministerial Education at TCU, 1873–1914

1. "Origin and History of Christian University," *Dallas Morning News*, September 11, 1910.
2. *Brite College of the Bible Caller* (May 1944): 9, Special Collections, Mary Couts Burnett Library, Texas Christian University, Fort Worth, TX.
3. The Stone-Campbell Movement refers to the nomenclatural origins of what is now three distinct streams of religious thought and practice identified as the Christian Church (Disciples of Christ); the Churches of Christ; and the Christian Churches/ Churches of Christ, sometimes known as independent Christian Churches. In 1832, two independent frontier religious groups—the "Christians" led by Barton W. Stone and the "Reformers" or "Disciples of Christ" led by Alexander and Thomas Campbell—merged based on a commitment to church unity resting on essential truths found in the restoration of primitive Christianity as expressed in Scripture rather than in human opinion. Eventually, two schisms (one in 1906 and the other in 1968) exposed the underlying tensions found in the principles of Christian unity and the restoration of the primitive church. For more on the history of the Stone-Campbell Movement, see *The Encyclopedia of the Stone-Campbell Movement*, ed. Douglas A. Foster, Paul M. Blowers, Anthony L. Dunnavant, and D. Newell Williams (Grand Rapids, MI: William B. Eerdmans Publishing, 2004).
4. The labels merely serve as a typology. Variants existed within each category. The principles of restoration and unity created much of the tension. By 1906, churches separated from the Christian Church (Disciples of Christ) and became known as the Churches of Christ, which attempted to focus solely on the restoration of the primitive church. See also Mark G. Toulouse, *Joined in Discipleship: The Shaping of Contemporary Disciples Identity* (St. Louis: Chalice Press, 1997), for a more in-depth historical view of these principles.
5. M. Eugene Boring, *Disciples and the Bible: A History of Disciples Biblical Interpretation in North America* (St. Louis: Chalice Press, 1997), 5–6. Boring's periodization of Disciples biblical scholarship includes five generations, divided unequally in terms of the major scholars and representative figures of each generation who "set the agenda for Disciples theology in their time, in both content and method. These representative figures both shaped and reflected the way Disciples thought about the faith, themselves, and their role in the world" (4).
6. At that time, the town was called Thorp's Spring. See "TCU Celebrating 75th Anniversary," *Dallas Morning News*, January 9, 1948.
7. "Origin and History of Christian University," *Dallas Morning News*.
8. Randolph Clark, *Reminiscences: Biographical and Historical* (Wichita Falls, TX: Lee Clark, Publisher, 1919), 13–15.

9. Ibid., 21–22.
10. Both Addison and Randolph served as soldiers in the Confederate forces. Clark, *Reminiscences*, 29–31.
11. Kenneth McKinley Hay, *The Life and Influence of Charles Carlton, 1821–1902* (Fort Worth: Christian Courier, 1940), 22–23, 30.
12. Colby D. Hall, *History of Texas Christian University: A College of the Cattle Frontier* (Fort Worth: Texas Christian University Press, 1947), 24.
13. Hay, *Life and Influence of Charles Carlton*, 16–18. Moses Lard was also a member of his class. John W. McGarvey also attended there at the same time, and he and Charles formed a life-long friendship.
14. Richard F. Selcer, *Hell's Half Acre: The Life and Legend of a Red-Light District* (Fort Worth: Texas Christian University Press, 1991), 48.
15. Chalmers McPherson, *Disciples of Christ in Texas* (Cincinnati: Standard Publishing Company, 1920), 90.
16. Selcer, *Hell's Half Acre*, 48. See also Clark, *Reminiscences*, 41, for his views on "Hell's Half Acre."
17. E.B. Bynum, *These Carried the Torch: Pioneers of Christian Education in Texas* (Dallas: Walter F. Clark Company, 1946), 17.
18. Carter E. Boren, *Religion on the Texas Frontier* (San Antonio: Naylor Company, 1968), 225.
19. *Add-Ran College Catalogue* (1874–1875): 12–13, Special Collections, Mary Couts Burnett Library, Texas Christian University, Fort Worth, TX. AddRan was the name of Addison Clark's first-born child, a son who died of diphtheria at age three. The name came from the first syllable of each of the brother's names.
20. Clark, *Reminiscences*, 49.
21. Lester G. McAllister and William E. Tucker, *Journey in Faith: A History of the Christian Church (Disciples of Christ)* (St. Louis: Chalice Press, 1975), 164.
22. Conrad Cherry, *Hurrying Toward Zion: Universities, Divinity Schools, and American Protestantism* (Bloomington: Indiana University Press, 1995), 187.
23. *Add-Ran College Catalogue* (1876–1877): 13–14.
24. *Add-Ran College Catalogue* (1883–1884): 26.
25. Lester G. McAllister, *Bethany: The First 150 Years* (Bethany, WV: Bethany College Press, 1991), 8. He lists and summarizes the threads of Campbell's educational philosophy as identified by D. Duane Cummins, *The Disciples Colleges: A History* (St. Louis: CBP Press, 1987). The hallmarks of Campbell's philosophy include: (1) Wholeness of Person; (2) Moral Formation of Character, believing that "moral excellence was the overall purpose of education;" (3) Biblical Studies, considering the "Bible as the great moral instructor;" (4) Nonsectarian; (5) the Perfectibility of Individuals; and (6) Lifelong Learning. "Campbell's educational philosophy was years ahead of its time. As the 19th century progressed and other colleges were founded, many of his ideas were expressed in curriculum and program" (McAllister, *Bethany*, 9). Addison and Randolph Clark reflected many of the tenets of Campbell's philosophy in their own approach to education.
26. Ibid, 30–31.
27. *Add-Ran College Catalogue* (1874–1875): 10–11.
28. *Add-Ran College Catalogue* (1875–1876): 10.
29. Clark, *Reminiscences*, 49–50.
30. *Add-Ran College Catalogue* (1874–1875): 3.

31. Ibid. The seven trustees named in the original charter were J.A. Clark, A. Clark, R. Clark, J.H. Harbison, James Brock, H.D. Bantau, and A.M. Arnot.
32. *Add-Ran College Catalogue* (1876–1877): 3.
33. Dwight E. Stevenson, *Lexington Theological Seminary, 1865–1965* (St. Louis: Bethany Press, 1964), 125.
34. *Add-Ran College Catalogue* (1875–1876): 14.
35. Virginia Lieson Brereton, "Disciples Higher Education in the Age of the University," in *A Case Study of Mainstream Protestantism: The Disciples' Relation to American Culture 1880–1989*, ed. D. Newell Williams (St. Louis: Chalice Press, 1991), 303.
36. *Add-Ran College Catalogue* (1874–1875): 11. Robert Milligan published *Reason and Revelation* in 1867 as "a systematic introduction to the nature, design, inspiration, content, and interpretation of the Bible." See W. Dennis Helsabeck, Jr., "Robert Milligan," in *The Encyclopedia of the Stone-Campbell Movement*, 519. Boring, in *Disciples and the Bible*, summarizes the key arguments in this work as: (1) The Bible is the "Inspired Word of God, the only infallible rule of faith and practice;" (2) It must be so, for reason demands it; (3) There is one system of doctrine that pervades the entire; (4) Reason can demonstrate that all this is the case; (5) The original inspired canonical books have been preserved in our Bible (meaning the Protestant canon of 66 books) and no others; and (6) It is possible and necessary to "prove the plenary inspiration of these sacred writings" (Boring, *Disciples and the Bible*, 149–153). Boring also notes this work outlined the presuppositions leading to the publication of Milligan's *The Scheme of Redemption* in 1868. This work "came as close to anything Disciples have ever had to being the official 'systematic' theology for a denomination that disavowed having either theology or creed. The volume is essentially a guide to reading the Bible and appropriating its doctrine in the perspective of second-generation Campbellism" (Boring, *Disciples and the Bible*, 142). Gary Hall notes, "Milligan stood squarely in the tradition of the Common Sense/Baconian model of biblical interpretation, clinging to the view . . . that the Bible is inherently a grand scheme of evidences logically designed to point the believer toward the lordship of Christ and the plan of salvation." See Gary H. Hall, "The Scheme of Redemption," in *The Encyclopedia of the Stone-Campbell Movement*, 671.
37. *Add-Ran College Catalogue* (1884–1885): 20.
38. *Add-Ran College Catalogue* (1886–1887): 18. Boring describes John W. McGarvey as a conservative biblical scholar and Christian apologist of the Disciples of Christ. McGarvey's *Evidences of Christianity* (1886) "was not a philosophical defense of Christianity, but a book about the New Testament. The 'evidences of Christianity' are the books of the New Testament. The first volume dealt with 'The Integrity of the New Testament Text,' subdivided into 'Integrity of the Text' and 'Genuineness.' Volume two also contained two parts, 'The Credibility of the New Testament Books,' dealing with objections to the historical veracity of New Testament events and explaining alleged contradictions, and 'The Inspiration of the New Testament Books,' arguing his theory of inspiration with regard to each of the New Testament documents" (Boring, *Disciples and the Bible*, 227–228).
39. *Add-Ran College Catalogue* (1877–1878): 12.
40. Ibid., 11.
41. Boring, *Disciples and the Bible*, 240.
42. *Add-Ran College Catalogue* (1888–1889): 19. The rhetorical change from "department" to "school" appeared in the catalog of 1883–1884.
43. *Add-Ran College Catalogue* (1880–1881): 3.

44. *Add-Ran College Catalogue* (1881–1882): 2.
45. Clark, *Reminiscences*, 46–49.
46. Hall, *History of Texas Christian University*, 36–37.
47. Clark, *Reminiscences*, 52–53.
48. Ibid., 57–58.
49. For J.W. Holsapple's account of this transfer, see Hall, *History of Texas Christian University*, 44.
50. *Add-Ran Christian University Catalogue* (1890–1891): 4.
51. *Add-Ran Christian University Catalogue* (1894–1895): 7.
52. "Charter of Add-Ran Christian University," September 27, 1889, in the Records of the Jarvis-Van Zandt Family, Special Collections, Mary Couts Burnett Library, Texas Christian University, Fort Worth, TX.
53. Ibid.
54. Ibid. The following persons were elected to serve as members of the Board of Trustees: J.J. Jarvis, J.P. Smith, J.N. Votaw, J.J. Collins, W.H. Lemmon, E.C. Smith, A. Clark, R. Clark, Charles Carlton, H.M. Bandy, T.A. Wyth, A.S. Henry, and A. Irby. The financial changes included policies governing the establishment of an endowment fund for the university.
55. The trustees did vote to confer the degree of L. D.on Addison Clark in 1893. See Add-Ran Christian University Board of Trustees Meeting Minutes (April 5, 1893), Special Collections, Mary Couts Burnett Library, Texas Christian University, Fort Worth, TX.
56. *Add-Ran Christian University Catalogue* (1892–1893): 34.
57. Add-Ran Christian University Board of Trustees Meeting Minutes (April 5, 1893).
58. "James William Lowber," *Handbook of Texas Online*, accessed February 15, 2008, http://www.tshaonline.org/handbook/online/articles/LL/flo40.html
59. *Add-Ran Christian University Catalogue* (1894–1895): 27.
60. "Add-Ran University, Texas," *The Christian Evangelist* 30, no. 26 (June 29, 1893): 409.
61. *Add-Ran Christian University Catalogue* (1892–1893): 44.
62. J.J. Jarvis and his wife, Ida Van Zandt Jarvis, would later be responsible for the gift of land in Hawkins, Texas, where Jarvis Christian College would open on January 14, 1913, to provide education for African Americans. See Colby D. Hall, *Texas Disciples* (Fort Worth: Texas Christian University Press, 1953), 333–338, for a more detailed account of the founding of this institution. See also Add-Ran Christian University Board of Trustees Meeting Minutes (June 10, 1895) for more on the board's instruction to Jarvis and Sweeney to explore a charter for the Bible College.
63. The minutes reflect that these bylaws were to be included in the book of bylaws for Add-Ran Christian University.
64. "Bible Colleges and the Bible," *The Christian Courier* 25, no. 23 (August 22, 1912): 6.
65. Add-Ran Christian University Board of Trustees Meeting Minutes (September 4, 1895, and December 5, 1895). Later minutes refer to shift from the title of "President" to "Dean."
66. *Brite College of the Bible Caller* (May 1944): 9.
67. Add-Ran Christian University Board of Trustees Meeting Minutes (September 13, 1895).
68. Ibid.
69. Add-Ran Christian University Board of Trustees Meeting Minutes (November 22, 1895).

70. J.Z. Miller to J.B. Sweeney, November 14, 1896, in the Records of the Jarvis–Van Zandt Family, Special Collections, Mary Couts Burnett Library, Texas Christian University, Fort Worth, TX. See also letter from J.B. Sweeney to J.J. Jarvis, November 25, 1896, in the Records of the Jarvis–Van Zandt Family.
71. Add-Ran Christian University Board of Trustees Meeting Minutes (March 15, 1898).
72. *Add-Ran Christian University Catalogue* (1898–1899): 6.
73. *Add-Ran Christian University Catalogue* (1896–1897): 39–41.
74. Boring, *Disciples and the Bible*, 255.
75. Cherry, *Hurrying Toward Zion*, 24–25.
76. *Add-Ran Christian University Catalogue* (1896–1897): 39–40.
77. Glenn T. Miller, *Piety and Profession: American Protestant Theological Education, 1870–1970* (Grand Rapids, MI: William B. Eerdmans Publishing, 2007), 157.
78. McAllister and Tucker, *Journey in Faith*, 286.
79. *Add-Ran Christian University Catalogue* (1897–1898): 40–41.
80. *Add-Ran Christian University Catalogue* (1898–1899): 4.
81. Add-Ran Christian University Board of Trustees Meeting Minutes (March 14, 1899).
82. Ibid.
83. Fay Bond–Hinrichs, "Clinton Lockhart: Cultural and Religious Pioneer" (MA thesis, Texas Christian University, 1939), 116–117.
84. Add-Ran Christian University Board of Trustees Meeting Minutes (March 15, 1899).
85. *Add-Ran Christian University Catalogue* (1899–1900): 32–33.
86. James O. Duke, "Theology: Nineteenth Century," in *The Encyclopedia of the Stone-Campbell Movement*, 731–732.
87. Add-Ran Christian University Board of Trustees Meeting Minutes (April 11, 1899).
88. Add-Ran Christian University Board of Trustees Meeting Minutes (March 12, 1900).
89. *Add-Ran Christian University Catalogue* (1901–1902): 6.
90. *Add-Ran Christian University Catalogue* (1900–1901): 33–34.
91. *Add-Ran Christian University Board of Trustees Meeting Minutes* (September 4, 1900).
92. Miller, *Piety and Profession*, 292.
93. Texas Christian University Board of Trustees Meeting Minutes (March 14, 1902).
94. *Texas Christian University Catalogue* (1903–1904): 11, Special Collections, Mary Couts Burnett Library, Texas Christian University, Fort Worth, TX.
95. Hall, *History of Texas Christian University*, 119–120.
96. Zollars earned the AB degree from Bethany College in 1875 and an AM degree from Bethany in 1876. Later he received an honory doctorate from Hiram College. See Records of Ely Vaughan Zollars, in the Biographical Files, Disciples Historical Society, Nashville, TN.
97. Ely Zollars, "President Zollars and Texas Christian University," *The Christian Courier* 15, no. 19 (April 24, 1902): 7.
98. Cherry, *Hurrying Toward Zion*, 2.
99. Ibid., 24–25.
100. "President E.V. Zollars Inaugural Address," *The Skiff*, March 7, 1903, Special

Collections, Mary Couts Burnett Library, Texas Christian University, Fort Worth, TX.

101. Boring, *Disciples and the Bible*, 255.

102. Dr. James Eskridge was on leave studying at the University of Chicago. See "Texas Christian University," *The Christian Evangelist* 60, no. 21 (May 21, 1903): 412.

103. *Texas Christian University Catalogue* (1903–1904): 53–63.

104. *Texas Christian University Catalogue* (1904–1905): 56, 65–66.

105. *Texas Christian University Catalogue* (1905–1906): 64.

106. Ibid., 68. *The Christian System* "served as the first systematic theology of the young movement, intended to deflect misrepresentations and misconceptions by opponents. It was foundational to the theology of the Stone–Campbell Movement." See John Mark Hicks, "The Christian System" in *The Encyclopedia of the Stone–Campbell Movement*, 199.

107. *The Horned Frog* (1905–1906), Special Collections, Mary Couts Burnett Library, Texas Christian University, Fort Worth, TX.

108. *The Horned Frog* (1904–1905).

109. Hall, *History of Texas Christian University*, 122.

110. Ronald E. Osborn, *Ely Vaughn Zollars: Teacher of Preachers, Builder of Colleges* (St. Louis: CBP Press, 1947), 194–195.

111. Ibid., 195–196. After leaving Texas Christian University, Ely Zollars founded Oklahoma Christian University, which later became Phillips University. The only remaining school once associated with the university is the separately incorporated Phillips Theological Seminary located in Tulsa, Oklahoma. Dr. Frank Marshall also resigned and went with Zollars to teach at Phillips University.

112. *The Horned Frog* (1906–1907): 8.

113. M. Eugene Boring, "The Disciples and Higher Criticism: The Crucial Third Generation," in *A Case Study of Mainstream Protestantism: The Disciples' Relation to American Culture, 1880–1989*, 56.

114. Bond-Hinrichs, "Clinton Lockhart," 70–72.

115. This institution originally began as Transylvania University but merged with Kentucky University and Bacon College in 1865. In 1908, it resumed its historic name of Transylvania University. See James Stephen Wolfgang, "Transylvania University," in *The Encyclopedia of the Stone-Campbell Movement*, 745.

116. Hinrichs, "Clinton Lockhart," 87–88

117. For a more detailed analysis of the Bible Chair movement, see Ronald B. Flowers, "The Bible Chair Movement in the Disciples of Christ Tradition: Attempts to Teach Religion in State Universities," (PhD diss., University of Iowa, February 1967). Flowers notes, "In the national convention of the Christian Woman's Board of Missions [CWBM] meeting in Nashville, Tennessee, in October 1892, Mrs. O.A. Burgess, the national president, made a speech in which she proposed and advocated that a Bible Chair be established at the University of Michigan. . . . At the conclusion of Mrs. Burgess' speech, a resolution was proposed that the idea of the Bible Chairs be studied seriously" (62–63). The CWBM would take up the cause of raising endowment funds to establish Bible Chairs for religious instruction in state–sponsored institutions.

118. Willett studied under William Rainey Harper and received a PhD from the University of Chicago in 1896. He was considered a "prominent liberal in controversies over higher criticism and open membership among the Disciples of Christ in the

early twentieth century." His work occasioned debate with conservatives, such as J.W. McGarvey, through editorials in *The Christian Evangelist* and *The Christian Standard*. See Larry D. Bouchard, "Willett, Herbert Lockwood" in *The Encyclopedia of the Stone-Campbell Movement*, 774. See also Chapter 6 in M. Eugene Boring, *Disciples and the Bible*, and Leo G. Perdue, "The Disciples and Higher Criticism: The Formation of an Intellectual Tradition," in *A Case Study of Mainstream Protestantism: The Disciples Relation to American Culture, 1880–1989*.

119. *The Horned Frog* (1906–1907): 8.

120. See Samuel C. Pearson, "Campbell Institute," in *The Encyclopedia of the Stone-Campbell Movement*, 142. See also, Edward Scribner Ames, "History of the Campbell Institute," in *Progress; Anniversary Volume of the Campbell Institute on the Completion of Twenty Years of History*, ed. Herbert L. Willett, Orvis F. Jordan, and Charles M. Sharpe (Chicago: The Christian Century Press, 1917), 36–37.

121. Bond-Hinrichs, "Clinton Lockhart," 164.

122. *The Horned Frog* (1906–1907): 71.

123. Boring, *Disciples and the Bible*, 206.

124. McAllister, *Bethany*, 229–230.

125. This reflects a trend to seek advanced education outside of Disciples schools that was beginning to appear in the third generation of Disciples. See Toulouse, *Joined in Discipleship*, in which he quotes a study by Edwin L. Becker, *Yale Divinity School and the Disciples of Christ, 1872–1989* (Nashville: Disciples Historical Society, 1990), concluding, "By 1920, 105 Disciples ministers had received the seminary degree from the divinity school at Yale University, and 48 more had received the degree from the University of Chicago Divinity School". Ellsworth Faris was the son of G.A. Faris, a member of the board of trustees and editor of *The Christian Courier*. Ellsworth was a former missionary to Africa and had recently completed his AB degree from the University of Chicago.

126. *Texas Christian University Catalogue* (1906–1907): 54.

127. *Texas Christian University Catalogue* (1907–1908): 55. The catalog for 1908–1909 lists her as Clyde Batsell Reaves. See *Texas Christian University Catalogue* (1908–1909): 64.

128. *The Horned Frog* (1907–1908): 112.

129. Bond-Hinrichs, "Clinton Lockhart," 170.

130. Hall, *History of Texas Christian University*, 140.

131. Ibid., 142.

132. Bond-Hinrichs, "Clinton Lockhart," 174.

133. Ibid., 173.

134. Miller, *Piety and Profession*, 88–89.

135. Cherry, *Hurrying Toward Zion*, 173.

136. Miller, *Piety and Profession*, 112.

137. Egbert Smyth, William J. Tucker, J.W. Churchill, George Harris, and E.V. Hincks of Andover Seminary in 1886; Crawford Toy of Southern Baptist Theological Seminary in 1879; Charles Briggs of Union Seminary in 1893; Henry Preserved Smith of Cincinnati's Lane Seminary in 1893; and Hinckley Mitchell of Boston University in 1905. See Miller, *Piety and Profession*, 92–112, 134–153, for a detailed description of each of these cases.

138. "The Christian Lectureship," *Dallas Morning News*, November, 18, 1898.

139. Ellsworth Faris, "Is Higher Criticism Infidelity?" *The Christian Courier* 15, no.15

(March 27, 1902): 9.
140. J.W. McGarvey, "A Young Apologist," *The Christian Standard* 83, no.15 (April 12, 1902): 533.
141. Hall notes that Fleming was a professor of Bible and dean of Southwestern Christian College, "a young institution of the conservative brethren" in Denton, who was fired for his "too–liberal views expressed at the Texas Christian Lectureship," held in Denton in 1905, and his "fraternizing with the enemy." Fleming apparently concurred publicly with some of the remarks made by Chalmers McPherson in a speech he gave at the lectureship concerning individual contributions to a missionary society. After his firing, Fleming became pastor of the Christian Church at Forney. See Hall, *Texas Disciples*, 154–156.
142. See "Biblical Criticism," *The Christian Standard* 64, no. 21 (May 23, 1908): 886–887, and "Biblical Criticism," *The Christian Standard* 64 no.22 (May 30, 1908): 926–927.
143. Chalmers McPherson, "Clinton Lockhart and Texas Christian University," *The Christian Standard* 64, no.35 (August 29, 1908): 1470.
144. G.A. Faris to Chalmers McPherson, November 6, 1908, in the Records of T.E. Tomlinson, Special Collections, Mary Couts Burnett Library, Texas Christian University, Fort Worth, TX.
145. "The Ministerial Institute," *The Skiff*, January 29, 1909.
146. Clinton Lockhart, "Some Misunderstandings," *The Christian Standard* 65, no.13 (March 27, 1909): 558.
147. Chalmers McPherson, "Texas Christian University," *The Christian Standard* 65, no. 29 (July 17, 1909): 1259.
148. L.C. Brite to Chalmers McPherson, November 13, 1909, in the Records of T.E. Tomlinson.
149. Boring, "The Disciples and Higher Criticism," 33.
150. Chalmers McPherson to Ellsworth Faris, November 26, 1909, in the Records of T.E. Tomlinson.
151. Ellsworth Faris to Chalmers McPherson, November 27, 1909, in the Records of T.E. Tomlinson.
152. Faris indicated that it was not intended for the entire Bible to be taken as history.
153. Chalmers McPherson to Ellsworth Faris, December 1, 1909, and Ellsworth Faris to Chalmers McPherson, December 6, 1909, in the Records of T.E. Tomlinson.
154. Chalmers McPherson to Ellsworth Faris, December 15, 1909, in the Records of T.E. Tomlinson.
155. Ellsworth Faris to Chalmers McPherson, December 19, 1909, in the Records of T.E. Tomlinson.
156. Chalmers McPherson to G.A. Faris, February 2, 1910, in the Records of T.E. Tomlinson.
157. G.A. Faris refers to his position as a member of the board of trustees and as Ellsworth's father.
158. G.A. Faris to Chalmers McPherson, February 17, 1910, in the Records of T.E. Tomlinson.
159. See "Lockhart Criticizes Present Bible Study," *Dallas Morning News*, November 21, 1910; "Baptist Workers Answer Lockhart," *Dallas Morning News*, December 21, 1910; and "Carroll Says Bible as Whole Inspired," *Dallas Morning News*, January 02,

1911.
160. Bond-Hinrichs, "Clinton Lockhart," 174.
161. "Dr. Lockhart's Resignation," *The Christian Courier* 24, no.4 (February 2, 1911): 13.
162. Texas Christian University Board of Trustees Meeting Minutes (February 21, 1911).
163. J.J. Hart to Colby Hall, March 10, 1911, in the Records of T.E. Tomlinson.
164. Colby Hall to J.J. Hart, March 15, 1911, in the Records of T.E. Tomlinson.
165. J.C. Mason to various individuals, March 7, 1911, in the Records of T.E. Tomlinson. The school has yet to create the chair. His language suggested that the trustees hoped to fund the chair.
166. Homer Magee to J.C. Mason, March 13, 1911, in the Records of T.E. Tomlinson.
167. J.S. Stockard to the trustees, March 11, 1911, in the Records of T.E. Tomlinson.
168. Colby Hall to T.E. Tomlinson, March 15, 1911, in the Records of T.E. Tomlinson.
169. *Texas Christian University Catalogue* (1911–1912): 66–67.
170. Charles M. Ashmore to T.E. Tomlinson, March 7, 1911, in the Records of T.E. Tomlinson.
171. D.A. Leak to the Board of Trustees at Texas Christian University, March 11, 1911, in the Records of T.E. Tomlinson.
172. G.A. Faris to T.E. Tomlinson, April 15, 1911, in the Records of T.E. Tomlinson.
173. "Dr. F.D. Kershner," *The Christian Courier* 24, no. 39 (October 5, 1911): 2.
174. "Statements of Brethren Concerning Possible Materials, " in the Records of T.E. Tomlinson. McPherson has three categories ("A," "B," and "C") of potential candidates, though his specific criterion for classification is not known. In Class "A," he lists the names and comments concerning Donald McCollum, Brother Snoddy, H. H. Guy, H. H. Peters, F.M. Rains, and Charles S. Medbury. In Class "B," he lists Hugh McLellan, Sherman Kirk, R.E. Hieronymous, and W.A. Fortune as potential candidates. In Class "C," McPherson names Vernon Stauffer, Peter Ainslie, T.E. Cramblett, Miner Lee Bates, H.L. Calhoun, and F.D. Kershner as candidates for the position. The two names eventually presented to the TCU Board of Trustees came from Class "C."
175. Vernon Stauffer, "Vita," in *New England and the Bavarian Illuminati* (New York: Columbia University Press, 1918): 37. See also Texas Christian University Board of Trustees Meeting Minutes (September 19, 1911).
176. "Frederick D. Kershner, A Biographical Sketch," *The Christian Evangelist* (April 6, 1916): 418.
177. "Our Congratulations to Texas," *The Christian Standard* 67, no. 40 (October 7, 1911): 1628.
178. F.D. Kershner, "An Open Letter to the Brotherhood in Texas," *The Christian Courier* 24, no. 46 (November 23, 1911): 2.
179. Texas Christian University Board of Trustees Meeting Minutes (October 26, 1911).
180. "L.C. Brite Bible Chair," *The Christian Courier* 25, no. 14 (July 3, 1912): 10.
181. The board of trustees also made L.C. Brite a trustee in February 1912; see Texas Christian University Board of Trustees Meeting Minutes (February 14, 1912).
182. G.A. Faris to T.E. Tomlinson, October 24, 1911, in the Records of T.E. Tomlinson.

183. *The Horned Frog* (1913–1914): 69.
184. Kershner received an honorary doctorate from Bethany College in 1913 and another from Transylvania College, Lexington, KY, in 1916; see *Biographical Records*, Disciples Historical Society, Nashville, TN. See also *Texas Christian University Catalogue* (1913–1914): 50.
185. Texas Christian University Board of Trustees Meeting Minutes (June 6, 1914).
186. "New Building for Bible College," *The Skiff*, May 27, 1910.
187. Letter from Colby Hall to T.E. Tomlinson, March 15, 1911, in the Records of T.E. Tomlinson.
188. "Brite Bible College," *The Christian Courier* 27, no. 12 (June 25, 1914): 5.
189. "Brite College of the Bible," *The Christian Courier* 27, no. 17 (July 30, 1914): 12.
190. McPherson also sent the same article, published in *The Christian Evangelist* (September 24, 1914): 1241. The terms of the charter were also printed in *The Christian Standard* (July 18, 1914): 1243.
191. J.C. Mason, "Letter to the Editor," *The Christian Courier* 27, no. 18 (August 6, 1914): 16.
192. A.E. Ewell, "Our Latest Venture in Creeds," *The Christian Courier* 27, no. 22 (September 3, 1914): 15. On the controversy over creeds within Protestant denominations, see Miller, *Piety and Profession*.
193. Chalmers McPherson, "Brite College of the Bible," *The Christian Standard* 69, no. 27 (July 4, 1914): 1186.
194. F.D. Kershner, "The Brite Charter—Its Creedal Character," *The Christian Courier* 27, no. 23 (September 10, 1914): 13.
195. "Reversion to Type," *The Christian Evangelist* 50, no. 39 (September 24, 1914): 1227–1228. The "Restoration Movement" is a reference to the early founders of the Disciples of Christ, referring to their efforts to restore the contemporary church to the beliefs and practices of the church founded at Pentecost.
196. McAllister and Tucker, *Journey in Faith*, 383–384.
197. F.D. Kershner, "Texas Christian University," *The Christian Standard* 69, no.30 (July 25, 1914): 1311–1312.
198. Miller, *Piety and Profession*, 97.
199. Ibid., 138.
200. Hall, *History of Texas Christian University*, 225.

Chapter Two
A Professional Curriculum: Educating Preacher Boys, 1914–1939

1. Brite Professor Colby Hall frequently used the term "Preacher Boys" to describe the students of the Brite College of the Bible.
2. "Feb. 9 A Big Day; Brite College of Bible Dedicated," *The Skiff*, February 12, 1915, Special Collections, Mary Couts Burnett Library, Texas Christian University, Fort Worth, TX.
3. Conrad Cherry, *Hurrying Toward Zion: Universities, Divinity Schools, and American Protestantism* (Bloomington: Indiana University Press, 1995), 127.
4. Glenn T. Miller, *Piety and Profession: American Protestant Theological Education, 1870–1970* (Grand Rapids, MI: William B. Eerdmans Publishing, 2007), 113–133.
5. Brite College of the Bible Board of Trustees Meeting Minutes (June 17, 1914), in the Board of Trustees File, Historical Archives, Brite Divinity School, Fort Worth, TX.

6. Colby D. Hall, "Brite College of the Bible," in Chalmers McPherson, *Disciples of Christ in Texas* (Cincinnati: Standard Publishing, 1920), 95.
7. Frederick D. Kershner to L.C. Brite, January 26, 1924, in the Records of the Brite History Project, Correspondence Files, Historical Archives, Brite Divinity School, Fort Worth, TX.
8. *Brite College of the Bible Catalogue* (1939–1940), Special Collections, Mary Couts Burnett Library, Texas Christian University, Fort Worth, TX.
9. "An Interesting Situation," *The Christian Evangelist* (July 2, 1914): 84.
10. *Texas Christian University Catalogue* (1913–1914): 51, Special Collections, Mary Couts Burnett Library, Fort Worth, TX.
11. Lewis Howard Grimes, *A History of the Perkins School of Theology* (Dallas: Southern Methodist University Press, 1993): 8.
12. Brite Divinity School Board of Trustees Meeting Minutes (February 8, 1921).
13. *Texas Christian University Catalogue* (1917–1918): 56.
14. "Dean Hall Returns From Trip to East," *The Skiff*, October 31, 1928.
15. *Texas Christian University Catalogue* (1915–1916): 69.
16. Ibid., 71.
17.Conrad Cherry, *Hurrying Toward Zion: Universities, Divinity Schools, and American Protestantism* (Bloomington: Indiana University Press, 1995), 140.
18. Ibid., 151.
19. Miller, *Piety and Profession*, 316.
20. *Texas Christian University Catalogue* (1915–1916): 67.
21. Miller, *Piety and Profession*, 318.
22. Stephen J. Corey, "The Brotherhood and the Challenge of World Conquest," in *One Hundredth Anniversary of the Disciples of Christ*, published by Disciples of Christ Centennial Convention (Cincinnati: Standard Publishing, 1909).
23. *Texas Christian University Catalogue* (1914–1915): 3.
24. Ibid., 42.
25. Ibid., 152.
26. Corey, "The Brotherhood and the Challenge of World Conquest."
27. Miller, *Piety and Profession*, 31.
28. Winfred E. Garrison and Alfred T. DeGroot, *The Disciples of Christ: A History* (St Louis: Christian Board of Publication Press, 1948), 372.
29. E.M. Waits, "Thinking White," undated and unattributed essay, in the Records of E.M. Waits, Special Collections, Mary Couts Burnett Library, Texas Christian University, Fort Worth, TX.
30. "Chapel Optional for all Seniors First Semester," *The Skiff*, October 1, 1937.
31. Brite College of the Bible Faculty Meeting Minutes (October 20, 1937), in the Faculty Meeting Files, Historical Archives, Brite Divinity School, Fort Worth, TX.
32. "Ministerial Club Has 25 Members," *The Skiff* , March 5, 1930.
33. *Texas Christian University Catalogue* (1915–1916): 67.
34. *Texas Christian University Catalogue* (1914–1915): 79.
35. "Biographical Sketch," October 2007, in the Records of E.M. Waits.
36. Colby D. Hall, *History of Texas Christian University: A College of the Cattle Frontier* (Fort Worth: Texas Christian University Press, 1947), 162.
37. Edward McShane Waits, "Texas Christian University," in Chalmers McPherson, *Disciples of Christ in Texas* (Cincinnati: Standard Publishing, 1920), 79.
38. Texas Christian University Board of Trustees Meeting Minutes (June 6, 1927),

Special Collections, Mary Couts Burnett Library, Texas Christian University, Fort Worth, TX.
39. Edward McShane Waits, *A College Man's Religion* (Fort Worth: Stafford-Lowdon Publishing, 1929), 242.
40. Hall, *History of Texas Christian University*, 165.
41. Texas Christian University Board of Trustees Meeting Minutes (March 12, 1918). See also "Position Offered to TCU Medics in US Army Corps," *The Skiff*, February 2, 1917.
42. "S.A.T.C.," *The Skiff*, October 12, 1918.
43. Texas Christian University Board of Trustees Meeting Minutes (September 5, 1918).
44. "President Kershner Draws Lessons from old Year Says Militarism is Folly; Nationalism is Wrong," *The Skiff*, January 8, 1915.
45. Lester G. McAllister and William E. Tucker, *Journey in Faith: A History of the Christian Church (Disciples of Christ)* (St Louis: Christian Board of Publication Press, 1989), 267.
46. *Texas Christian University Alumni Bulletin* (1919), Special Collections, Mary Couts Burnett Library, Texas Christian University, Fort Worth, TX.
47. Ibid.
48. Ibid.
49. The slogan of the Men and Millions campaign was: "To secure 1,000 men and women and more than $6,000,000 for the work of the cooperating societies and colleges of the Disciples of Christ and the every-member canvass in every church."
50. McAllister and Tucker, *Journey in Faith*, 267.
51. "World Missionary Leaders visit TCU." *The Skiff*, February 3, 1919.
52. Hall, "Brite College of the Bible,"
53. Colby D. Hall, *Texas Disciples* (Fort Worth: Texas Christian University Press, 1953), 196.
54. *Texas Christian University Catalogue* (1920–1921): 111.
55. Cherry, *Hurrying Toward Zion*, 21.
56. Hall, *History of Texas Christian University*, 222.
57. Cherry, *Hurrying Toward Zion*, 40.
58. *Texas Christian University Catalogue* (1920–1921).
59. Brite College of the Bible Board of Trustees Meeting Minutes (June 9, 1920).
60. Hall, *History of Texas Christian University*, 227
61. L.C. Brite to F.D. Kershner, December 30, 1923, in the Records of the Brite History Project, Correspoondence Files.
62. F.D. Kershner to L.C. Brite, January 8, 1924, in the Records of the Brite History Project, Correspondence Files.
63. "Medical School Closes," *The Skiff*, May 11, 1918.
64. "Dept. of Law of University is Abolished," *The Skiff*, September 17 , 1920.
65. Ibid.
66. Robert A. Baker, *Tell the Generations Following: A History of Southwestern Baptist Theological Seminary, 1908–1983* (Nashville: Broadman Press, 1983), 169.
67. Texas Christian University Board of Trustees Meeting Minutes (February 16, 1926).
68. Texas Christian University Board of Trustees Meeting Minutes (June 3, 1921).
69. Texas Christian University Board of Trustees Meeting Minutes (February 13,

1923).
70. Hall, *History of Texas Christian University*, 174.
71. Texas Christian University Board of Trustees Meeting Minutes (September 23, 1927).
72. "The Burnett Trust: Some Inside Stories for Future Record," in the Records of Colby Hall, Special Collections, Mary Couts Burnett Library, Texas Christian University, Fort Worth, TX.
73. Milliard Patterson Will, October 5, 1934, in the Records of the Brite History Project, Documents Files, Historical Archives, Brite Divinity School, Fort Worth, TX.
74. Ibid.
75. Brite College of the Bible Audit Report, September 28, 1939, Special Collections, Mary Couts Burnett Library, Texas Christian University, Fort Worth, TX.
76. Hall, *History of Texas Christian University*, 228.
77. Ibid.
78. F.D. Kershner to L. C. Brite, April 30, 1924, in the Records of the Brite History Project, Correspondence Files.
79. L.C. Brite to F.D. Kershner, April 22, 1924, in the Records of the Brite History Project, Correspondence Files.
80. L.C. Brite to F.D. Kershner, January 25, 1924, in the Records of the Brite History Project, Correspondence Files.
81. F.D. Kershner to L.C. Brite, January 26, 1924, in the Records of the Brite History Project, Correspondence Files.
82. William Morro to L.D. Anderson, June 12, 1926, in the Records of the Brite History Project, Correspondence Files.
83. L.C. Brite to L.D. Anderson, June 19, 1926, in the Records of the Brite History Project, Correspondence Files.
84. Ibid.
85. Colby Hall to John Kearns, June 23, 1926, in the Records of the Brite History Project, Correspondence Files.
86. Chalmers McPherson to L.C. Brite, June 24, 1926, in the Records of the Brite History Project, Correspondence Files.
87. John W. Kerns to Colby Hall, June 25, 1926, in the Records of the Brite History Project, Correspondence Files.
88. L.C. Brite to Mr. Chalmers McPherson, June 26, 1926, in the Records of the Brite History Project, Correspondence Files.
89. Lewis Howard Grimes, *A History of the Perkins School of Theology* (Dallas: Southern Methodist University Press, 1993), 46.
90. L.C. Brite to F.D. Kershner, January 25, 1924, in the Records of the Brite History Project, Correspondence Files.
91. Keith Watkins, *Christian Theological Seminary, Indianapolis: A History of Education for Ministry* (Zionsville, IN: Guild Press, 2001), 21.
92. Garrison and DeGroot, *Disciples of Christ*, 331.
93. William Morro to L.D. Anderson, July 1, 1926, in the Records of the Brite History Project, Correspondence Files.
94. William Morro to L.D. Anderson, July 8, 1926, in the Records of the Brite History Project, Correspondence Files.
95. Brite College of the Bible Board of Trustees Meeting Minutes (February 6, 1936).
96. Ibid., 215.

97. Chalmers McPherson to L.C. Brite, June 24, 1926, in the Records of the Brite History Project, Correspondence Files.
98. Brite College of the Bible Board of Trustees Meeting Minutes (September 23, 1925).
99. Brite College of the Bible Board of Trustees Meeting Minutes (February 10, 1933).
100. Hall, *History of Texas Christian University*, 227.
101. Cherry, *Hurrying Toward Zion*, 189.
102. *Texas Christian University Catalogue* (1928–1929): 178.
103. *Texas Christian University Catalogue* (1926–1927): 191.
104. Cherry, *Hurrying Toward Zion*, 129.
105. *Texas Christian University Catalogue* (1929–1930): 204.
106. Texas Christian University Board of Trustees Meeting Minutes (February 9, 1933). See also Texas Christian University Board of Trustees Meeting Minutes (May 30, 1932).
107. Brite College of the Bible Board of Trustees Meeting Minutes (February 3, 1937).
108. Texas Christian University Board of Trustees Meeting Minutes (June 11, 1928).
109. Hall, *Texas Disciples*, 248.
110. "Brite College of the Bible," *The Christian Evangelist* (January 19, 1933): 98.
111. Robert T. Miller, quoted in Robert T. Handy, *The American Religious Depression, 1925–1935* (Minneapolis: Fortress, 1968).
112. *Disciples of Christ Year Book* (1920–1939), to the International Convention of Disciples of Christ (Indianapolis: United Christian Missionary Society).
113. Stephen J. Corey, *Fifty Years of Attack and Controversy* (St Louis: Christian Board of Publications Press, 1953), 96.
114. *Disciples of Christ Year Book* (1920–1939).
115. Corey, *Fifty Years*, 143.
116. Cherry, *Hurrying Toward Zion*, 194.
117. Corey, *Fifty Years*, 165.
118. *Texas Christian University Catalogue* (1930–1931): 170.
119. Ibid., 171.
120. Ibid., 172.
121. *Texas Christian University Catalogue* (1930–1931): 183.
122. Hall, *History of Texas Christian University*, 209.
123. Texas Christian University Board of Trustees Meeting Minutes (February 12, 1931).
124. Texas Christian University Board of Trustees Meeting Minutes (September 18, 1936).
125. Texas Christian University Board of Trustees Meeting Minutes (February 10, 1936).
126. *Texas Christian University Catalogue* (1937–1938): 86.
127. *Texas Christian University Catalogue* (1936–1937): 74.
128. *Brite College of the Bible Catalogue* (1939): 5.
129. "Brite College of the Bible Report to the American Association of Theological Schools," October 18, 1939, in the AATS Files, Historical Archives, Brite Divinity School, Fort Worth, TX.
130. Hall, *History of Texas Christian University*, 228.

131. "Votes for Women Advocates Form Suffrage League," *The Skiff*, March 3, 1916.
132. "Pastor Ridicules the Suffragette," unknown newspaper, author, and date, in the Records of E. M. Waits.
133. *Texas Christian University Catalogue* (1928–1929): 202.
134. For the interest in training women for careers in the mission field, see Miller, *Piety and Profession*, 202.
135. Hall, *Texas Disciples*, 324.
136. "Ordination Service of Katherine Schutze," 1927, in the Records of the Brite History Project, Documents Files.
137. Hall, *Texas Disciples*, 323.
138. *Texas Christian University Catalogue* (1931–1932): 189.
139. "College Presidents Clash in Fist Fight," *Fort Worth Record*, December 15, 1921.
140. Brite College of the Bible Faculty Meeting Minutes (January 18, 1932).
141. Brite College of the Bible Faculty Meeting Minutes (February 15, 1932).
142. "Students Aided by T.C.U. with Ministerial Scholarships," November 1937, in the Records of E.M. Waits.
143. Hall, *Texas Disciples*, 199.
144. Joseph R. Jeter Jr., "Brite Divinity School: An Historical Sketch, 1914–1989" (Fort Worth: Brite Divinity School, 1989), 10, in the Records of the Brite History Project, Documents Files.
145. Ibid.
146. Ibid.
147. "Lockhart Attributes Success of University to 'Alertness.'" *The Skiff*, May 15, 1936.
148. Corey, *Fifty Years*, 48.
149. H. Richard Niebuhr, *The Purpose of the Church and its Ministry: Reflections on the Aims of Theological Education* (New York: Harper and Brothers, 1956), 5.
150. Garrison and DeGroot, *Disciples of Christ*, 419.
151. Cherry, *Hurrying Toward Zion*, 32.
152. Ibid., 164.
153. Miller, *Piety and Profession*, 481.
154. US Census Bureau, accessed online December 3, 2007, http://www.census.gov/.
155. "Brite College of the Bible Report to the American Association of Theological Schools," October 18, 1939.
156. "More Degrees Conferred," *Dallas Morning News*, November 26, 1929, accessed online via NewsBank November 20, 2007.
157. Note that the College of the Bible in Lexington was already accredited in 1938.
158. "Brite College to Issue Own Catalogue in June," *The Skiff*, June 2, 1939.

Chapter Three
Accreditation and Change: From Brite College of the Bible to Brite Divinity School, 1939–1963

1. Glenn T. Miller, *A Community of Conversation: A Retrospective of the Association of Theological Schools and Ninety Years of North American Theological Education* (Pittsburgh: Association of Theological Schools, 2008), 4.
2. See Mark May, William Brown, and Frank Shuttleworth, *The Education of American Ministers* (New York: Institute of Social and Religious Research, 1934).
3. Lewis J. Sherrill to Theological Schools in the United States and Canada, July 6,

1936, in the Records of the Brite History Project, Correspondence Files, Historical Archives, Brite Divinity School, Fort Worth, TX.

4. Colby Hall to Lewis J. Sherrill, October 5, 1936, in the Records of the Brite History Project, Correspondence Files.

5. Lewis J. Sherrill to Colby Hall, October 12, 1936, in the Records of the Brite History Project, Correspondence Files.

6. Jerome Moore, "Retirement Years of Colby Hall," in the Records of Jerome A. Moore, Special Collections, Mary Couts Burnett Library, Texas Christian University, Fort Worth, TX.

7. "Accrediting Theological Schools," *The Christian Evangelist* (October 20, 1938): 1143.

8. There is no extant record of this letter other than the reference to it by Charles Pyatt in his response. See Letter from Charles Lynn Pyatt to Colby Hall, November 2, 1938, in the Records of the Brite History Project, Correspondence Files.

9. Ibid.

10. Charles Lynn Pyatt to Colby Hall, March 23, 1939, in the Records of the Brite History Project, Correspondence Files.

11. Brite College of the Bible Faculty Meeting Minutes (November 21, 1938), in the Faculty Meeting Files, Historical Archives, Brite Divinity School, Fort Worth, TX.

12. Brite College of the Bible Faculty Meeting Minutes (December 19 1938).

13. E.H. Roberts to Colby Hall, November 8, 1939, in the Records of the Brite History Project, Correspondence Files.

14. Colby Hall to E.H. Roberts, November 13, 1939, in the Records of the Brite History Project, Correspondence Files.

15. E.H. Roberts to Colby Hall, December 22, 1939, in the Records of the Brite History Project, Correspondence Files.

16. Colby Hall to E.H. Roberts, January 2, 1940, in the Records of the Brite History Project, Correspondence Files. Hall included a visit to Southwestern Baptist Theological Seminary in Robert's trip to Fort Worth, which resulted in their interest to join AATS as well. See also letter from E.H. Roberts to Colby Hall, February 14, 1940, in the Records of the Brite History Project, Correspondence Files.

17. Brite College of the Bible Faculty Meeting Minutes (January 15, 1940).

18. Brite College of the Bible Board of Trustees Meeting Minutes (February 14, 1940), in the Board of Trustees Files, Historical Archives, Brite Divinity School, Fort Worth, TX.

19. E.H. Roberts to Colby Hall, February 24, 1941, in the Records of the Brite History Project, Correspondence Files.

20. E.H. Roberts to Colby Hall, January 5, 1942, in the Records of the Brite History Project, Correspondence Files.

21. Texas Christian University Board of Trustee Meeting Minutes (September 22, 1939), Special Collections, Mary Couts Burnett Library, Texas Christian University, Fort Worth, TX.

22. Colby Hall to E.H. Roberts, January 10, 1942, in the Records of the Brite History Project, Correspondence Files.

23. Colby D. Hall, *History of Texas Christian University: A College of the Cattle Frontier* (Fort Worth: Texas Christian University Press, 1947), 221.

24. *Brite College of the Bible Catalogue* (1939): 7, Special Collections, Mary Couts Burnett Library, Texas Christian University, Fort Worth, TX.

25. Brite College of the Bible Faculty Meeting Minutes (December 19, 1938).
26. "Brite College of the Bible Application to AATS," October 18, 1939, in the Records of the Brite History Project, Documents Files. There is no mention or reasoning for titling the third field doctrinal rather than theological. The curriculum changes were made by a separate committee of the faculty with no extant minutes to explain their decisions.
27. Miller, *A Community of Conversation*, 457.
28. D. Duane Cummins, *The Disciples Colleges: A History* (St. Louis: Christian Board of Publication Press, 1987), 116.
29. Brite College of the Bible Faculty Meeting Minutes (September 20, 1943).
30. "Agreement No 344 between the United States of America and Brite College of the Bible," February 1, 1944, in the Records of the Brite History Project, Documents Files.
31. Colby D. Hall, *History of Texas Christian University: A College of the Cattle Frontier* (Fort Worth: Texas Christian University Press, 1947), 223.
32. "The Navy V–12 Chaplain Program in Texas Christian University and Brite College of the Bible," undated, in the Records of the Brite History Project, Documents Files.
33. *Brite College of the Bible Caller* (1944): 13, Special Collections, Mary Couts Burnett Library, Texas Christian University, Fort Worth, TX.
34. Brite College of the Bible Faculty Meeting Minutes (April 17, 1944).
35. Colby Hall to Jerome Moore and S.W. Hutton, April 21, 1944, in the Records of the Brite History Project, Correspondence Files.
36. Richard Cabot, "A Plea for a Clinical Year in the Course of Theological Study," quoted in Miller, *A Community of Conversation*, 595.
37. *Brite College of the Bible Caller* (1948): 13, Special Collections, Mary Couts Burnett Library, Texas Christian University, Fort Worth, TX.
38. See Texas Christian University Board of Trustees Meeting Minutes (November 11, 1941) and also Texas Christian University Board of Trustees Meeting Minutes (February 19, 1942).
39. D. Ray Lindley, "Recommendations," in Brite College of the Bible Board of Trustees Meeting Minutes (January 18, 1948).
40. "Annual Report to the Board of Trustees," Brite College of the Bible Board of Trustees Meeting Minutes (October 21, 1949).
41. See *Brite College of the Bible Caller* (1948 and 1949).
42. Noel Keith, *The Brites of Capote* (Fort Worth: Texas Christian University Press, 1950), 198.
43. Ibid., 177.
44. R.H. Foster to L.D. Anderson, Dan D. Rogers, D.C. Reed, L.C. Brite, and W. S. Cooke, February 25, 1941, in the Records of L.D. Anderson, box 5, folder 3, Disciples of Christ Historical Society, Nashville, TN, states that "at the meeting of the Board of Trustees of Texas Christian University, held on Thursday, the 20th of this month, President Waits submitted his resignation as president, to become effective when his successor could be elected and installed. A committee of us appointed recommended to the Board that a committee of five be selected by the President of the Board of Trustees and that this committee be directed to make an investigation of men who might be available and who might be deemed proper persons to fill this office, and to pursue the subject to the point of making a recommendation to the Board as to who

the successor of President Waits should be. I have appointed you gentlemen as the members of this committee of five." Foster went on to say, "I am confident that, if any group of men not only from our trustees but in our brotherhood is capable of handling this important problem in a satisfactory manner, it is your particular group."
45. "Desirable Qualifications," in the Records of L.D. Anderson, box 5, folder 3.
46. "Names suggested," in the Records of L.D. Anderson, box 5, folder 3. This document lists the following people: Dr. Kelly O'Neal, Dr. Eugene S. Briggs, Dr. H.G. Harmon, Dr. M.E. Sadler, Rev. Perry Gresham, Dr. Joseph U. Yarborough, Dr. Riley B. Montgomery, Dr. Colby Hall, Dr. O.L. Shelton, Dean Luther Stalnaker, Hon. Fritz Lanham, and Rev. Joe R. Babb.
47. See "Desirable Qualifications" in the Records of L.D. Anderson.
48. Brite seminary students to L.D. Anderson, April 4, 1941, in the Records of L.D. Anderson, box 5, folder 3. This letter endorses O'Neall, "a man who we fear may be overlooked," and adds that "this suggestion is made humbly and sincerely in order that his name may not be overlooked, and that due consideration may be given to his possibilities, in the deliberations of the committee." It is signed by twenty–five Brite seminary students.
49. L.D. Anderson from R.C. Snodgrass, March 4, 1941, in the Records of L.D. Anderson, box 5, folder 3.
50. L.D. Anderson from E.D. Henson, March 1, 1941, in the Records of L.D. Anderson, box 5, folder 3.
51. E.M. Waits to M.E. Sadler, April 10, 1922, in the Records of E.M. Waits, Special Collections, Mary Couts Burnett Library, Texas Christian University, Fort Worth, TX. Waits wrote, "My dear Mr. Sadler: I am writing you in regard to the probability of securing you to fill a position in the Department of Sociology and Political Science at Texas Christian University next year. You have been highly recommended to me by Dr. Pritchard and Professor Raymond Smith, who is the head of our department of education."
52. Ibid.
53. "Presidential Search" files in the Records of L.D. Anderson, Box 5, Folder 3. In the file of saved recommendation letters, only one letter was from students, and that was from a group of Brite College of the Bible students in support of Dr. Kelly O'Neall.
54. Chancellor Emeritus James M. Moudy, interview, August 18, 1989, transcripts in the Records of James M. Moudy, box 2, folder 17, Special Collections, Mary Couts Burnett Library, Texas Christian University, Fort Worth, TX.
55. Elmer Henson to Rev. Oliver Harrison, October 23, 1946, in the Records of the Brite History Project, Correspondence Files.
56. Ibid.
57. Ibid.
58. Elmer Henson to Rev. Oliver Harrison, October 23, 1946, in the Records of the Brite History Project, Correspondence Files.
59. See correspondence between H.H. Philllips and M.E. Sadler, December 1946, in the Records of M.E. Sadler, Special Collections, Mary Couts Burnett Library, Texas Christian University, Fort Worth, TX.
60. M.E. Sadler to H.H. Phillips, December 23, 1946, in the Records of M.E. Sadler, box 18.
61. H.H. Phillips to M.E. Sadler, December 30, 1946, in the Records of M E. Sadler,

box 18.

62. Ibid. Interestingly, Lindley would become vice president of TCU four years later.

63. Ibid.

64. H.H. Phillips to M.E. Sadler, December 30, 1946, in the Records of M. E. Sadler, box 18.

65. Ibid. In actuality, the funds raised for this "living endowment" were split fifty–fifty between Brite and TCU.

66. Ibid.

67. Note from M.E. Sadler to H.H. Phillips, December 31, 1946, in the Records of M. E. Sadler, box 18.

68. Elmer Henson to M.E. Sadler, December 23, 1946, in the Records of the Brite History Project, Correspondence Files.

69. Ibid.

70. Brite College of the Bible Board of Trustees Meeting Minutes (January 2, 1947).

71. Telegram message from M.E. Sadler to H.H. Phillips, January 3, 1947, in the Records of M.E. Sadler, box 18.

72. Brite College of the Bible Board of Trustees Meeting Minutes (October 4, 1940).

73. Brite College of the Bible Board of Trustees Meeting Minutes (February 21, 1941).

74. *Brite College of the Bible Caller* (1941).

75. Brite College of the Bible Board of Trustees Meeting Minutes (February 18, 1942).

76. Bulletin, the Sixteenth Biennial Meeting of the American Association of Theological Schools, held at Bonebrake Theological Seminary, June 15–16, 1948. It is interesting to note that Christian Theological Seminary was not listed among accredited Theological Schools. The notations of 7 & 9 after Brite College of the Bible mean that Brite's library and library support were inadequate.

77. E. Brooks Holifield, *God's Ambassadors: A History of the Christian Clergy in America* (Grand Rapids, Michigan: William B. Eerdmans Publishing, 2007) 236.

78. Ibid.

79. Winfred Ernest Garrison and Alfred T. DeGroot, *The Disciples of Christ: A History* (St. Louis: Bethany Press, 1958), 502; James O. Duke and Joseph D. Driskell, "Disciples Theologizing amid Currents of Mainstream Protestant Thought, 1940–1980," in *A Case Study of Mainstream Protestantism: The Disciples' Relation to American Culture, 1880–1989*, ed. Douglas A. Foster, Paul M. Blowers, Anthony L. Dunnavant, and D. Newell Williams (Grand Rapids, MI: William B. Eerdmans Publishing, 1991), 140. In this essay, Duke and Driskell make the claim that "shortly after the end of World War II, the United States experienced a phenomenal upsurge of interest in religion. To mainline Protestants the postwar boom brought, along with much else, a 'theological renaissance.'"

80. Memo to Dean D. Ray Lindley from President M.E. Sadler, June 7, 1947, in the Records of the Brite History Project, Correspondence Files.

81. Elmer Henson from Granville Walker, May 14, 1948, in the Records of the Brite History Project, Correspondence Files.

82. "Report of the Dean to the Board of Trustees," November 12, 1948, Historical Archives, Brite Divinity School, Fort Worth, TX.

83. Ibid.

84. Ibid., 229.

85. "Report of the President to the Board of Trustees," Texas Christian University

Board of Trustees Meeting Minutes (November 5, 1943).
86. Brite College of the Bible Board of Trustees Meeting Minutes (February 16, 1944; March 1, 1945; and December 20, 1945).
87. Texas Christian University Board of Trustees Meeting Minutes (January 26, 1946) and Brite College of the Bible Board of Trustees Meeting Minutes (December 20, 1945).
88. Brite College of the Bible Board of Trustees Minutes (October 17, 1946).
89. "Report of the President to the Board of Trustees," Texas Christian University Board of Trustees Meeting Minutes (February 24, 1948).
90. Brite College of the Bible Board of Trustees Meeting Minutes (October 21, 1949).
91. Conrad Cherry, *Hurrying Toward Zion: Universities, Divinity Schools, and American Protestantism* (Bloomington: Indiana University Press, 1995), 270–76.
92. *Texas Christian University Bulletin: Ex-Student edition* XLV, no. 9 (November 1949), Documents Files, Historical Archives, Brite Divinity School, Fort Worth, TX.
93. Brite College of the Bible Faculty Meeting Minutes (December 9, 1949).
94. Dean Lindley from President Sadler, March 7, 1950 in the Records of the Brite History Project, Correspondence Files.
95. For an example, see Lindley's resignation letter, in the Records of the Brite History Project, Documents Files.
96. Dean Lindley from President Sadler, March 24, 1950, in the Records of the Brite History Project, Correspondence Files.
97. Ibid.
98. Brite College of the Bible Board of Trustees Meeting Minutes (February 15, 1950).
99. Ibid.
100. Sadler was continually frustrated by churches and pastors who referred to "Brite College of the Bible and TCU." He insisted that they were not two separate institutions. For example, see M.E. Sadler to D.R. Lindley, March 24, 1950, in the Records of Denton Ray Lindley, box 3.
101. President Sadler to Mrs. R.S. Wetherell, secretary to the dean, July 5, 1950, in the Records of the Brite History Project, Correspondence Files.
102. Dean Roy Snodgrass to President Sadler, September 18, 1950, in the Records of the Brite History Project, Correspondence Files.
103. Dean Snodgrass to President Sadler, January 19, 1951, in the Records of the Brite History Project, Correspondence Files.
104. Records of Denton Ray Lindley, Box 2, "Snodgrass" File, Special Collections, Mary Couts Burnett Library, Texas Christian University, Fort Worth, TX.
105. Correspondence found with theTexas Christian University Board of Trustees Meeting Minutes (March 26, 1955), Special Collections, Mary Couts Burnett Library, Texas Christian University, Fort Worth, TX. Valerie Kuykendall–Rogers discovered this document in her research for the class on Brite history.
106. *Brite College of the Bible Catalogue* (1939): 10.
107. *Brite College of the Bible Caller* (1944): 12.
108. Miller, A *Community of Conversation*, 582.
109. President Sadler to Dean Snodgrass, September 25, 1950, in the Records of the Brite History Project, Correspondence Files.
110. Roy Snodgrass to M.E. Sadler, September 30, 1950, in the Records of the Brite History Project, Correspondence Files.
111. Brite College of the Bible Faculty Meeting Minutes (October 20, 1950).

112. Ibid. Although it is not clear what was meant by "handled appropriately," Dean Snodgrass and the faculty at Brite interpreted it to mean that they would be admitted.
113. Brite College of the Bible Board of Trustees Meeting Minutes (October 20, 1950).
114. Brite College of the Bible Faculty Meeting Minutes (Nov. 16, 1950).
115. Letter to Dean Snodgrass from President Sadler, June 19, 1952, in the Records of the Brite History Project, Correspondence Files. There is no extant copy of the letter Sadler referred to.
116. Brite College of the Bible Faculty Meeting Minutes (June 20, 1952).
117. Brite College of the Bible Board of Trustees Meeting Minutes (September 3, 1952).
118. Brite College of the Bible Faculty Meeting Minutes (September 19, 1952).
119. See Merrimon Cuninggim, *Perkins Led the Way: The Story of Desegregation at Southern Methodist University* (Dallas: Perkins School of Theology Southern Methodist University, 1994), 10, and Robert A. Baker, *Tell the Generations Following: A History of Southwestern Baptist Theological Seminary 1908–1983* (Nashville: Broadman Press, 1983), 313. Valerie Kuykendall–Rogers dealt with this topic in her paper for the Brite history class and brought the class's attention to issues related to these other schools.
120. Amilcar Shabazz, *Advancing Democracy: African Americans and the Struggle for Access and Equity in Higher Education in Texas* (North Carolina: University of North Carolina Press, 2007), 130.
121. Vada Felder interview by Brite history team, November 7, 2007, audio recording in the Records of the Brite History Project: Archived Interviews, Digital Interviews Files, Historical Archives, Brite Divinity School, Fort Worth, TX.
122. Vada P. Felder, *20 Years of Service: The United Christian Leadership School, 1954–1974* (published by author, no date), 52.
123. M.E. Sadler to Elmer Henson, May 25, 1955, in the Records of the Brite History Project, Correspondence Files.
124. In 1946, the C.H. Harris Foundation established a college of nursing affiliated with the Harris Memorial Methodist Hospital and Texas Christian University with the agreement that "should the Hospital or Texas Christian University refuse to operate according to the agreement or cease to so operate, then the directors shall have the right and duty to affiliate same with some other hospital and/or college." See Executive Committee of Board of Trustees of Texas Christian University Meeting Minutes (May 30, 1946), Special Collections, Mary Couts Burnett Library, Texas Christian University, Fort Worth, TX.
125. E.D. Henson to M.E. Sadler, June 27, 1955, in the Records of Denton Ray Lindley, box 3.
126. M.E. Sadler to E.D. Henson, June 28, 1955, in the Records of Denton Ray Lindley, box 3.
127. M.E. Sadler to E.D. Henson, October 25, 1955, in the Records of the Brite History Project, Correspondence Files.
128. C.O. Hawley to E.D. Henson, November 4, 1955, in the Records of the Brite History Project, Correspondence Files. See also letter from E.D. Henson to M.E. Sadler, December 13, 1955, in the Records of the Brite History Project, Correspondence Files.
129. There is no mention of a decision that Brite would have only 40 percent equity in the new Brite building in any of the minutes of the Executive Committee of TCU,

the TCU Board of Trustees, or the Brite Board of Trustees up to that time, including the November meeting that year of the TCU Board.
130. Letter from E.D. Henson to M.E. Sadler, December 13, 1955, in the Records of the Brite History Project, Correspondence Files.
131. Letter from M.E. Sadler to E.D. Henson, December 15, 1955, in the Records of the Brite History Project, Correspondence Files.
132. E.D. Henson to M.E. Sadler, January 20, 1956, in the Records of D. Ray Lindley, box 3.
133. Ibid.
134. M.E. Sadler to E.D. Henson (letter no. 1), January 23, 1956, in the Records of Denton Ray Lindley, box 3.
135. M.E. Sadler to E.D. Henson (letter no. 2), January 23, 1956, in the Records of Denton Ray Lindley, box 3.
136. Ibid.
137. Ibid.
138. M.E. Sadler to Jerome Moore, January 30, 1956, in the Records of Denton Ray Lindley, box 3.
139. M.E. Sadler to Noel Keith, February 1, 1956, in the Records of Denton Ray Lindley, box 3.
140. M.E. Sadler to Reverend Clarence Saint and to Reverend. Wilbur Mindel, February 2, 1956, in the Records of Denton Ray Lindley, box 3, and M.E. Sadler to Elmer Henson, February 3, 1956, also in the Records of Denton Ray Lindley, box 3.
141. Brite College of the Bible Board of Trustees Meeting Minutes (October 31, 1957).
142. M.E. Sadler to Colby Hall, October 21, 1957, in the Records of the Brite History Project, Correspondence Files.
143. Brite College of the Bible Board of Trustees Meeting Minutes (June 14, 1958). Until 1946, all money coming from the churches went to Brite exclusively.
144. Ibid.
145. M.E. Sadler to Denton Ray Lindley, January 31, 1961, in the Records of the Brite History Project, Correspondence Files.
146. "Restated Articles of Incorporation (With Amendments) of Brite College of the Bible," 1963, as filed in Tarrant County.
147. Brite College of the Bible Board of Trustees Meeting Minutes (March 6, 1963). For more information on the different understandings of seminaries and divinity schools, see David H. Kelsey, *Between Athens and Berlin: The Theological Education Debate* (Grand Rapids, MI: William B. Eerdmans Publishing, 1993), 1–28; Miller, *Piety and Profession*, 43–60; and Cherry, *Hurrying Toward Zion*, 102–122 and 156–182.
148. "Restated Articles of Incorporation," 1963.
149. Ibid.

Chapter Four
Culture and Education: Social Awakening at Brite, 1964–1977

1. "50 Years To Be Celebrated," *The Skiff*, May 1, 1964, Special Collections, Mary Couts Burnett Library, Texas Christian University, Fort Worth, TX.
2. "Brite '50th Marked,'" *The Skiff*, May 5, 1964.
3. Texas Christian University Board of Trustees Meeting Minutes (November 5, 1965), Special Collections, Mary Couts Burnett Library, Texas Christian University, Fort Worth, TX.

4. Walter Naff, interview by Brite History team, February 13, 2008, audio recording in the Records of the Brite History Project: Archived Interviews, Digital Interviews Files, Historical Archives, Brite Divinity School, Fort Worth, TX.
5. *Brite Divinity School Bulletin* (1965–1966 and 1966–1967), Special Collections, Mary Couts Burnett Library, Texas Christian University, Fort Worth, TX.
6. Gilbert Davis, interview by Brite History team, 30 October 2007, audio recording in the Records of the Brite History Project: Archived Interviews, Digital Interviews Files.
7. *Brite Divinity School Catalogue* (1964–1965).
8. *Brite Divinity School Catalogue* (1963–1964).
9. *Brite Divinity School Catalogue* (1965–1966 and 1966–1967).
10. "Resolution," March 1962, in the Records of the Brite History Project, Documents Files, Historical Archives, Brite Divinity School, Fort Worth, TX.
11. Dean Elmer Henson to President M.E. Sadler, April 13, 1962.
12. Texas Christian University Board of Trustees Meeting Minutes (November 1, 1963).
13. Texas Christian University Board of Trustees Meeting Minutes (January 23, 1964).
14. Ibid.
15. "Trustees Drop Racial Barriers," *The Skiff*, February 4, 1964.
16. Texas Christian University Board of Trustees Meeting Minutes (January 23, 1964).
17. "Jeter Discusses Jail, Rights Work," *The Skiff*, October 1964.
18. "Communist Influence Felt in Negro 'Rights' Drive," *The Skiff*, May 1, 1964.
19. "Psalm for All Races," *Brite Divinity School Newsletter*, in the Records of the Brite History Project, Documents Files, Historical Archives, Brite Divinity School, Fort Worth, TX.
20. "Memorandum of Understanding Between Texas Christian University and Jarvis Christian College," March 17, 1964, Special Collections, Mary Couts Burnett Library, Texas Christian University, Fort Worth, TX.
21. "Chancellor's Report," Texas Christian University Board of Trustees Meeting Minutes (November 1969).
22. "TCU Receives 'Soul' Evaluation in TCU-Jarvis Exchange," *The Skiff*, November 8, 1968.
23. Brite College of the Bible Steering Committee of the Lay School of Theology Meeting Minutes (December 20, 1962), in the Records of the Brite History Project, Documents Files. The UCMS, formed in the early twentieth century, served as the arm of the Disciples concerned with foreign and domestic missions.
24. Albert C. Hofrichter, "Concern for Developing Lay Schools of Theology: A Background Paper," United Christian Missionary Society, [ca. 1962], in the Records of the Brite History Project, Documents Files.
25. "600 March in Protest," *The Skiff*, March 19, 1965.
26. As in "White Anglo-Saxon Protestant" values.
27. Texas Christian University Board of Trustees Meeting Minutes (April 14, 1965).
28. Jerome A. Moore, *Texas Christian University: A Hundred Years of History* (Fort Worth: Texas Christian University Press, 1974), 230.
29. James M. Moudy, "The Inaugural Address, Education Without Magic," November 19, 1965, Special Collections, Mary Couts Burnett Library, Texas Christian Univer-

sity, Fort Worth, TX.
30. *Brite Divinity School Catalogue* (1963–1964).
31. *Brite Divinity School Bulletin* (1977–1978).
32. "Biographical Data Concerning James M. Moudy," October 1968, in the Records of James M. Moudy, Special Collections, Mary Couts Burnett Library, Texas Christian University, Fort Worth, TX.
33. Chancellor Emeritus James M. Moudy, interview, August 18, 1989, transcripts in the Records of James M. Moudy, box 2, folder 17.
34. Ibid.
35. Ibid.
36. Brite Divinity School Board of Trustees Meeting Minutes (November 5, 1965), in the Board of Trustees Files, Historical Archives, Brite Divinity School, Fort Worth, TX.
37. "Dean's Report," Brite Divinity School Board of Trustees Meeting Minutes (March 9, 1966).
38. Brite Divinity School Board of Trustees Meeting Minutes (March 9, 1966).
39. "Report of the AATS Reevaluation of Brite Divinity School," October 1967, in the Records of the Brite History Project, Documents Files.
40. "Brite Receives New Faculty," *Brite Divinity School Newsletter*, March 31, 1966, in the Documents Files, Historical Archives, Brite Divinity School, Fort Worth, TX. Also available in Microfilm Archives, Mary Couts Burnett Library, Texas Christian University, Fort Worth, TX.
41. "Dr. William Baird joins faculty as professor of New Testament," *Brite Divinity School Newsletter*, April 28, 1967.
42. Marcus Bryant, interview by Brite History team, October 10, 2007, audio recording in the Records of the Brite History Project: Archived Interviews, Digital Interviews Files.
43. "DeGroot publishes three more," *Brite Divinity School Newsletter*, November 1, 1968.
44. Bryant, interview.
45. "Report of the AATS Reevaluation of Brite Divinity School," October 1967.
46. Robert Olsen, interview by Brite History Team, February 6, 2008, audio recording in the Records of the Brite History Project: Archived Interviews, Digital Interviews Files.
47. Moore, *Texas Christian University*, 206.
48. Gilbert Ferrell, interview by the Brite History team, October 17, 2007, audio recording in the Records of the Brite History Project: Archived Interviews, Digital Interviews Files.
49. "Proposal for a Master of Divinity Degree," Brite Divinity School, [ca. 1968], in the Records of the Brite History Project, Documents Files.
50. "A Statement of Policy and Procedure for Field Service Education," Brite Divinity School, Fall 1966, in the Records of the Brite History Project, Documents Files.
51. *Brite Divinity School Catalog/Bulletin* (1967–1968 and 1968–1969): 779.
52. Naff, interview.
53. "Brite," *Brite Divinity School Newsletter*, May 1973.
54. Lance Morrow, "1968, Like a Knife Blade, the Year that Severed Past from Future," *Time*, January 11, 1988, 16.
55. Ibid.

56. Ferrell, interview.
57. Glenn T. Miller, Piety and Profession: American Protestant Theological Education, 1870–1970 (Grand Rapids, MI: William B. Eerdmans Publishing, 2007), 739.
58. Lewis Howard Grimes, *A History of the Perkins School of Theology* (Dallas: Southern Methodist University Press, 1993), 139.
59. "Report of the AATS Reevaluation of Brite Divinity School," October 1967.
60. Howard G. Wible to J.M. Moudy, March 6, 1967, in the Records of James M. Moudy.
61. Texas Christian University Board of Trustees Meeting Minutes (May 9, 1969).
62. "Nation's Protests Find Campus," *The Skiff*, May 12, 1969.
63. "An Important Message to TCU Students and Parents," August 15, 1969, Special Collections, Mary Couts Burnett Library, Texas Christian University, Fort Worth, TX.
64. "Campus ROTC Fires Investigated," *Dallas Morning News*, May 14, 1969, accessed online via Dallas Morning News Archive.
65. "Fire Guts ROTC Buildings," *The Skiff*, May 12, 1969.
66. "Chancellor's Remarks," Texas Christian University Board of Trustees Meeting Minutes (November 21, 1969).
67. Miller, *Piety and Profession*, 747.
68. "Authority on Vietnam to speak at Brite May 13," *Brite Divinity School Newsletter*, May 9, 1969.
69. "Vietnamese Author is Fireside Speaker," *Brite Divinity School Newsletter*, February 9, 1968.
70. "James Cone: Brite Series Lecturer," *Brite Divinity School Newsletter*, March 17, 1972.
71. J.M. Moudy to Mr. C. Mile Thelin, March 6, 1968, in the Records of James M. Moudy.
72. Glenn Routt, interview by Brite History team, September 12, 2007, in the Records of the Brite History Project: Archived Interviews, Digital Interviews Files.
73. Conrad Cherry, *Hurrying Toward Zion: Universities, Divinity Schools, and American Protestantism* (Bloomington: Indiana University Press, 1995), 214.
74. "Viet Moratorium Day Dawns," *Dallas Morning News*, October 15, 1969, accessed online via Dallas Morning News Archive.
75. Bill Baird, interview by the Brite History team, October 29, 2007, audio recording in the Records of the Brite History Project: Archived Interviews, Digital Inteviews Files.
76. "Dean's Report," Brite Divinity School Board of Trustees Meeting Minutes (November 30, 1969).
77. E. Brooks Holifield, *God's Ambassadors: A History of the Christian Clergy in America* (Grand Rapids, MI: William B. Eerdmans Publishing, 2007), 261.
78. "Christian Churches in Texas, Capital Development Program," [ca. 1971], Special Collections, Mary Couts Burnett Library, Texas Christian University, Fort Worth, TX.
79. *Brite Divinity School Bulletin* (1972–1973).
80. "The Comprehensive Examinations," 1968, in the Records of the Brite History Project, Documents Files.
81. "Reprint of Prayer in Memorial Service," *Brite Divinity School Newsletter*, April 26, 1968.
82. "Student Council Responds to Dr. King's Death," *Brite Divinity School Newsletter*,

April 12, 1968.
83. "Brite Receives Response From Rep. Jim Wright," *Brite Divinity School Newsletter*, April 19, 1968.
84. Miller, *Piety and Profession*, 738.
85. Routt, interview.
86. Baird, interview.
87. "Kansas City Convention Adopts Restructure Proposal," *Brite Divinity School Newsletter*, October 4, 1968.
88. Lester G. McAllister and William E. Tucker, *Journey in Faith: A History of the Christian Church (Disciples of Christ)* (St. Louis: Chalice Press, 1975), 443.
89. *The Book of Discipline of the United Methodist Church* (Nashville: United Methodist Publishing House, 2008).
90. Miller, *Piety and Profession*, 753.
91. Grimes, *History of the Perkins School*, 135.
92. Proposal for a Doctor of Ministry Degree, Brite Divinity School, [ca. 1968], in the Records of the Brite History Project, Documents Files.
93. *Brite Divinity School Bulletin*, (1977–1978 and 1978–1979).
94. Brite Divinity School Board of Trustees Meeting Minutes (March 26, 1976).
95. Miller, *Piety and Profession*, 775.
96. Robert G. Duffett, "The Future of Pastoral Counseling as a Profession," in *The Future of Pastoral Counseling: Whom, How and For What Do We Train*, ed. James McHolland (Fairfax, VA: American Association of Pastoral Counselors, 1993), 11.
97. Cy Rowell, interview by the Brite History team, November 14, 2007, in the Records of the Brite History Project: Archived Interviews, Digital Interviews Files.
98. *Brite Divinity School Catalogue* (1963–1964): 12.
99. *Brite Divinity School Catalogue* (1965–1966 and 1966–1967): 117.
100. Holifield, *God's Ambassadors*, 330.
101. Rodney J. Hunter, "Pastoral Theology, Graduate Education In," in *Dictionary of Pastoral Care and Counseling*, ed. Rodney J. Hunter (Nashville: Abingdon Press, 2005), 865.
102. Cherry, *Hurrying Toward Zion*, 144.
103. Charles A. Van Wagner, *AAPC in Historical Perspective* (Fairfax, VA: American Association of Pastoral Counselors, 1992), 15.
104. Pamela Couture, "The Identity of the Pastoral Counselor," in *The Future of Pastoral Counseling: Whom, How and For What Do We Train*, 24.
105. *Brite Divinity School Bulletin* (1977–1978 and 1978–1979).
106. "Brite," *Brite Divinity School Newsletter*, May 1973.
107. "Pastoral Care and Training Center Begins Operation," *Brite Divinity School Newsletter*, October 25, 1968.
108. "Pastoral Care and Training Center," *Brite Divinity School Newsletter*, November 2007.
109. "Pastoral Care and Training Center Begins Operation," *Brite Divinity School Newsletter*, October 25, 1968.
110. "PC joins poverty work," *Brite Divinity School Newsletter*, November 4, 1970.
111. "Annual Report, Pastoral Care and Training Center," [ca. 1973], in the Records of the Brite History Project, Documents Files.
112. "State of the University Address," Texas Christian University Trustees, September 11, 1970, Special Collections, Mary Couts Burnett Library, Texas Christian

University, Fort Worth, TX.
113. Texas Christian University Board of Trustees Meeting Meeting (November 13, 1970).
114. J.M. Moudy to L. W. Pollard, November 25, 1970, in the Records of James M. Moudy.
115. "A Self Look at Brite," *This is TCU*, Winter 1971, in the Records of the Brite History Project, Documents Files.
116. "Dean Henson Speaks Out on Worship," *Brite Divinity School Newsletter*, March 29, 1968.
117. William E. Tucker, interview by Brite History team, December 5, 2007, in the Records of the Brite History Project: Archived Interviews, Digital Interviews Files.
118. Brite Divinity School Board of Trustees Meeting Minutes (November 17, 1971).
119. By the early twenty-first century, TCU found it difficult to identify members of its board willing to serve on the Brite board. In 2010, two members of the TCU board (one ex officio) also served on Brite's board.
120. Brite Divinity School Board of Trustees Meeting Minutes (November 17, 1971).
121. Gilbert Davis, interview by Brite History team, October 30, 2007, in the Records of the Brite History Project: Archived Interviews, Digital Interviews Files.
122. Brite Divinity School Board of Trustees Meeting Minutes (March 24, 1975).
123. *Brite Divinity School Bulletin* (1977–1978): 22.
124. *Brite Divinity School Bulletin* (1977–1978): 39.
125. Cherry, *Hurrying Toward Zion*, 253.
126. Miller, *Piety and Profession*, 741.
127. "The Acting Dean's Report," *Brite Divinity School Newsletter*, November 9, 1973.
128. Holifield, *God's Ambassadors*, 263.
129. "Women Ministers Work to Beat Stereotypes," *Fort Worth Star-Telegram*, December 5, 1973, Special Collections, Mary Couts Burnett Library, Texas Christian University, Fort Worth, TX.
130. Walter Naff, interview by Brite History team, February 13, 2008, in the Records of the Brite History Project: Archived Interviews, Digital Interviews Files.
131. "Dean's Report," Brite Divinity School Board of Trustees Meeting Minutes (November 21, 1975).
132. William E. Tucker to Dr. William L. Miller, May 31, 1971, in the Records of the Brite History Project, Correspondence Files, Historical Archives, Brite Divinity School, Fort Worth, TX.
133. Holifield, *God's Ambassadors*,260.
134. Grimes, *History of the Perkins School*, 155.
135. "Brite," *Brite Divinity School Newsletter*, January 1974.
136"Brite," *Brite Divinity School Newsletter*, January 1975.
137. "Brite," *Brite Divinity School Newsletter*, January 1976.
138. *Brite Divinity School Bulletin* (1977–1978 and 1978–1979): 34.
139. Brite Divinity School Faculty Meeting Minutes (November 16, 1970), in the Faculty Meeting Files, Historical Archives, Brite Divinity School, Fort Worth, TX.
140. Ibid.
141. "Report of the Acting Dean," November 12, 1976, in the Records of the Brite History Project, Documents Files.
142. Holifield, *God's Ambassadors*, 267.
143. Dale A. Johnson, ed., *Vanderbilt Divinity School* (Nashville: Vanderbilt Univer-

sity Press, 2001), 182.
144. "Dean's Report," Brite Divinity School Board of Trustees Meeting Minutes (November 21, 1975).
145. "Christian Churches in Texas, Capital Development Program," [ca. 1971], Special Collections, Mary Couts Burnett Library, Texas Christian University, Fort Worth, TX.
146. Texas Christian University Board of Trustees Meeting Minutes (November 21, 1975.
147. "Dean's Report," Brite Divinity School Board of Trustees Meeting Minutes (March 26, 1976).
148. "Fall 1975 Enrollment,"[ca. 1975], in the Records of the Brite History Project, Documents Files.
149. Miller, *Piety and Profession*, 778.
150. Brite Divinity School Board of Trustees Meeting Minutes (September 10, 1976).
151. "State of the University," September 8, 1972, in the Records of the Brite History Project, Documents Files.
152. "Brite," *Brite Divinity School Newsletter*, May 1976 and 1978.

Chapter Five
The Suggs Era: Church and Academy, 1977–1989

1. He had been acting dean at Brite since August 1976.
2. "Suggs New Brite Dean," *Brite Divinity School Newsletter*, May 1977, in the Documents Files, Historical Archives, Brite Divinity School, Fort Worth, TX. Suggs's scholarly works include being "New Testament editor for a major Oxford Press publication, the 1976 annotated version of the New English Bible, and publications such as *The Layman Reads His Bible*, *The Gospel Story*, *Studies in the History and Text of the New Testament*, *Wisdom, Christology and Law in Matthew's Gospel*, and 'Book of Wisdom' for *Encyclopedia Britannica*" (ibid.).
3. This would be a phrase that Suggs would use often during his time as dean.
4. *Brite Divinity School Bulletin* (1977–1978 and 1978–1979): 5, in the Documents File, Historical Archives, Brite Divinity School, Fort Worth, TX.
5. *Brite Divinity School Bulletin* (1978–1979): 5–6, in the Documents Files, Historical Archives, Brite Divinity School, Fort Worth, TX.
6. Texas Christian University Board of Trustees Meeting Minutes (March 20, 1981), Special Collections, Mary Couts Burnett Library, Texas Christian University, Fort Worth, TX.
7. "Dean's Report," Brite Divinity School Board of Trustees Meeting Minutes (March 22, 1984), in the Board of Trustees Files, Historical Archives, Brite Divinity School, Fort Worth,TX.
8. "Dean's Report and Swan Song," Brite Divinity School Board of Trustees Meeting Minutes (March 30, 1989).
9. Conrad Cherry, *Hurrying Toward Zion: Universities, Divinity Schools, and American Protestantism* (Indianapolis: Indiana University Press, 1995), 66.
10. Ibid., 197.
11. Ibid., 266–267.
12. "Dean's Report," Brite Divinity School Board of Trustees Meeting Minutes (November 8, 1979).
13. Ibid., 211.

14. "Dean's Report," Brite Divinity School Board of Trustees Meeting Minutes (March 30, 1979).
15. "Dean's Report," Brite Divinity School Board of Trustees Meeting Minutes (March 19, 1981).
16. "Dean's Report," Brite Divinity School Board of Trustees Meeting Minutes (March 30, 1979).
17. *Brite Divinity School Institutional Self-Study for the Association of Theological Schools in the United States and Canada,* May 1, 1978, 6, in the Documents Files, Historical Archives, Brite Divinity School, Fort Worth, TX.
18. Brite Divinity School Board of Trustees Meeting Minutes (March 27, 1980).
19. Bryant had already received tenure in 1971.
20. *Brite Divinity School Bulletin* (1979–1980 and 1980–1981): 63. Bryant earned his PhD in 1958 from the University of Nebraska. Two of the other faculty members possessed DD degrees, one had two master's degrees, and the other two faculty members held bachelor of divinity degrees. The other faculty member with a PhD was planning to retire in 1981.
21. *Brite Divinity School Institutional Self-Study for the Association of Theological Schools in the United States and Canada,* May 1, 1978, 225.
22. Duke was a prolific scholarly writer, active in professional organizations, and many activities associated with the Christian Church (Disciples of Christ). See *Brite Divinity School Institutional Self-Study*, May 1, 1978, 226. See also, "Duke Tenured," *Brite Divinity School Newsletter*, April 1981, and *Brite Divinity School Bulletin* (1981–1982 and 1982–1983): 65.
23. *Brite Divinity School Institutional Self-Study*, May 1, 1978, 18. "A normal teaching load for full–time faculty is eighteen hours spread over two semesters. . . . Assignment to three Brite committees is the usual faculty load and . . . most Brite faculty members are also on one University committee. . . . Leaves of absence for study and research are not granted automatically as sabbatical years, but upon approval of a specific proposal submitted usually after an interval of at least seven years. Full salary is granted for one semester's leave; one–half salary is granted for two semester's leave. . . . By custom, Brite extends assistance of one–hundred dollars per year toward the expenses of each faculty member who attends a professional meeting in his discipline. If the faculty member is an officer in the organization, or makes a major presentation on the program, his expenses for attendance are paid by the University" (ibid., 7–10).
24. *Brite Divinity School Institutional Self-Study for the Association of Theological Schools in the United States and Canada,* January 15, 1989, 28, 30, in the Documents File, Historical Archives, Brite Divinity School, Fort Worth, TX.
25. Ibid., 36.
26. "Dean's Report," Brite Divinity School Board of Trustees Meeting Minutes (November 1, 1984).
27. "Dean's Report," Minutes of the Brite Board of Trustees (March 19, 1981).
28. E. Brooks Holifield, *God's Ambassadors: A History of the Christian Clergy in America* (Grand Rapids, MI: William B. Eerdmans Publishing, 2007), 330.
29. Brite Divinity School Board of Trustees Meeting Minutes (November 11, 1983).
30. "Dean's Report," Brite Divinity School Board of Trustees Meeting Minutes (November 11, 1983).
31. "Dean's Report," Brite Divinity School Board of Trustees Meeting Minutes (March 28, 1985).
32. Brite Divinity School Faculty Meeting Minutes (March 16, 1987), in the Faculty

Meeting Files, Historical Archives, Brite Divinity School, Fort Worth, TX. See also *Brite Divinity School Institutional Self-Study*, January 15, 1989, 97, 100. The new grading scale reflects the following: A+, A is 4.0, A– is 3.7, B+ is 3.3, B is 3.0, B– is 2.7, C+ is 2.3, C is 2.0, C– is 1.7, D+ is 1.3, D is 1.0, and D– is .7, and "the Committee's expectation is that it will probably result in a slightly lower, but statistically more accurate GPA for students" (ibid.).

33. *Brite Divinity School Institutional Self-Study*, January 15, 1989, 114–115. The recommendations made resulted from grade distribution reports that indicated, "Field Education and Choir tend to skew the percentage of A grades upward. This becomes even more obvious when one considers that A grades in these two courses of study account for 21% of all A grades given in spring, 1987, 19% of all A grades given in fall, 1987, and 16% of all A grades given in spring, 1988" (ibid., 102).

34. Brite Divinity School Faculty Meeting Minutes (March 16, 1987).

35. Brite Divinity School Faculty Meeting Minutes (August 17, 1987).

36. Brite Divinity School Faculty Meeting Minutes (October 26, 1987).

37. Memo from Jack Suggs to Don Pittman, January 30, 1989, in the Records of the Brite History Project, Correspondence Files, Historical Archives, Brite Divinity School, Fort Worth, TX.

38. *Brite Divinity School Institutional Self-Study*, May 1, 1978, 18.

39. Holifield, *God's Ambassadors*, 323.

40. Cherry, *Hurrying Toward Zion*, 253.

41. "Adjunct Faculty Enrich Brite Program," *Brite Divinity School Newsletter*, October 1978.

42. Brite Divinity School Board of Trustees Meeting Minutes of the Brite Board of Trustees (March 27, 1980).

43. "Old Testament Appointment Made," *Brite Divinity School Newsletter*, April 1980.

44. Brite Divinity School Board of Trustees Meeting Minutes (March 28, 1985, and March 27, 1986).

45. Brite Divinity School Board of Trustees Meeting Minutes (March 21, 1984).

46. "Native Texans Return as Faculty at Brite," *Brite Divinity School Newsletter*, June 1984. Her PhD was in systematic theology.

47. "Dean's Report," Brite Divinity School Board of Trustees Meeting Minutes (March 22, 1984).

48. Brite Divinity School Board of Trustees Meeting Minutes (March 28, 1985).

49. "Adjunct Professor of Black Studies Named," *Brite Divinity School Newsletter*, October 1979. Truvillion graduated from Bishop College with a BA and received his master of divinity degree from Drew Theological Seminary. His honorary DD was from Northern Baptist School of Religion.

50. "Dr. James Cone to Do Brite Series," *Brite Divinity School Newsletter*, April 1980.

51. "Dean's Report," Brite Divinity School Board of Trustees Meeting Minutes (November 17, 1988).

52. *Brite Divinity School Institutional Self-Study*, January 15, 1989, 377.

53. Ibid., 49.

54. "Longsworth Is New Ethics Professor," *Brite Divinity School Newsletter*, October 1977. He was scheduled to receive his PhD from Yale University later that year.

55. "New Testament Post Filled," *Brite Divinity School Newsletter*, April 1979.

56. "Pastoral Care Appointment Made," *Brite Divinity School Newsletter*, April 1979.

57. Virginia McCarter, Assistant Secretary, Brite Board of Trustees, to Dr. Harold Rhea, Secretary, Brite Board of Trustees, April 3, 1979, in the TCU/Brite Records,

Disciples Historical Society, Nashville, TN.
58. "Dean's Report," Brite Divinity School Board of Trustees Meeting Minutes (November 18, 1982).
59. See "Gouwens Ordained," *Brite Divinity School Newsletter*, June 1986.
60. "Brite Calls Three Davids to Challenge Secular Goliath," *Brite Divinity School Newsletter*, May 1983.
61. See "Native Texans Return as Faculty at Brite," *Brite Divinity School Newsletter*, June 1984.
62. Brite Divinity School Board of Trustees Meeting Minutes (November 1, 1984).
63. Brite Divinity School Board of Trustees Meeting Minutes (November 15, 1985).
64. "Toulouse Called in Church History," *Brite Divinity School Newsletter*, June 1986.
65. *Brite Divinity School Institutional Self-Study*, May 1, 1978, 137, 138.
66. "A Look at This Year's Student Body," *Brite Divinity School Newsletter*, October 1978.
67. *Brite Divinity School Institutional Self-Study*, January 15, 1989, 165–167.
68. Cornwall Collective, *Your Daughters Shall Prophesy: Feminist Alternatives in Theological Education* (New York: Pilgrim Press, 1980), 4–5.
69. Cherry, *Hurrying Toward Zion*, 253–254.
70. Sandra Lydick to Dean M. Jack Suggs, March 14, 1987, in the Records of the Brite History Project, Correspondence Files.
71. Brite Divinity School Faculty Meeting Minutes (August 19, 1986).
72. Brite Divinity School Faculty Meeting Minutes (October 26, 1987).
73. *Brite Divinity School Institutional Self-Study*, January 15, 1989, 185.
74. *Brite Divinity School Institutional Self-Study*, May 1, 1978, 157–158.
75. "Grant Received for Minority Field Ed," *Brite Divinity School Newsletter*, January 1979.
76. Brite Divinity School Human Relations Committee Meeting Minutes (January 24, 1980), in the Faculty Meeting Files, Historical Archives, Brite Divinity School, Fort Worth, TX.
77. Brite Divinity School Faculty Meeting Minutes (November 3, 1986).
78. Brite Divinity School Faculty Meeting Minutes (January 23, 1987).
79. *Brite Divinity School Institutional Self-Study*, May 1, 1978, 180–181.
80. Brite Divinity School Human Relations Committee Meeting Minutes (January 24, 1980).
81. Memo from Human Relations Committee to Recruitment and Admissions Committee, October 13, 1980, in the Records of the Brite History Project, Correspondence Files.
82. Brite Divinity School Faculty Meeting Minutes (February 23, 1987).
83. *Brite Divinity School Institutional Self-Study*, January 15, 1989, 187.
84. Cherry, *Hurrying Toward Zion*, 65.
85. Richard Hoehn to the Brite Faculty Committee, January 1980, in the Records of the Brite History Project, Documents Files, Historical Archives, Brite Divinity School, Fort Worth, TX.
86. James Duke to the Brite Faculty Committee, May 22, 1980, in the Records of the Brite History Project, Documents Files.
87. "Hispanic Theologian: Distinguished Visiting Professor," *Brite Divinity School Newsletter*, January 1982.
88. "Japanese Theologian Visiting Professor for the Year," *Brite Divinity School News-*

letter, October 1982.
89. "Faculty Welcomes Bolivian Churchman," *Brite Divinity School Newsletter*, January 1984.
90. "Dean's Report," Brite Divinity School Board of Trustees Meeting Minutes (November 1, 1984).
91. Brite Divinity School Board of Trustees Meeting Minutes (March 28, 1985).
92. Nancy Duff to David Gouwens, Chair of the Brite Curriculum Committee (November 16, 1987), in the Records of the Brite History Project, Documents Files.
93. Cherry, *Hurrying Toward Zion*, 85.
94. *Brite Divinity School Institutional Self-Study*, (May 1, 1978), 16.
95. "New Position Announced," *Brite Divinity School Newsletter*, April 1978.
96. "First Funded Professorship Given," *Brite Divinity School Newsletter*, April 1979.
97. "Fully Endowed Brown Professorship Established," *Brite Divinity School Newsletter*, May 1983.
98. Fully Endowed Brown Professorship Established," *Brite Divinity School Newsletter*, May 1983.
99. Cherry, *Hurrying Toward Zion*, 148.
100. *Brite Divinity School Institutional Self-Study*, January 15, 1989, 142.
101. Ibid., 143.
102. "New Field Ed Program at Hand," *Brite Divinity School Newsletter*, April 1979.
103. "Dean's Report," Brite Divinity School Board of Trustees Meeting Minutes (November 19, 1981).
104. "DMin in Pastoral Care and Counseling Proposal," Attachment to Brite Faculty Minutes, November 19, 1984, in the Faculty Meeting Files, Historical Archives, Brite Divinity School, Fort Worth, TX.
105. Brite Divinity School Faculty Meeting Minutes (November 3, 1986).
106. *Brite Divinity School Institutional Self-Study*, May 1, 1978, 50–51.
107. *Brite Divinity School Institutional Self-Study*, January 15, 1989, 66–69.
108. Cherry, *Hurrying Toward Zion*, 175.
109. Holifield, *God's Ambassadors*, 333–334.
110. Brite Divinity School Board of Trustees Meeting Minutes (November 18, 1982).
111. "Dean's Report," Brite Divinity School Board of Trustees Meeting Minutes (March 27, 1986).
112. Ibid., March 26, 1987.
113. Preliminary Announcement of New Programs of Study, April 1987, in the Records of the Brite History Project, Documents Files.
114. Brite Divinity School Board of Trustees Meeting Minutes (March 26, 1987).
115. "Dean's Report," Brite Divinity School Board of Trustees Meeting Minutes (March 24, 1988).
116. Daniel Luby, Director of the Office of Continuing Pastoral Formation for the Diocese of Fort Worth, to M. Jack Suggs, October 29, 1986, in the Records of the Brite History Project, Correspondence Files.
117. "Investment in Ministry Program off to Good Start," *Brite Divinity School Newsletter*, January 1977.
118. Brite Divinity School Board of Trustees Meeting Minutes (March 27, 1980).
119. Brite Divinity School Board of Trustees Meeting Minutes (November 13, 1980). Brite was one of eleven schools in the nation receiving a grant like this one from Lilly; see Texas Christian University Board of Trustee Minutes (November 14, 1980).

120. "Dean's Report," Brite Divinity Board of Trustees Meeting Minutes (November 18, 1982).
121. Cherry, *Hurrying Toward Zion*, 291.
122. Joint Resolution of Texas Christian University and Brite Divinity School, March 1978, in the Records of the Brite History Project, Documents Files.
123. *Brite Divinity School Institutional Self–Study*, January 15, 1989, 213–214.
124. Cherry commented that "one of the most venerable legacies of the divinity schools is a long, ardent commitment to social justice"; see Cherry, *Hurrying Toward Zion*, 298.
125. Faculty of Brite Divinity School to Brite Divinity School Board of Trustees, February 23, 1987, in the Faculty Meeting Files, Historical Archives, Brite Divinity School, Fort Worth, TX.
126. Brite Divinity School Board of Trustees Executive Committee Meeting Minutes (March 26, 1987).
127. Brite Divinity School Board of Trustees Executive Committee Meeting Minutes (March 26, 1987).
128. Brite Divinity School Board of Trustees Meeting Minutes (March 26, 1987).
129. Brite Divinity School Board of Trustees Meeting Minutes (November 17, 1988).
130. Ibid.

Chapter Six
Living into Brite's Incorporation, 1989–2009

1. *Brite Divinity School Report to the American Association of Theological Schools*, January 15, 1989, 212.
2. M. Jack Suggs to Joe Enochs and Leo Perdue, May 1, 1989, in the Records of the Brite History Project, Correspondence Files, Historical Archives, Brite Divinity School, Fort Worth, TX.
3. Jack Suggs to Joe Enochs and Leo Perdue, May 1, 1989, in the Records of the Brite History Project, Correspondence Files.
4. Ibid.
5. "Restated Articles of Incorporation (with Amendments) of Brite College of the Bible," 1953, as filed in Tarrant County, see Article VI, Section 2.
6. Mark G. Toulouse, "A Brief History of Brite's Governance Documents," November 18, 1998, n. 2, 4, in the Records of the Brite History Project, Documents Files.
7. See Article VI, Section 2.
8. "Board of Trustees Statement," November 17, 1988, in the Records of the Brite History Project, Documents Files.
9. Mr. Joe Enochs to Robert Leibrock, May 22, 1989, in the Records of the Brite History Project, Correspondence Files.
10. H. Richard Niebuhr, *The Purpose of the Church and Its Ministry: Reflecttion on the Aims of Theological Education* (New York: Harper and Brothers, 1956).
11. "1991 Mission, Philosophy and Goals Statement," in the Records of the Brite History Project, Documents Files.
12. "Brite Divinity School Enrollment Statistics," Fall, 1985; and "Brite Divinity School Enrollment Statistics," Fall, 1989; these reports are available in the Associate Dean's office at Brite.
13. "Dean's Report," November 3, 1989, 3, in the Records of the Brite History Project, Documents Files.

14. Brite Divinity School Board of Trustees Meeting Minutes (November 7, 1991), in the Board of Trustees Files, Historical Archives, Brite Divinity School, Fort Worth, TX.
15. "Dean's Report," November 3, 1989, 3; and Brite Divinity School Board of Trustees Meeting Minutes (November 1, 1990).
16. Brite Divinity School Board of Trustees Meeting Minutes (November 4, 1993).
17. Cherry, *Hurrying Toward Zion: Universities, Divinity Schools and American Protestantism* (Bloomington: Indiana University Press, 1995) 254–255.
18. "Twelfth Day Report on Enrollment Statistics for Fall 2002," September 13, 2002; this report is available in the Associate Dean's office at Brite.
19. Don Browning, quoted in Cherry, *Hurrying Toward Zion*, 65.
20. "1991 Mission, Philosophy and Goals," in the Records of the Brite History Project, Documents Files.
21. "2000 Mission Statement," in the Records of the Brite History Project, Documents Files.
22. Brite Divinity School Board of Trustees Meeting Minutes (November 5, 1992).
23. Brite Divinity School Faculty Meeting Minutes (April 27, 1992), Historical Archives, Brite Divinity School, Fort Worth, TX.
24. On Brown–May, see Glenn T. Miller, *Piety and Profession: American Protestant Theological Education, 1870–1970* (Grand Rapids, MI: William B. Eerdmans Publishing, 2007), 470–489. On lingering complaints about admissions standards among ATS schools, see E. Brooks Holifield, *God's Ambassadors: A History of the Christian Clergy in America* (Grand Rapids, MI: William B. Eerdmans Publishing, 2007), 330.
25. "Twelfth Day Report of Enrollment Statistics for Spring 2008," January 30, 2008; this report is available in the Associate Dean's office at Brite.
26. Brite Divinity School Faculty Meeting Minutes (September 28, 1992).
27. Brite Divinity School Board of Trustees Meeting Minutes (November 7, 1996).
28. Cherry, *Hurrying Toward Zion*, 34–38.
29. *Brite Divinity School Bulletin* (1987–1988 and 1988–1989): 51, in the Records of the Brite History Project, Documents Files, Historical Archives, Brite Divinity School.
30. *ATS Bulletin*, "Degree Program Standards," E.1 – E.2, in the Records of the Brite History Project, Documents Files.
31. Brite Divinity School Board of Trustees Meeting Minutes (March 30, 1989, and March 25, 1999).
32. Brite Divinity School Board of Trustees Meeting Minutes (March 26, 1998).
33. Brite Divinity School Board of Trustees Meeting Minutes (November 6, 1997).
34. Brite Divinity School Board of Trustees Meeting Minutes (November 7, 1991).
35. Mark G. Toulouse, "Talking Points for Governance Related to Section 8, ATS Standards: November 18, 1998," in the Records of the Brite History Project, Documents Files.
36. Ibid., 2.
37. Ibid.
38. Ibid., 3
39. Ibid., 4–5.
40. Ibid., 7.
41. Mark Toulouse to Michael Ferrari, December 14, 1998, private collection. Toulouse sent the letter to summarize the nature of the conversation held three days

earlier.
42. Michael Ferrari, phone interview with the author, March 11, 2009.
43. Ibid.
44. *Brite Divinity School Report to the American Association of Theological Schools* (2000).
45. Brite Divinity School Board of Trustees Meeting Minutes (November 18, 1999).
46. Daniel O. Aleshire, Earthen Vessels: Hopeful Reflections on the Work and Future of Theological Schools (Grand Rapids, MI: William B. Eerdmans Publishing, 2008), 95.
47. "Statement from TCU's Chancellor Victor J. Boschini, Jr. regarding Brite Divinity School's award for Reverend Jeremiah Wright," March 17, 2008.
48. "Statement from TCU," March 19, 2008.
49. Nancy J. Ramsay and Eugene Brice, "Why Brite Divinity School is honoring the Rev. Dr. Wright," *Fort Worth Star-Telegram*, March 23, 2008.
50. Michael Ferrari emphasized his intentions in 1998–1999, in a phone interview with the author on March 11, 2009, to avoid grounding the agreement in a cost analysis.
51. Victor J. Boschini to Newell Williams, June 5, 2009, private collection.
52. "Memorandum of Preferential Rights to Purchase/Lease Real Estate and Agreements Concerning Mortgages," 1–6.
53. Total headcount during this period dropped from 247 to 241 (2.4 percent). Enrollment in the MDiv program dropped from 175 to 127.
54. Holifield, *God's Ambassadors*, 330.
55. For general overviews of the debates on and approaches to MDiv education in the late nineteenth and early twentieth century, see Aleshire, *Earthen Vessels*, Jackson W. Carroll, et. al., *Being There: Culture and Formation in Two Theological Schools* (New York: Oxford University Press, 1997); Cherry, *Hurrying Toward Zion;* Holifield, *God's Ambassadors;* and David Kelsey, *Between Athens and Berlin: The Theological Education Debate* (Grand Rapids, MI: William B. Eerdmans Publishing, 1993).
56. Holifield, *God's Ambassadors*, 330.
57. Between 2000 and 2008, enrollment in the DMin program declined from twenty-seven to seventeen.
58. Miller, *Piety and Profession*, 35.
59. Katherine E. Amos, "Report of the Survey of ATS Schools on Educational Technology and Distance Education," *Theological Education* 36, no. 1 (Autumn 1999): 125–140.
60. "Houston Program Review Report," Brite Divinity School Faculty Meeting Minutes (April 25, 2005).
61. Linda Cannell, "A Review of Literature on Distance Education," *Theological Education* 36, no. 1 (Autumn 1999): 1–72. Meri MacLeod, "Distance Hybrid Master of Divinity: A Course-Blended Program Developed By Western Theological Seminary," *Theological Education* 43, no. 2 (2008): 1–72. For a helpful, though somewhat dated, bibliography on distance education in theological education see, Charles Bellinger, "Theological Education and Distance Learning: A Working Bibliography," http://www.libnt4.lib.tcu.edu/staff/bellinger/theo_distance_bib.htm.
62. The standard is usually interpreted as the equivalent of at least one year's worth of courses rather than one calendar year. See ATS General Institutional Standards, 10.3.4.2, and Degree Program Standards, A.3.2, B.3.2, C.3.2, D.3.2, L.3.2

63. Bethel Seminary, Asbury Theological Seminary, and Fuller Theological Seminary are among the leaders in online delivery of theological education. For a summary of Bethel's online program see, Jimmy Dukes and Gregory W. Bourgand, "Summaries of Two Experimental Distance Education Programs," *Theological Education* vol. 36:1 (Autumn 1999): 122–124, and Kristin M. Anderson, "A Case Narrative of Bethel Seminary's In Ministry Program," *Theological Education* 42, no. 2 (2007): 67–78.
64. Tuition for MBA students at TCU's Neeley School of Business and Harris School of Nursing and Health Sciences in 2008–2009 was $935 per credit hour as opposed to $725 per credit hour at Brite.
65. Anthony Ruger, Sharon Miller, and Kim Maphis Early, "The Gathering Storm: The Educational Debt of Theological Students," *Auburn Studies* (September 2005): 3–5.
66. Aleshire, *Earthen Vessels*, 127.

Selected Bibliography

Add-Ran Christian University Board of Trustees Meeting Minutes, 1893–1900. Special Collections. Mary Couts Burnett Library, Texas Christian University. Fort Worth, TX.

Add-Ran College Catalogue, 1874–1889. Special Collections. Mary Couts Burnett Library, Texas Christian University. Fort Worth, TX.

Add-Ran Christian University Catalogue, 1889–1902. Special Collections. Mary Couts Burnett Library, Texas Christian University. Fort Worth, TX.

Aleshire, Daniel O. *Earthen Vessels: Hopeful Reflections on the Work and Future of Theological Schools*. Grand Rapids, MI: William B. Eerdmans Publishing, 2008.

Ames, Edward Scribner. "History of the Campbell Institute." *In Progress: Anniversary Volume of the Campbell Institute on the Completion of Twenty Years of History*, edited by Herbert L. Willett, Orvis F. Jordan, and Charles M. Sharpe, 35–43. Chicago: Christian Century Press, 1917.

Amos, Katherine E. "Report of the Survey of ATS Schools on Educational Technology and Distance Education." *Theological Education* 36, no. 1 (Autumn 1999): 125–140.

Anderson, Kristin M. "A Case Narrative of Bethel Seminary's InMinistry Program." *Theological Education* 42, no. 2 (2007): 67–68.

Baker, Robert A. *Tell the Generations Following: A history of Southwestern Baptist Theological Seminary, 1908–1983*. Nashville: Broadman Press, 1983.

Becker, Edwin L. *Yale Divinity School and the Disciples of Christ, 1872–1989*. Nashville: Disciples Historical Society, 1990.

Bellinger, Charles. "*Theological Education* and Distance Learning: A Working Bibliography." http://www.libnt4.lib.tcu.edu/staff/bellinger/theo_distance_bib.htm.

Bond-Hinrichs, Fay. "Clinton Lockhart: Cultural and Religious Pioneer." MA thesis, Texas Christian University, 1939.

Book of Discipline of the United Methodist Church. Nashville: United Methodist Publishing House, 2008.

Boren, Carter E. *Religion on the Texas Frontier*. San Antonio: The Naylor Company, 1968.

Boring, M. Eugene. *Disciples and the Bible: A History of Disciples Biblical Interpretation in North America*. St. Louis: Chalice Press, 1997.

__________. "The Disciples and Higher Criticism: The Crucial Third Generation." In *A Case Study of Mainstream Protestantism: The Disciples' Relation to American Culture, 1880–1989*, edited by D. Newell Williams, 29-70. St. Louis: Chalice Press, 1991.

Bouchard, Larry D. "Willett, Herbert Lockwood." In *The Encyclopedia of the Stone-Campbell Movement*, edited by Douglas A. Foster, Paul M. Blowers, Anthony L. Dunnavant, and D. Newell Williams, 774. Grand Rapids: William B. Eerdmans Publishing, 2004.

Brereton, Virginia Lieson. "Disciples Higher Education in the Age of the University." *In A Case Study of Mainstream Protestantism: The Disciples' Relation to American Culture, 1880–1989*, edited by D. Newell Williams, 299-317. St. Louis: Chalice Press, 1991.

"Brite College of the Bible Application to AATS," October 18, 1939. AATS Files. Historical Archives, Brite Divinity School. Fort Worth, TX.

Brite College of the Bible Board of Trustees Meeting Minutes, 1893–1963. Board of Trustee Files. Historical Archives, Brite Divinity School. Fort Worth, TX.

Brite College of the Bible Caller, 1946–1952. Special Collections, Mary Couts Burnett Library, Texas Christian University. Fort Worth, TX.

Brite College of the Bible Catalogue, 1939–1963. Special Collections, Mary Couts Burnett Library, Texas Christian University. Fort Worth, TX.

Brite College of the Bible Committee on Registration and Counseling Meeting Minutes, 1950–1955. Faculty Meeting Files. Historical Archives, Brite Divinity School. Fort Worth, TX.

Brite College of the Bible Faculty Meeting Minutes, 1924v1963. Faculty Meeting Files. Historical Archives, Brite Divinity School. Fort Worth, TX.

"Brite College of the Bible Report to the American Association of Theological Schools," October18, 1939. AATS Files. Historical Archives, Brite Divinity School. Fort Worth, TX.

Brite Divinity School Board of Trustees Meeting Minutes, 1964–2008. Board of Trustees Files. Historical Archives, Brite Divinity School. Fort Worth, TX.

Brite Divinity School Bulletin, 1964–2006. Special Collections. Mary Couts Burnett Library, Texas Christian University. Fort Worth, TX.

Brite Divinity School Faculty Meeting Minutes, 1964-2008. Faculty Meeting Files. Historical Archives, Brite Divinity School. Fort Worth, TX.

Brite Divinity School Institutional Self-Study for the Association of Theological Schools in the United States and Canada, May 1, 1978. AATS Files. Historical Archives, Brite Divinity School. Fort Worth, TX.

Brite Divinity School Institutional Self-Study for the Association of Theological Schools in the United States and Canada, January 15, 1989. AATS Files. Historical Archives, Brite Divinity School. Fort Worth, TX.

Brite Divinity School Newsletter, 1964–1989. Document, Files. Historical Archives, Brite Divinity School. Fort Worth, TX.

Burris, Ronald II. "My Dusky Children: Race, Paternalism and Reform in the Founding and Emergence of Jarvis Christian College." Unpublished. Written in partial fulfillment of course requirement for Disciples History at Brite Divinity School. Fort Worth, TX.

Bynum, E.B. *These Carried the Torch: Pioneers of Christian Education in Texas*. Dallas, TX: Walter F. Clark Company, 1946.

Cannell, Linda. "A Review of Literature on Distance Education." *Theological Education* 36, no.1 (Autumn 1999): 1–72.

Carroll, Jackson W., et al. *Being There: Culture and Formation in Two Theological Schools*. New York: Oxford University Press, 1997.

Cherry, Conrad. *Hurrying Toward Zion: Universities, Divinity Schools, and American Protestantism*. Bloomington: Indiana University Press, 1995.

"Christian Churches in Texas, Capital Development Program," [ca. 1971]. Special Collections. Mary Couts Burnett Library, Texas Christian University. Fort Worth, TX.

The Christian Courier, 1902–1953.

The Christian Evangelist, 1893–1939.

The Christian Standard, 1902–1914.

Clark, Randolph. *Reminiscences*. Wichita Falls, TX: Lee Clark, 1919.

Corey, Stephen J. *Fifty Years of Attack and Controversy*. St Louis: Christian Board of Publication, 1953.

__________. "The Brotherhood and the Challenge of World Conquest." In *One Hundredth Anniversary of the Disciples of Christ*, published by Disciples of Christ Centennial Convention. Standard Publishing: Cincinnati, OH, 1909.

Cornwall Collective. *Your Daughters Shall Prophesy: Feminist Alternatives in Theological Education*. New York: Pilgrim Press, 1980.

Couture, Pamela. "The Identity of the Pastoral Counselor." In *The Future of Pastoral Counseling: Whom, How and For What Do We Train*, edited by James McHolland. Fairfax, VA: America Association of Pastoral Counselors, 1993.

Cummins, D. Duane. *The Disciples Colleges: A History*. St. Louis: Christian Board of Publications Press, 1987.

Cuninggim, Merrimon. Perkins *Led the Way: The Story of Desegregation at Southern Methodist University*. Dallas: Perkins School of Theology, Southern Methodist University, 1994.

Duffett, Robert G. "The Future of Pastoral Counseling as a Profession." In *The Future of Pastoral Counseling: Whom, How and For What Do We Train*, edited by James McHolland. Fairfax, Va: American Association of Pastoral Counselors, 1993.

Duke, James O. "Theology: Nineteenth Century." In *The Encyclopedia of the Stone-Campbell Movement*, edited by Douglas A. Foster, Paul M. Blowers, Anthony L. Dunnavant, and D. Newell Williams, 731–736. Grand Rapids, MI: William B. Eerdmans Publishing, 2004.

Dukes, Jimmy, and Bourgand, Gregory W. "Summaries of Two Experimental Distance Education Programs." *Theological Education* 36, no. 1 (Autumn, 1999): 122–124.

Fisher, Lucy. "The Stained Glass Ceiling." *Time*, (July 17, 2000).

Flowers, Ronald B. "The Bible Chair Movement in the Disciples of Christ Tradition: Attempts to Teach Religion in State Universities." PhD diss., University of Iowa, 1967.

Garrison, Winfred E., and Alfred T. DeGroot. *The Disciples of Christ: A History*. St Louis: Christian Board of Publication, 1948.

Gates, Errett. *The Story of the Churches: The Disciples of Christ*. New York: Baker & Taylor, 1905. http://www.mun.ca/rels/restmov/ texts/egates/tdoc/TDOC00A.HTM.

Grimes, Lewis Howard. *A History of the Perkins School of Theology*. Dallas: Southern Methodist University Press, 1993.

Hall, Colby D. *History of Texas Christian University: A College of the Cattle Frontier*. Fort Worth, TX: Texas Christian University Press, 1947.

Hall, Colby D. Texas Disciples. Fort Worth: Texas Christian University Press, 1953.

Hall, Gary H. "The Scheme of Redemption." In *The Encyclopedia of the Stone-Campbell Movement*, edited by Douglas A. Foster, Paul M. Blowers, Anthony L. Dunnavant, and D. Newell Williams, 671-672. Grand Rapids, MI: William B. Eerdmans Publishing, 2004.

The Handbook of Texas Online. http://www.tshaonline.org/handbook/online/articles/LL/flo40.html .

Hay, Kenneth McKinley. *The Life and Influence of Charles Carlton, 1821–1902*. Fort Worth: Christian Courier, 1940.

Helsabeck, W. Dennis, Jr. "Milligan, Robert (1814–1878)." In *The Encyclopedia of the Stone-Campbell Movement*, edited by Douglas A. Foster, Paul M. Blowers,

Anthony L. Dunnavant, and D. Newell Williams, 518-520. Grand Rapids, MI: William B. Eerdmans Publishing, 2004.

Hicks, John Mark. "The Christian System." In *The Encyclopedia of the Stone-Campbell Movement*, edited by Douglas A. Foster, Paul M. Blowers, Anthony L. Dunnavant, and D. Newell Williams, xx-xx. Grand Rapids, MI: William B. Eerdmans Publishing, 2004.

Holifield, E. Brooks. *God's Ambassadors: A History of the Christian Clergy in America*. Grand Rapids, MI: William B. Eerdmans Publishing, 2007.

The Horned Frog, 1904–1914. Special Collections. Mary Couts Burnett Library, Texas Christian University. Fort Worth, TX.

Hunter, Rodney J., ed. "Graduate Education in Pastoral Theology." In *The Dictionary of Pastoral Care and Counseling*. Nashville: Abingdon Press, 2005.

Jeter, Joseph R. Jr. *Brite Divinity School: An Historical Sketch, 1914–1989*. Fort Worth: Brite Divinity School, 1989. In the Records of the Brite History Project. Documents Files. Historical Archives, Brite Divinity School. Fort Worth, TX.

Johnson, Dale A., ed. *Vanderbilt Divinity School*. Nashville: Vanderbilt University Press, 2001.

"Joint Resolution of Texas Christian University and Brite Divinity School," March 1978. Documents Files. Historical Archives, Brite Divinity School. Fort Worth, TX.

Keith, Noel L. *The Brites of Capote*. Fort Worth: Texas Christian University Press, 1950.

MacLeod, Meri. "Distance Hybrid Master of Divinity: A Course-Blended Program Developed by Western Theological Seminary." *Theological Education* 43, no. 2 (2008): 1–72.

Marty, Martin E. *Modern American Religion: Under God, Indivisible, 1941–1960*. 3. Chicago: University of Chicago Press, 1996.

McAllister, Lester G. *Bethany: The First 150 Years*. Bethany, WV: Bethany College Press, 1991.

McAllister, Lester G., and William E. Tucker. *Journey in Faith: A History of the Christian Church (Disciples of Christ)*. St. Louis: Chalice Press, 1975.

__________. *Journey in Faith: A History of the Christian Church (Disciples of Christ)*. St Louis: Christian Board of Publication Press, 1989.

McPherson, Chalmers. Disciples of Christ in Texas. Cincinnati: Standard Publishing, 1920.

Miller, Glenn T. *Piety and Profession: American Protestant Theological Education, 1870–1970*. Grand Rapids, MI: William B. Eerdmans Publishing, 2007.

Moore, Jerome A. *Texas Christian University: A Hundred Years of History*. Fort Worth: Texas Christian University Press, 1974.

Morrow, Lance. "1968, Like a Knife Blade, the Year that Severed Past from Future." *Time*, January 11, 1988.

Niebuhr, H. Richard. *The Purpose of the Church and its Ministry: Reflections on the Aims of Theological Education*. New York: Harper and Brothers, 1956.

Osborn, Ronald E. *Ely Vaughn Zollars: Teacher of Preachers, Builder of Colleges*. St. Louis: Christian Board of Publication Press, 1947.

Pearson, Samuel C. "Campbell Institute." In *The Encyclopedia of the Stone-Campbell Movement*, edited by Douglas A. Foster, Paul M. Blowers, Anthony L. Dunnavant, and D. Newell Williams, 142. Grand Rapids, MI: William B. Eerdmans Publishing, 2004.

Perdue, Leo G. "The Disciples and Higher Criticism: The Formation of an Intellectual Tradition." In *A Case Study of Mainstream Protestantism: The Disciples Relation to American Culture, 1880–1989*, edited by D. Newell Williams, 71-106. St. Louis: Chalice Press, 1991.

"Pre-Seminary Curriculum." American Association of Theological Schools, 1940. AATS Files. Historical Archives, Brite Divinity School. Fort Worth, TX.

Records of the Brite History Project. Archived Interviews. Digital Interviews, Files. Historical Archives, Brite Divinity School. Fort Worth, TX.

Records of the Brite History Project. Correspondence Files. Historical Archives, Brite Divinity School. Fort Worth, TX.

Records of the Brite History Project. Documents Files. Historical Archives, Brite Divinity School. Fort Worth, TX.

Records of Colby Hall. Special Collections. Mary Couts Burnett Library, Texas Christian University. Fort Worth, TX.

Records of Denton Ray Lindley. Special Collections. Mary Couts Burnett Library, Texas Christian University. Fort Worth, TX.

Records of Ely Vaughan Zollars. Biographical File. Disciples of Christ Historical Society. Nashville, TN.

Records of E.M. Waits. Special Collections. Mary Couts Burnett Library. Texas Christian University. Fort Worth, TX.

Records of Frederick Doyle Kershner. Biographical File. Disciples Historical Society. Nashville, TN.

Records of James M. Moudy. Special Collections. Mary Couts Burnett Library, Texas Christian University. Fort Worth, TX.

Records of Jarvis-Van Zandt Family. Special Collections. Mary Couts Burnett Library, Texas Christian University. Fort Worth, TX.

Records of Jerome A. Moore. Special Collections. Mary Couts Burnett Library, Texas Christian University. Fort Worth, TX.

Records of L.D. Anderson. Disciples of Christ Historical Society. Nashville, TN.

Records of M.E. Sadler. Special Collections. Mary Couts Burnett Library, Texas Christian University. Fort Worth, TX.

Records of T.E. Tomlinson. Special Collections. Mary Couts Burnett Library, Texas Christian University. Fort Worth, TX.

"Restated Articles of Incorporation (With Amendments) of Brite College of the Bible," 1963, as filed in Tarrant County, TX.

Ruger, Anthony, Sharon Miller, and Kim Maphis Early. "The Gathering Storm: The Educational Debt of Theological Students." *Auburn Studies* (September 2005): 3–5.

Selcer, Richard F. *Hell's Half Acre: The Life and Legend of a Red-Light District*. Fort Worth: Texas Christian University Press, 1991.

The Skiff, 1903–1977. Special Collections. Mary Couts Burnett Library, Texas Christian University. Fort Worth, TX.

Stauffer, Vernon. "Vita." *New England and the Bavarian Illuminati*. New York: Columbia University Press, 1918.

Stevenson, Dwight E. *Lexington Theological Seminary, 1865–1965*. St. Louis: Bethany Press, 1964.

Swaim, Joan H. *Walking TCU: A Historical Perspective*. Fort Worth: Texas Christian

University Press, 1992.

Texas Christian University 1919 Alumni Bulletin. Special Collections. Mary Couts Burnett Library, Texas Christian University. Fort Worth, TX.

TCU/Brite Records. Disciples Historical Society. Nashville, TN.

Texas Christian University Bulletin: Ex-Student edition, 1948–1956. Special Collections. Mary Couts Burnett Library. Fort Worth, TX.

Texas Christian University Board of Trustees Minutes, 1939–2008. Special Collections. Mary Couts Burnett Library, Texas Christian University, and TCU Chancellor's office.

Texas Christian University Catalogue, 1902–1989. Special Collections. Mary Couts Burnett Library, Texas Christian University. Fort Worth, TX.

Texas Christian University 1919 Alumni Bulletin. Special Collections. Mary Couts Burnett Library. Texas Christian University. Fort Worth, TX.

Texas Christian University Catalogue, 1902–1939. Special Collections. Mary Couts Burnett Library, Texas Christian University. Fort Worth, TX.

"The Navy V-12 Chaplain Program in Texas Christian University and Brite College of the Bible," undated. Documents Files. Historical Archives, Brite Divinity School, Fort Worth, TX.

Toulouse, Mark G. *Joined in Discipleship: The Shaping of Contemporary Disciples Identity*. St. Louis: Chalice Press, 1997.

US Census Bureau. Accessed online December 3, 2007. http://www.census.gov/.

Van Wagner, Charles A. *AAPC in Historical Perspective*. Fairfax, VA: American Association of Pastoral Counselors, 1992.

Waits, Edward McShane. *A College Man's Religion*. Fort Worth: Stafford-Lowdon Publishing, 1929.

Watkins, Keith. *Christian Theological Seminary, Indianapolis: A History of Education for Ministry*. Zionsville, IN: Guild Press, 2001.

Williams, D. Newell, ed. *A Case Study of Mainstream Protestantism: The Disciples' Relation to American Culture, 1880–1989*. St. Louis: Chalice Press, 1991.

Wolfgang, James, Steven. "Transylvania University." In *The Encyclopedia of the Stone-Campbell Movement*, edited by Douglas A. Foster, Paul M. Blowers, Anthony L. Dunnavant, and D. Newell Williams, 745-746. Grand Rapids, MI: William B. Eerdmans Publishing, 2004.

Woolery, W.K. *Bethany Years: The Story of Old Bethany From Her Founding Years Through a Century of Trial and Triumph*. Huntington, WV: Standard Printing & Publishing, 1941.

Index

About the Contributors

Lisa Barnett is an ordained minister of the Christian Church (Disciples of Christ). She received her MDiv degree from Brite Divinity School in 2008.

Dyan M. Dietz is a Commissioned Elder in the North Texas Conference of the United Methodist Church, serving as Associate Pastor at Lake Cities United Methodist Church in Lake Dallas, TX. She is currently enrolled in the PhD program in Biblical Interpretation at Brite Divinity School.

Blaine Hamilton received his ThM from Brite Divinity School in 2008. He is currently enrolled in the PhD program in History at Rice University.

Gregory S. Henneman serves as Associate Pastor at Central United Methodist Church in Albuquerque, New Mexico. With a background as an Air Force historian, he received his MDiv from Brite Divinity School in 2009.

Dr. Mark G. Toulouse is the Principal and Professor of the History of Christianity at Emmanuel College of Victoria University in the University of Toronto. From 1986 to 2008, he taught American Religious History at Brite Divinity School.

Dr. Jeffrey Williams arrived at Brite Divinity School in 2005. He is the Associate Dean for Academic Affairs and teaches American Religious History.